# BELIEVING AGAIN

# BELIEVING AGAIN

Stories of Leaving and Returning to Faith

DANIEL TAYLOR

CASCADE Books • Eugene, Oregon

BELIEVING AGAIN
Stories of Leaving and Returning to Faith

Copyright © 2025 Daniel Taylor. All rights reserved. Except for brief quotations in critical publications or reviews, no part of this book may be reproduced in any manner without prior written permission from the publisher. Write: Permissions, Wipf and Stock Publishers, 199 W. 8th Ave., Suite 3, Eugene, OR 97401.

Cascade Books
An Imprint of Wipf and Stock Publishers
199 W. 8th Ave., Suite 3
Eugene, OR 97401

www.wipfandstock.com

PAPERBACK ISBN: 979-8-3852-1154-8
HARDCOVER ISBN: 979-8-3852-1155-5
EBOOK ISBN: 979-8-3852-1156-2

*Cataloguing-in-Publication data:*

Names: Taylor, Daniel, author.

Title: Believing again : stories of leaving and returning to faith / Daniel Taylor.

Description: Eugene, OR: Cascade Books, 2025 | Includes bibliographical references.

Identifiers: ISBN 979-8-3852-1154-8 (paperback) | ISBN 979-8-3852-1155-5 (hardcover) | ISBN 979-8-3852-1156-2 (ebook)

Subjects: LCSH: Christianity—United States. | Spirituality—Christianity—United States. | Spiritual pilgrimage—Christianity—United States.

Classification: BV4501.2 T2745 2025 (paperback) | BV4501.2 (ebook)

VERSION NUMBER 022025

Paula Huston's essay "A Love Story" was originally published in *Dappled Things*, Pentecost 2023.

For Wanderers and Yearners everywhere. May you find home.

And for Ted Lewis—reconciler and friend (1958–2024)

# CONTENTS

INTRODUCTION | ix

## I. LEAVING: THE NUMBERS

CHAPTER 1: THE GREAT EXODUS | 3

## II: RETURNING: STORIES OF BELIEVING AGAIN

TALES FROM THE STORYTELLERS

CHAPTER 2: KATHLEEN NORRIS: THE POETRY OF BELIEVING AGAIN | 17

CHAPTER 3: LECRAE MOORE: REFORMATION RAPPER | 39

CHAPTER 4: CHRISTIAN WIMAN: REVENANT BELIEVER AND POET | 57

CHAPTER 5: DAN WAKEFIELD: WAKING UP SCREAMING | 89

SHORTER STORIES OF OTHER PUBLIC FIGURES

CHAPTER 6: ANNE RICE: FROM JESUS TO VAMPIRES AND BACK AGAIN | 107

CHAPTER 7: ROSARIA BUTTERFIELD: THE COST OF COMING OUT CHRISTIAN | 120

CHAPTER 8: A. N. WILSON: THE FAILURE OF ALTERNATE EXPLANATIONS | 129

HEARING FROM THE COMMON FOLK

CHAPTER 9: A LOVE STORY by PAULA HUSTON | 137

CHAPTER 10: TED LEWIS: REDISCOVERING THE LYRICS OF FAITH | 148

CHAPTER 11: BRAD GERMANY: BAD TO WORSE TO BEST | 154

CHAPTER 12: RETURNERS by LESA ENGELTHALER | 161

## III. WHAT THESE STORIES TELL US

CHAPTER 13: COMMON THEMES IN STORIES OF RETURN | 177

CHAPTER 14: KEEPING THEM WITH US, DRAWING THEM BACK: SOME THOUGHTS FOR THE CHURCH | 197

EPILOGUE: A WORD TO POTENTIAL RETURNERS | 207

SUGGESTED READING | 211

# INTRODUCTION

> "Nothing is more common in the pages of religious autobiography than the way in which seasons of lively and of difficult faith are described as alternating."
>
> —WILLIAM JAMES, *THE VARIETIES OF RELIGIOUS EXPERIENCE*

A POPULAR NARRATIVE OF our time says that people are leaving religious faith and the Christian church in America at a precipitous rate, especially young adults. Social scientists have both supported and contested this story. They have, for instance, documented a steep rise in the percentage who say they have no religious affiliation—with labels such as the Nones, some of whom are also atheists, though most are not. They have studied the popular identification, fairly or not, of conservative religion with conservative politics and linked it to a move away, even by believers, from church attendance—the so-called Dones (as in "done with church"). They have reported on the growing number of young people who have never have been exposed to religion at all—the Unchurched (or what could be called the Never-Weres). What is much less studied—if at all—is why so many of those who leave faith and the church eventually come back (one estimate is 20 percent, some say higher, but this has not been rigorously established). Those people are the subject of this book.

Into the soup of names used for categories of belief and nonbelief and ambivalent belief—Believers, True Believers, Atheists, New Atheists, Agnostics, Unaffiliated, Nones, Dones, Dechurched, Unchurched, Nonverts, Exvangelicals—each with a different shade of meaning or emotional freight, please allow me to add two more: Leavers and Returners. Neither of these terms is synonymous with the previous terms, since one can be in any of those categories and not be a Leaver or Returner.

I use both terms neutrally. A Leaver in this book is someone who once consciously self-identified as a believer in some form of Christianity—and then testifies consciously and expressly to leaving it. A Returner is simply one who, after time away from faith, returns to it and usually to the church, though often to a different expression of the church than the one they left. Many people are Leavers—especially in recent decades—but a significant number of those become Returners.

(I will use capital letters throughout when referring to these categories, and lower case with "church," though some groups of course capitalize it when referring to themselves.)

As long as I'm naming categories—as Adam named the animals—let me suggest one more: Yearners. In an interview with Dan Wakefield, the writer Leonard Kriegel says the following: "I wouldn't call myself a believer but a man yearning for belief—which is why I also wouldn't call myself a nonbeliever." This is a position for which I have great respect—and empathy. In fact, I've been something of a Yearner myself at times in my life.

Yearners live in the borderlands between fully committed faith and disbelief—just inside the border or just outside—only God knows which. They want more belief, more faith, more of God than they have, but obstacles stand in the way—some external, some internal. Scholars have largely ignored these border dwellers. The conservative church traditionally calls these people "doubters," mistakenly equating doubt with disbelief and suggesting they should simply "get over it." Yearners deserve better. God calls to them and the church needs them.

This book is not expressly about Yearners (though others of my books have been), but yearning is a stage that most Returners go through before they find they can believe again.

The biblical parable often titled "the return of the prodigal son" is one of the best known and loved stories in Western culture. It's a story about leaving and returning—and it's crucial that the place left and returned to is home. The idea of home is so deeply engrained in us in a generally positive sense—even for many whose home experience was painful—that any reference to returning home is likely to appeal both to the heart and to the mind. It is a basic human instinct that home is, or should be, where we are loved, protected, and valued, the place where we thrive, where we are meant to be.

The bias of this book is that returning home after a time away, even a long time, is a good and desirable thing. Within that bias is another one—that a return to a healthy religious faith after absence is a good and desirable thing. If you don't think so, you will not enjoy this book.

Although the insights from the stories that follow can apply to a return to any religion—or to any defining set of beliefs and values—the focus of this book is on Christianity, particularly American Christianity. Its preliminary, contextual question is "who is leaving faith and why?" But its major question is "who is returning to faith and why?" It is not a book about folks who come to faith for the first time, nor who leave the Christian faith and don't return, nor about those who leave for another religion, including an eclectic spirituality of their own making. It is about those who at one time in their life sincerely self-identified with faith in the biblical God and with the Christian church, who then consciously abandoned that faith, and who later openly returned to faith and to some expression of the church.

After telling some of these stories and exploring common themes in why people say they leave and why they come back, *Believing Again* suggests key characteristics of how Christians can tell and live the story of faith so as to make it believable, compelling, and desirable.

This book is not objective or scientific. It is a reflective and story-focused book, not another social science study. It will present a brief overview of the statistics associated with religious life in America, but is more interested in personal stories than in numbers. The stories are drawn from the written accounts of well-known writers, artists, and intellectuals, but also from regular folk who are sometimes telling their story for the first time.

Its goal is to be helpful and encouraging—to people of faith, to individuals exploring a return to faith, and to Christian organizations trying to understand the state of faith in America at the moment, and what might be needed to strengthen it.

# I. LEAVING: THE NUMBERS

# Chapter 1

## THE GREAT EXODUS

> "Be kind; for everyone you meet is fighting a great battle."
> —Philo of Alexandria

The focus of this book is on Returning, but you can't return to anything or anywhere or anyone unless you have previously left. So we need to address, even if only briefly, the phenomenon of people leaving God, faith, and the church. For better and worse, this is something the social scientists have investigated thoroughly and for a long time.

I say "for better" because data is usually helpful. It puts measurement underneath too often vague and imprecise generalizations, anecdotes, speculations, and hunches. For many people, the more numbers (and graphs, and charts, and databases) we have, the better they feel about the validity of any assertion.

I also say "and worse" because measurement is often misleading—hiding presuppositions, biases, faulty methodologies, misguided interpretations of data, and the like. And many important aspects of being human do not lend themselves to measurement. Most significant human experience is carried in stories, and stories deal with the complexity and even mystery of those experiences better than numbers do.

My hat is off to those social scientists who start with stories and then try to quantify them, but this book will offer stories and interpretation (both by the original storyteller and by me) and forego the numbers and graphs.

One challenge for measurers is clearly identifying what they are trying to measure. A lot of confusion about what is being measured has resulted from people measuring different things that are taken as more or less the same thing. The social sciences in recent decades, for instance, have explored and tried to measure all of the following sometimes overlapping phenomena, sometimes without making clear distinctions between them:

— those who participate meaningfully in a recognized expression of organized religion (the great majority of people in the past), as measured by things like self-identification, church attendance, and other beliefs and behaviors.

— those who once participated in organized religion and no longer do so, but still retain core beliefs of the religion and still at times engage in religious practices (sometimes called the Dones or a specific subset of the Dechurched).

— those who have left one major religion and joined another.

— those who no longer participate in an established religion but have developed an eclectic set of beliefs they consider spiritual, as in the popular refrain, "I'm spiritual but not religious."

— those who once participated meaningfully in a recognized religious expression of organized religion but no longer do so *and* also reject religious beliefs as unfounded.

— those who have never affiliated with any religion or religious belief, but do not oppose or belittle it.

— those who believe all reality is solely material and are aggressively anti-religion (sometimes called the New Atheists).

— those who were raised without any religious experience (the Unchurched or Never-Weres, who could fall into a number of the above categories).

Depending on the choices offered on any given survey, those from the above groups who indicate no current religious or spiritual identification are often lumped together as the Nones or the Unaffiliated, though they can be very different from each other.

Given this wide range of categories, it is not surprising that the statistics bandied about regarding who has faith and who doesn't, who is leaving religion and the church and who isn't—and the like—are often conflicting and confusing. Yesterday's numbers and interpretations are likely to be outdated and contradicted by tomorrow's new data and new interpretations.

Someone, for instance, who has left the Christian church, and has not joined any other religion, is not likely an atheist or even a non-Christian.

They might well argue, and some do, that they are *more* Christian than those who remain in a dead or corrupt institutional church. Even if they have left Christianity completely, they may well have embarked on an alternative spiritual quest they consider as valid as any traditional religion, something the survey instrument may not measure.

None of the above caveats regarding polls, surveys, and measurement generally should be taken to suggest that the overall trend is not clear. It is. People are leaving faith in God, in Christianity (and other religions) generally, and the church in higher numbers than at any time in American history. (The low point of church membership in America was actually the late eighteenth century, but that's another story). It's something that Christians and church leaders need to think about, and many are doing so. (My hope is that this book will be of help.)

Sociologists distinguish between three different aspects of religion: belief, belonging, and behavior—what do you say you believe, what specific group do you belong to, and what practices and behaviors do you engage in. What we call "faith" includes, but also transcends, all of these. Beliefs, belongings, and behaviors can be listed and measured. Faith is less quantifiable.

Only God knows who has faith—even among those who testify to it—but participation in religion is more measurable. And by almost all measures, participation in religion is in significant decline—many say steep and unprecedented decline. (See "Suggested Reading" at the end of this book for a general indication of sources for the following statistics.)

Here are some numbers from various sources, none of which should be taken as irrefutable (they change from year to year), but all of which contribute to the widely documented perception that religious participation is waning in America (following earlier trends in much of the Western world).

Lyman Stone claims "since peaking in 1960, the share of American adults attending any religious service in a typical week has fallen from 50 percent to about 35 percent," much of that decline occurring in recent years. And "the share of Americans who self-identify . . . with any religion has fallen from over 95 percent to about 75 percent." A very high percentage of Americans say they believe in God, but their behaviors suggest that such belief often does not translate into any significant religious practice or specific, related beliefs.

The Barna Group reported that 48 percent of Americans attended church weekly in 2009, but that number had fallen to 29 percent *before* the pandemic in 2020. Millennial church attendance dropped by 22 percent in that same time. Gallup indicates that while 87 percent of American adults believe in God, just under 50 percent of Americans claim they are a member of any specific religious body. (It was always above 70 percent until the 1990s.) Even the majority of self-identified Evangelicals do not attend church on any given Sunday.

Ryan Burge and Perry Bacon cite a major social science survey in claiming that those who affiliate with no religion—the Nones—are the fastest growing group in the religiosity surveys: "the nones went from 12 percent of American adults in 1998 to 16 percent in 2008, to 24 percent in 2018." Other recent surveys put the number as high as 32 percent. According to polling by Barna, 61 percent of young adults who were involved in church during their teen years are now spiritually disengaged.

So who are these "Nones"? Burge and Bacon describe them as follows, contradicting some common stereotypes (such as that they are largely young, educated, white, liberal elites): "The average age of a none is 43 (so plenty are older than that). About one-third of nones (32 percent) are people of color. More than a quarter of nones voted for Trump in 2020. And about 70 percent don't have a four-year college degree." (Burge points out that the Nones are not primarily disaffected former churchgoers, but rather are younger adults who were never churched at all when young and are replacing older and more religious Boomers who are dying off.)

It used to be thought that those who leave the church as young people return when they marry and start having children. Burge claims the "life cycle effect" no longer exists for most who leave. Even for those who raise their children in the church, one finds that some will stop going to church themselves once the children have left and they have "done their duty."

Other studies, including from church denominations themselves, paint an even starker picture. The following data is relatively old and the numbers are contestable, but even if overstated they are startling to the average person in the pew.

— An Assemblies of God study reported that between 50 percent and 67 percent of Assemblies of God young people who attend a non-Christian public or private university will have left the faith four years after entering college. (Which does not prove that college attendance itself causes the exodus; these are ripe years for changing beliefs no matter one's context.)

— A UCLA study says the number of students who described themselves as "born again" when entering college dropped by almost 60 percent by the time they left college.

— Lifeway Research claims that 70 percent of Christian students lose their faith in college, a longtime worry of religious conservatives. (A

Fuller Seminary study puts the number at 40 to 50 percent.) Burge, on the other hand, argues against the perception that higher education in itself results in mass exodus from faith by Christians, pointing out that the less educated leave the church at a higher rate.

— One scholar says that young Americans are leaving religion at five to six times the historic rate.

Many of these studies focus on young people, from the late teens to the mid-thirties. This affects the resulting numbers because it is in these years that people are most likely to make and change major commitments, including religious ones. Stone says, "Religiosity tends to be high as a child, fall in young adulthood, then rise until around age 40, when it stabilizes until retirement and then tends to rise still further."

Most people who leave faith and the church do so between the ages of sixteen and thirty. Commonly, many make a serious commitment to religious faith in their childhood and youth, it is tested in their early adulthood, and then either abandoned or carried on into middle age. (Or, as in the phenomenon we are exploring, abandoned and then later embraced again.) But according to Barna, some of the biggest declines in church attendance over the past three decades have been among adults fifty-five and older—though a decline in attendance does not necessarily mean a decline in belief.

And, of course, in our increasingly secular age, many—the Unchurched—are never exposed to religion or make commitments to religious faith at any point in their lives, a major factor within the Nones. Worldviews are self-perpetuating—both religious and secular. The more None parents there are, the more None children there will be. What they never knew and committed to—or were even asked to consider—they can never leave.

If answering the "what" question regarding people leaving faith and the church is problematic, answering the "why" question is even more so. That question is more complex, more human, and therefore less measurable. But, of course, that doesn't keep some people from trying. Following is a list, without much elaboration, of reasons scholars and others have given for why Leavers leave. (For fuller discussions, again, explore "Suggestions for Further Reading.")

I have generalized and combined various explanations people give for the decline in faith and religiosity in order to make the list shorter and clearer:

— the ongoing secularizing of culture over recent centuries and decades, from many sources.

- the rise in access (including via the internet) to a wide variety of alternate explanations of reality, including some that are actively hostile to religion.
- the pervading climate of relativism and skepticism that makes all truth claims suspect, especially value and faith claims.
- the incompatibility of religious values and widely shared social values, such as an emphasis on hyper-individuality, self-esteem, and self-fulfillment, creating one's own reality and value system, materialism (both popular and philosophical), instant gratification, and so on.
- church wounds, family wounds.
- growing faith in secular solutions to life challenges: scientism, technology, social engineering, and progress.
- the perception that the world outside faith is more fun and fulfilling.
- the desire to be accepted by the larger, secular world.
- increasing government determination to not be seen as favoring any one religion, or religion at all.
- increasing government policy decisions seen as devaluing religion, combined with government domination of education.
- government replacing religious institutions as a source of aid in difficult times.
- decreasing role of religion in providing a sense of identity, community, and mutual support.
- growing prosperity and the sense of self-sufficiency it engenders.
- simple busyness: too many demands on time and energy to spend them on religious participation, making religion feel increasingly irrelevant.
- the decline of marriage, marriage and the home traditionally being a primary location for religious identification and instruction.
- increasingly negative stereotypes of the church and religion (anti-modern, anti-reason and science, morally defective, etc.).
- the failure of the church to demand active commitment from its members.
- the perceived failure of the church to provide an attractive, intellectually respectable understanding of the life of faith and the Bible.

- a perceived failure in the church to distinguish between core doctrines and beliefs and less central ones: an all-or-nothing approach.
- the perceived failure of the church to be "good news" to the poor and marginalized.
- the perception of the church as hypocritical, judgmental, intolerant, and scandal-ridden.
- the association of large segments of the church with politics.
- unrealistic expectations on the part of the individual about the true nature of faith, the church, and the world.

To all these explanations, we must add one more: people leave because they freely choose to leave, not because they are the helpless victims of external forces. To suggest otherwise is to rob people of their freedom and agency. Human beings do a myriad of things from a myriad of motives, but except in very limited cases, they are responsible for what they do. Sometimes people are justified in leaving a specific church or expression of faith. Other times they are simply foolish, or immature, or confused, or selfish, or attracted to evil. In short, unwise. In theological terms, fallen.

In the stories that follow, we will see examples of many of the factors in this long list of why people leave, some that are not listed, and some self-admitted cases of poor choices and lack of wisdom. We also see that none of these has to be determinative. If we are free to leave God, faith, and the church—and we are—we are also free to return. These are the stories of some who did.

To sum up, at no time in Western history have more people left religious faith and religious practices than in the last thirty years. And increasing numbers of young people are never exposed to religion in the first place. The centuries-old expectation of secularists that religion would wither in the modern world has not happened, and does not appear likely to happen, but religion certainly has become less central in the West.

Not everyone in the church is alarmed by these trends. For some, the Christian faith is healthiest when society disapproves of it most. If the world as a whole is hostile to God, which the Bible claims, then a believer should expect hostility from the world as well. In fact, believers should perhaps be worried about the genuineness of their faith commitment if they do *not* face hostility. Atheist Terry Eagleton sums it up nicely, "Apparently, if you claim to be a follower of Jesus and don't end up dead, you've got some explaining to do."

The Bible itself is full of references to Leavers. In the Old Testament individual tribes and the whole nation of Israel are depicted as having abandoned God, often for other gods, or for prosperity or power. In the New Testament, it is more individuals or smaller groups who leave. The New Testament not only assumes that a person who identifies as a Christian *can* abandon faith, it repeatedly reports it happening, often calling it "falling away" or "turning away." And it indicates that it will continue in the future. Here are just a few examples (using the New Living Translation):

> "Then all his disciples deserted him [Jesus] and ran away" (Mark 14:50).

> "But I have this complaint against you. You don't love me or each other as you did at first!" (Revelation 2:4).

> "And many will turn away from me and betray and hate each other. . . . [A]nd the love of many will grow cold. But the one who endures to the end will be saved" (Matt 24:10–13).

> "At this point [after a hard-to-accept teaching from Jesus] many of his disciples turned away and deserted him" (John 6:66).

> "For a time is coming when people will no longer listen to sound . . . teaching. They will follow their own desires and will look for teachers who will tell them whatever their itching ears want to hear. They will reject the truth and chase after myths" (2 Tim 4:3–4).

And then there is that parable in Matthew 13 and Mark 4 that always worried me as a child—the parable of the sower, sowing seeds on different kinds of ground with different results. I always feared becoming the example of the shallow soil that receives the seed of the gospel and flourishes for a while but then withers, because its soil is thin. "But since they don't have deep roots, they don't last long. They fall away as soon as they have problems or are persecuted for believing God's word" (Mark 4:17).

So given this history, say those in the church undisturbed by contemporary trends, "What's the big deal?" People have left faith and following God from the beginning—in significant numbers. The present exodus is nothing new, even if the numbers are. The Bible says "narrow is the gate" that leads to life. God created the church and will maintain it, whatever its numbers.

In this view, the broader church is not withering, it's being pruned. If there is no social or economic advantage to being a believer (and even more so if there are distinct disadvantages), then believers are likely to be in the church because of genuine faith and a willingness to sacrifice for it. Social, political, and economic approval has always, in this view, been a debilitating narcotic for the church. Let those who think they've found a better story embrace it and see if it gives them a better life—and a better eternity.

Others are less sanguine about the declining participation in religious life and faith. It suggests that the church is failing in its mission to preach the gospel to all nations, to be the conveyor of the good news of reconciliation with God. If our own young people are leaving, we must be doing something wrong. We are not living God's story in a way that is attractive and believable. We need to live and worship in a way that makes it clear—especially to our own—that the gospel is genuinely "the greatest story ever told."

My own view? On a macro scale, it doesn't bother me that the church is slimming down. I am impressed by the strength, courage, and faithfulness of the persecuted church, in history and around the world presently, and find that wide social approval of the church in the past has often made it flabby and unfaithful to its own story.

At the same time, at the micro level, I have witnessed the suffering that results when individuals walk away from faith—in their own lives and in the lives of people of faith who love them. There are no blessings as great to believing parents and grandparents as having their children and grandchildren carry a healthy faith into the next generation, and few pains as sharp as seeing the next generation discard faith as without value.

So this is not an issue about which I believe we can be indifferent.

In all complex situations there are balancing truths. All heresies and much of human error come when a partial truth is taken as a whole truth and its balancing truth is ignored or suppressed. So it appears true that the social scientists and church historians are correct—people are leaving faith (or continuing to live without it) in record numbers, especially the young.

The balancing truth, also confirmed by social science, is that many who leave eventually return. That same LifeWay Research study that claims that 70 percent of Christian students abandon their faith in college also estimates that about half of those eventually return to faith, a number I find difficult to believe and higher (as we saw earlier) than estimates given for other categories of Leavers, but an indication that whatever the number, it is significant.

We will explore all this in stories rather than numbers. These are pilgrimage or journey or quest stories. They will include both reasons for stepping away from faith and reasons for returning, each often understood only in hindsight. After all the stories I will offer what seem to me common factors in both Leaving and Returning, and will suggest some things that leaders in the church and those who value it might consider as they seek to make it better reflect God's intention for those who seek him.

Why these particular stories? I relate these stories because they are the ones that have come my way—through reading over the years and through recommendations and from keeping my ears open. There is no great attempt to represent every category of human being, those categories being too many even to list—and multiplying like rabbits every day. I begin with chapters devoted to individual writers and artists who have told their stories publicly, sometimes in a single place, more often scattered here and there. Some are stories I have long known, others are new to me. I follow with briefer tellings of stories from others—vignettes—some of them writers and thinkers, others just folks.

I want to make clear this book's limited claims. *Believing Again* is a nonscientific exploration of a phenomenon to which the social scientists have paid insufficient attention. It looks into the common but under-investigated phenomenon of the journey out of faith and back. Specifically, it explores the contemporary journey within Christianity of those who at one time have a self-identified faith in God and are active in the church, who eventually leave faith and church—consciously and by their own description—and who later in life (after a shorter or much longer time) testify to returning to faith and to some expression of the Christian church.

The methodology for this study is simple: listen to people's stories. Allow them to tell their own stories in their own words. Also allow them to interpret their stories as they see fit. And then try, as a listener, to draw some conclusions from the stories they tell and the significance they find in them.

These stories and this book do not prove anything. The sample size is too small and the analysis too subjective to qualify as science or proof. Stories are powerful, but they are also unique. Their transferability from one life to another is uncertain. But human beings telling each other stories for the common good is an ancient practice that predates speech itself (a hunter in prehistory could act out a "killing the bear" story without having to use words).

Ultimately, each reader of this book will have to decide how significant and useful these stories are.

These are not conversion stories (though some of those will be included as part of the journey), but what could be called re-conversion stories (I acknowledge that the term is theologically suspect) or possibly reversion stories. They are narratives of Return, of finding a way back to something once valued, then discarded, then rediscovered—back to something that some people call home.

# II: RETURNING: STORIES OF BELIEVING AGAIN

# TALES FROM THE STORYTELLERS

Following are the stories of well-known public figures. In each case, they have told parts of their story in scattered places—books, memoirs, articles, interviews. Here those pieces are gathered for a linear retelling, often using their own words, with reflections on the aspects most relevant to the topic of Believing Again.

## Chapter 2

## KATHLEEN NORRIS: THE POETRY OF BELIEVING AGAIN

"'Salvation is far from sinners,' and such was I at that time. Yet little by little I was drawing closer to you, although I did not know it."

—St Augustine, *Confessions* (Cited in Kathleen Norris, *The Virgin of Bennington*)

"I came to understand that God hadn't lost me, even if I seemed to have misplaced God."

Kathleen Norris, *The Vocabulary of Faith*

Kathleen Norris is a widely read writer in various genres, especially memoir. Her pilgrimage carries her from "a radiant" Christian faith in childhood and adolescence to the abandonment of that faith in the aggressively secular world of an East Coast college, followed by an absorption into the New York literary scene, then by a surprising and very gradual return to faith after her move from New York to her grandmother's small town, house, and church in South Dakota. Details of and reflections on this journey are spread throughout her writing.

Because she writes so insightfully and specifically, Norris's life makes a good starting point for telling stories of faith embraced, abandoned, and then embraced again. In her story one can find many of the major factors in why so many leave faith, what they turn to instead, and why and how a significant number make their way back. We will use her life as a paradigm for this phenomenon, discovering later how others follow a similar path or forge a very different path of their own.

There are important common denominators in the experience of believing, leaving, and then believing again, but each story is also unique, demonstrating the variety of ways in which God meets and woos people in the specific details of their lives.

## BELIEVING: A FAITH ROOTED IN STORY AND SONG

"I had a radiant faith as a child, mostly related to song and story." Song later included poetry—and music, poetry, and story are central to her life throughout and play an important role in her return to faith. Church for her as a child meant "dressing up and singing." In fact, she "for a long time believed that singing was the purpose of religion."

A particular form of music was especially important. "One of my strongest memories of early childhood is of sitting on my mother's lap at our old, battered Steinway upright as she played the hymns and I sang." Hymns remained potent in her life decades later when she made her way back to the church.

As did stories—both from the Bible and from her family tree. Hers was a family of preachers. "My paternal great-grandfather was a Methodist circuit rider in West Virginia and a chaplain in the Confederate Army; his son, my grandfather Norris, became a minister as well. I count many Methodist and Presbyterian pastors among my distant relatives. . . . My father has traced clergy in our ancestry all the way back to Reformation England." That paternal grandfather and his wife "served twelve Methodist churches in South Dakota and several more in Iowa," and her brother and sister-in-law are, respectively, a Disciples of Christ pastor and Episcopal priest.

Her understanding of her faith came primarily through inhaling the stories of the Bible, as told over and over in the various churches her family attended in a variety of denominations. "My inheritance, my story, is of a Protestant Christianity—Methodist, Congregational, and Presbyterian—whose roots lie deep in Judaism."

It was only much later in life that Norris reflected on why stories were the primary shaper of her early faith. Essentially, stories are rooted in the messy particulars of life, where faith must live. They appeal to the whole person—mind, emotions, body, and will. Stories compel us toward belief—belief in the truth and significance and value of the characters and events related—at least during the moments of the story's telling, and often long after. It was a story-based faith—intertwining family and church and Bible—which formed Norris in her youth; it was a different set of stories that led her away from faith, and it was a story-based faith to which she returned.

More important to her story than any of the pastors were her grandmothers. Norris's early faith took its shape under the polar influences of two grandmothers, each pulling her in a different direction with different consequences. She sums it up this way: "my two grandmothers, reflecting two very different strains of American Protestantism that exist in me as a continual tension between curse and blessing, pietism and piety, law and grace, the God of wrath and the God of love."

The faith of her paternal grandmother Norris was fierce and legalistic. God made the rules. God blesses the folks who keep the rules and sends them to heaven. The rest go to hell—and deservedly so. In Norris's words: curse, pietism, law, and wrath. Her maternal grandmother Totten acknowledged the rules—seeing them as ultimately for our own good—but grounded her faith and her life differently: in blessing, piety, grace, and love.

Both grandmothers had their effect, but the harsh faith of the one was not easy to escape. "Fundamentalism is about control more than grace, and in effect my grandmother implanted the seed of fundamentalism within me . . . that has been difficult to overcome."

One could argue that the legalistic grandmother's understanding won out in the intermediate term because her expression of Christianity matched the stereotypes of religious people that Norris later encountered in her elite, East Coast college and in the elite literary world of New York in the years after. It was a kind of faith that was easy to reject, and she did. The story of her return to faith is in large part the story of the ultimate victory of her other grandmother's example. One expression of her religious heritage tells a story she feels she must reject, another expression tells a story that eventually calls her back.

## LEAVING: IF THE STORIES AREN'T TRUE, WHY HANG AROUND?

Kathleen Norris's faith lasted beyond her childhood, but not far beyond. More and more faith was presented to her as doctrines to be believed rather than a satisfying life to be lived. "Like many people of my 'baby boomer' generation, I drifted away from religion when catechism came to the fore, and the well-meaning adults who taught Sunday school and confirmation class seemed intent on putting the vastness of 'God' into small boxes of their own devising. Theirs was a scary vocabulary, not an inviting one."

Her faith had moments of respite and even growth. She says "my interest in religion deepened in adolescence" when she joined a politically active church, a place where she discovered some congruence between what people believed and how they lived. But more and more faith was presented to her in terms of abstract doctrine and rule keeping. The doctrines, taught to her by well-intending confirmation teachers, were hard to remember and she found little connection to her life. She did not directly judge them as false, only as irrelevant.

But soon she happened on learned folks who judged them both irrelevant *and* false. One turning point was a course she took in late adolescence on Rudolf Bultmann, a highly influential mid-twentieth-century theologian. Bultmann denied the historicity of the New Testament and argued that it had to be demythologized in order to sift out any valuable nuggets it had to offer. The young Norris had based her belief on the stories and came to the logical conclusion that if the stories of Jesus did not happen, the religious faith based on them was of little value. "Religion came to seem just one more childhood folly that I had to set aside as an adult." Whether her understanding of Bultmann was adequate is irrelevant, the effect was devastating to her faith. The experience "led me to conclude that there was little in the religion for me."

Norris later marveled at the swiftness of her transition from faith to disbelief. "I remembered how completely I had loved God, and church, as a child, and how easily I had drifted away as a young adult."

## THE VIRGIN OF BENNINGTON

Kathleen Norris journeyed away from faith at two different speeds: first rapidly, then precipitously. And her enrollment at Bennington College played a significant role in that journey. It is a staple of the fundamentalist perception of life that college is the place young believers go to lose their faith. That stereotype played itself out fully in Norris's life.

What waning faith she had when she went vanished like a morning mist under the hot sun of secularism. Her own description of that time in *The Virgin of Bennington* characterizes it as a place of rampant drug use, reckless sex, and aggressive secularism. And she characterizes herself as arriving as a complete naïf.

When she asks a young woman why she kept taking aspirin during a class, the response stunned her: "This isn't aspirin, it's speed." When she inquired of a dormmate about the boy the student had sex with in her room, the woman said she didn't know his name: "I never asked." Norris's initial response was to keep her distance from the frenetic self-indulgence, earning her mockery for her nunnishness. Her refraining was not from moral conviction—she prided herself on being nonjudgmental—but from simple shyness and caution.

Bennington was also a place that shaped her mind, offering her a prepackaged substitute for religion. She watched a religiously conservative classmate being treated condescendingly by a professor and took the lesson. College continued the direction set by her exposure to Bultmann's demythologizing. She describes her "heady first encounter with Enlightenment and modern humanistic philosophies. . . . The doctrines I'd memorized at confirmation had little existential meaning for me and were no match for my emerging know-it-all, sophomoric self."

The root meaning of "sophomoric," she points out, is "sophisticated fool," paralleling Alexander Pope's famous observation that "a little learning is a dangerous thing." It is a common disease of the elitely but lightly educated. She says, "I was sophisticated in the shallow way only a person in her twenties can be." "A dose of the Enlightenment, a bit of Bertrand Russell, a dollop of Marx, a dash of Camus, and away with God! I remained a sophomore for many years."

Bennington was also the place she discovered poetry as a serious passion, in fact as a handy substitute for faith. "Our religions," she says, "were the arts and psychology." She began writing poetry and involving herself in the college's artistic and literary world, saying she skipped anti-war demonstrations for literary activities. Later in her time there, she also entered into the world of drug use and cavalier sex, including with one of her professors. She was finally fully "sophisticated."

Norris says this about herself upon first coming to Bennington: "College was something I had strived and longed for, and yet I felt empty there, without resources." Empty yes, but waiting to be filled, and Bennington obliged, filling her with things both useful and toxic. As would the New York literary scene in the years thereafter.

## NEW YORK: ARTSY AND SPIRITUAL, BUT NOT RELIGIOUS

Kathleen Norris says she moved to New York after graduation because that kept her close to her predatory professor lover. She does not call him predatory, but I have no problem doing so. She was one in a long series of sex partners he found in his grade book. She used up all the modern rationalizations for why there was nothing wrong with the affair, including convincing herself that it didn't actually do any harm to his wife.

Eventually she discovered—surprise surprise—that he was a jerk. He disparaged her abilities as a poet, telling her boss that Norris "will never amount to anything" without him. And he resented it when her first book of poetry won a prize. Eventually, of course, he dumped her for the next coed in line.

Norris carved a spot for herself in the New York literary scene, primarily by working as an assistant at the Academy of American Poets to Betty Kray, a mover and shaker in that scene, and an important person in Norris's life. Among her jobs was organizing and attending endless poetry readings by the famous and the obscure.

Her relationships were almost entirely with people of like mind pursuing like goals. She discovered that this world is one of aggressive competition, self-absorption, and self-indulgence. She arrived in Manhattan steeped in Romantic poetry, "which meant becoming immersed in heady notions of the poet as mystic, seer, lover, hierophant, drunk and all-around screw-up, an identity just foolhardy enough to attract me at the time."

In an early poem offering a guide for angels coming to earth, she warns angels and herself of the kind of place into which they have entered:

> Be careful how you unfold your wings—
> there are some in the world who are not content
> unless their teeth are full of feathers.

Norris found no shortage of people with teeth full of feathers. She also indulged more fully in casual sex and drug use, finding that the harder stuff—including LSD and mescaline—was something neither her body nor her mind could handle.

Her religious past was still weakly influential, though far distant. "My life had become bifurcated. Part of me still wanted to be the good kid I had been brought up to be, the Sunday-school girl formed in the Protestant work ethic. But I had grown attracted to what was forbidden, all the things the good girl had been denied."

This sense of having been denied "real life" and its pleasures is a common theme among Leavers of religious faith. Religion is associated with the legalistic denial of earthly pleasures, and who would want to deny pleasure? She says, "we had indulged in the dangerous folly of thinking we had found a better way." That better way, for Norris, included both her way of seeing the world and her daily way of living within it.

And she thought she still retained the best part of religion—its spirituality.

"Like many . . . I had long claimed to be spiritual but not religious." She invoked John Dewey: "I had soaked up his notion that the educated person is religious, but against religions." The spiritual for her was conflated with the aesthetic. If one was creative and imaginative, one was clearly spiritual. She tried to use poetry and creativity and all the substitute values of the life of the mind and imagination to stand in for faith in God. And it didn't work.

She says she was in a city filled with churches, but never went to one, not even to admire the architecture. "Like many Americans of my baby boom generation, I had thought that religion was a constraint that I had overcome by dint of reason, learning, artistic creativity, sexual liberation. Church was for little kids or grandmas, a small-town phenomenon that one grew out of or left behind." For twenty years, when confronted with a form that asked for one's religious affiliation, she wrote "nothing"—a None before they had been named.

She had replaced the faith of her youth with a "secular world view, terribly sophisticated but of little use to me in the long run." It was of little use because it was simply too thin, too watered-down. Its world was too flat, too competitive, too self-absorbed and individualistic, too harried, too little rooted in things that were timeless and therefore meaningful.

Norris is not entirely negative about this period of her life. She prizes the tutelage and friendship of Betty Kray. She loved her immersion in poetry, calling it the anchor of her life at a precarious time. But she also says, "I had become increasingly reckless with my life" and "In my writing, as in my life, I was a girl adrift."

Much later she decides that while these were not healthy years for her, they were years God would use to bring her back to himself.

## RETURNING: GOING HOME

After six years in New York, much to the surprise of her friends and herself, Kathleen Norris returned to South Dakota—to live in her grandmother's small town, small house, and, eventually, small local church. She did not return in order to find God—that comes only in time, quite a long time actually—but returning was a key step in the process.

Norris herself didn't quite know why she was returning. "I was slow to articulate, even to myself why I felt I needed to go." In an important sense it was to come home—home to an "inheritance," a word she uses frequently. The New York life, with its closed circle of literary friends and lovers, seemed increasingly "a narrow, pinched existence." She told her astonished friends the move was to better concentrate on writing poetry, but she knew it was more than that. It was more a return to roots—to a landscape that had shaped her, to a way of doing life that she had left behind, to a family legacy of hardworking people whose values no longer seemed as distant as they once did.

And she came with a husband, David Dwyer, who had helped her settle her life. It was not intended as a permanent move, only a couple of years at most, but it was a move that changed everything. And therefore they stayed.

Norris's grandmother Totten had died. The family did not want to sell the home—a home Norris's own mother had been born in—and they were happy when Norris agreed to come live there for a time. It was a house in which she had spent many summers as a child. It felt like home because it had already been a home for her, occupied by a beloved grandmother.

It was also a home in a small town that she knew, both its strengths and its weaknesses. (She calls it "a dusty little town on the Plains," with only 1,600 souls at the time, fewer than 1,200 now.) It was a home associated with a specific church, a Presbyterian church, whose strengths and weaknesses she also knew. She visited the church initially out of nostalgia and politeness. Everyone knew and admired her recently passed grandmother, and most of them also remembered her and wished her well. She attended only sporadically, not ready for any quick return to an institution she had been taught not to value. She did not join it for ten years.

So began a long journey of her return to faith. During that time she discovered that while she had forgotten God, God had not forgotten or stopped loving her. "I came to understand that God hadn't lost me, even if I seemed . . . to have misplaced God."

## ACCEPTING AN INHERITANCE: THE FAILURE OF SUBSTITUTE STORIES

I say "so began," but a repeated theme in Norris's account is that God was as much at work in her life in the wandering years, unseen and undesired, as in the Returning years. In, for instance, a quasi-mystical experience while sitting in her New York apartment, three years before returning to South Dakota and much longer before returning to faith. She finds herself, out of nowhere, thinking about the concepts of goodness and sin. And then she has a visitation, you might call it, from her grandmother Totten, then still alive back in South Dakota.

"[O]n that afternoon my grandmother's presence struck me with a poignancy that made me feel as if she were whispering in my ear over a distance of thousands of miles. And I wondered whether I did have a conscience, after all. It had come to seem a useless appendage, but now I suspected that it had simply been dormant. I was a Sleeping Beauty awakened not by the kiss of a prince but by the resonant voice of my Presbyterian grandma."

A reawakened conscience is not the same as a return to faith, but it was a step toward it for Norris. And the leading, healing whispers of her grandmother's voice in her memory are central to the "inheritance" to which Norris believes she returned. Her grandmother represented a story about how to live one's life. Kathleen Norris had rejected that story to embrace other stories that promised a better life than the life of her grandmother. Those substitute stories were failing her, and the call of the stories of her inheritance grew stronger and stronger.

That inheritance, Norris came to understand, was far bigger than her grandmother and family. It was bigger than merely being a good person or living a simpler life. It wasn't only about life*style*, it was about the possibility of ultimate meaning and significance in her life. Being free and artsy and intellectual in New York hadn't provided that sense of a profound life. Perhaps there was something in her past—her own past and a much wider past—which would.

Norris didn't think all this at the time of her move back to South Dakota, or for years after, but it's an understanding she came to after returning to a life of "attending baptisms, weddings, and funerals on a regular basis"—after years in New York where she "had not witnessed a single one." And she was surprised to find that in her sporadic visits to church she "loved hearing Scripture read aloud." The hymns once again spoke to her, as they had when a child, including the lyrics "Jesus sought me when a stranger / Wandering from the fold of God"—words that still make her think of her time in New York.

Norris's New York friends were mostly "appalled" by her "counter-cultural decision to live in what the rest of the world considers a barren waste," an assessment both of the Dakota topography and of the views and values of the people who lived in it, not least their religious beliefs. They worried that she was returning to a darker past from which she had been liberated, which some thought "would ruin my writing."

"[P]eople tested me to see if I had become narrow-minded overnight. Others seemed to regard me as a drop-out from the grown-up world of Enlightenment rationalism and tried to argue me out of my fledgling faith." Norris observes that for many, "Conversion . . . can seem like a regression." As can, in this case, not an initial conversion, but a Return, a believing again.

There is a difference between "an inherited faith" and "an inheritance of faith." The former suggests a passive faith one picks up simply as a consequence of one's childhood context—growing up in a religious environment—whereas the latter suggests a rich and attractive history of lived faithfulness. The one is easily dispensed with, the latter can call to you for a lifetime. Norris chose to respond to that call.

## GUIDES AND MENTORS

God, especially in the Trinitarian understanding, seems to be big on relationships. One can rightly argue that it is the Holy Spirit who ultimately shepherds every Returner back to the fold. But it appears that the Spirit prefers to accomplish this by using human guides and mentors in the Returner's life. Kathleen Norris found them everywhere, usually recognized as such only in retrospect.

These guides share a number of common denominators in addition to being unrecognized by Norris: they often didn't see themselves as such, their influence was more often by example than by instruction, they were themselves less than saintly (and sometimes not even believers), and they included the dead (ancient and recent) as well as the living.

We have already looked at the influence of her grandmother Totten, who Norris explicitly calls her "guide" in her return to faith, but there is more to say. She was the one who modeled a faith that emphasized blessing, piety, grace, and love. While some of Norris's "difficult ancestors" were among "the religiously self-righteous who literally scared the bejesus out of me when I was little, or who murdered my spirit with words of condemnation," Charlotte Totten gave her the example of a woman with a "livable faith" that showed itself less importantly in her Bible teaching at church than in simple acts of kindness, including to her neighbor.

Norris says one of her own steps back to faith was also doing a simple act of kindness to that same neighbor. She noticed her neighbor's seventy-fifth birthday on her grandmother's calendar, so she took over to her a bouquet of her grandmother's columbines to celebrate. "I was not prepared for the emotional reaction I received. My grandmother had been her best friend, the woman tearfully explained, and after she died she did not expect that many people would remember her birthday."

God has given everyone, believer and skeptic alike, the ability to do acts of kindness, but in this case the act was based, perhaps unconsciously, on a legacy of kindness that grew from her grandmother's faith. Norris began doing some of the acts of faith before she acknowledged to herself that she had returned to faith. This one was more than a bit of do-goodism; it was something that grew out of who she was becoming—again—and her grandmother (and her grandmother's calendar) were the prompt.

Other guides, unbeknownst to themselves, helped her overcome her prejudices about the Bible. Feminism had trained her to see the Bible as misogynist and oppressive, but she says, "I was drawn to the strong old women in the congregation. Their well-worn Bibles said to me, 'there is more here than you know,' and made me take more seriously the religion that had caused my grandmother Totten's Bible to be so well used that its spine broke." Was it possible to be a person of faith and a strong woman at the same time? The strong, old women—who put on the potluck dinners, and the wedding showers, and decorated for the funerals—said "yes." "Jesus had told them they were worth a great deal, and it was as Christians that they embraced their human dignity."

While one might have guessed that grandmothers and local church folk could act as guides for Kathleen Norris, no one would have predicted the large role played in her return to faith by monks. Norris is almost genetically Protestant, claiming "this is who I am: a complete Protestant with a decidedly ecumenical bent." That "ecumenical bent" is largely due to her unforeseeable encounter with isolated Benedictine monks on the Dakota plains.

That encounter didn't begin because Norris was seeking God. It began because she was seeking poetry. Specifically, she first went to a monastery to hear the poet Carol Bly read and lecture. Norris says God used her love of poetry in various ways to woo her back to faith, adding with a smile, "my conversion is a perfect example of how literature can get a person into deep trouble." Trouble in this case is a return to church and to faith.

Eventually Norris would profit from the wisdom of the Benedictines, which she often cites in her writing, but initially she was drawn simply to their hospitality, a point to keep in mind for those who would like to help Leavers to Return. Benedict in the sixth century initiated their long history of welcoming strangers, insisting that they "receive all guests as Christ." Norris cites a Russian story of an old monk telling a younger one, "sometimes I see a stranger coming up the road and I say, 'Oh, Jesus Christ, is it you again?'" In this case, Christ's name was Kathleen.

That hospitality included offering a place of retreat and stillness as she sorted out her spiritual life, leavened with just enough direction and wisdom to be useful without being overbearing. She calls the Benedictines "a wise and ancient spiritual powerhouse," but it is a power that was exercised discreetly, often in silence.

The monastery, in many ways, offered a life that was the polar opposite of the one she had been living in New York. Rather than noise, stillness; rather than competition, community; rather than intellectualism, wisdom; rather than dissipating the body, cultivating the spirit; rather than the latest, the oldest.

In short, the Benedictines—and the life of faith generally—offered a different understanding of what is important in life and what isn't, what success consists of and what it doesn't, what is real and what illusion. "Monastic people," she observes, are "not easily suckered by the All-American myth of self-reliance and self-sufficiency." The monks exploded the stereotype of religious people as insufficiently educated and unintelligent. As one monk writes, "We may be crazy, but we are not necessarily stupid."

Her encounters with the Benedictines greatly broadened both her sense of community and the range of those—past and present—who could serve as guides and mentors. "I find it a blessing, now, to be able to invoke the saints who have formed me, a beloved grandmother, say, as well as St. Paul, St. Benedict, St Thérèse of Lisieux. I am blessed to be able to enjoy the worshipping assembly of any Christian church as including both those present and absent, both the living and the dead. When I come to the end of the Apostles' Creed, they are all there, in the 'communion of saints.'"

Also there is St. Gertrude, a thirteenth-century German Benedictine nun, recognized by both the Catholic and Episcopal churches. Gertrude's description of her life is hauntingly close to Norris's own. "I praise and glorify your great patience, which bore with me even though from my . . . childhood, adolescence, and early womanhood, until I was nearly twenty-six, I was always so blindly irresponsible. Looking back I see that but for your protecting hand I would have been quite without conscience in thought, word, or deed. But you came to my aid . . . and provided me with necessary correction from those among whom I lived."

Norris says similar things throughout her writing, including "I realized suddenly that I had been most fortunate in being given another chance" to experience genuine faith and genuine worship among people who loved her. She experienced that most directly through simple hospitality that made faith not only attractive again, but also believable.

A Returner usually needs to see examples of people who have lived and are living it well. The Benedictines, as with her other guides, not only provided that example from afar, they nurtured her from within. The "expansiveness of Benedictine hospitality . . . on more than one occasion has turned my Dakota desert into a garden." She goes further. "I have become convinced that hospitality is at the center of the Christian faith." (We will find others saying the same.)

It is worth noting that one of her important guides appears not to have shared the faith of the others. Betty Kray, her boss in New York, and a leader in its literary world, also played a part in Norris's eventual return to faith. She looked out for the young Norris, trying to steer her through the maze of opportunities and hazards of that place. She "was particularly sensitive to any self-destructive tendencies in me." She also gave Norris needed strength, repeatedly encouraging her that a writer must learn to "live by her wits," because a writer's life is not an easy one. Norris considered her move to the Dakotas and example of so doing.

But most importantly, Kray preached to Norris the possibility of transformation. Norris offers no indication that Kray was at all religious, but Norris drew hope from "Betty's faith that people have it within themselves to undergo profound and necessary change." Not long after moving to South Dakota, Norris sent Kray drafts of poems she was writing in her grandmother's house. Kray's response was eerily prophetic: "Change simply expresses the fact that one has been able to discover some new power in oneself. It was there all the time, but it needed a trail hacked open to find it." It is highly unlikely that the "power" she had in mind was the same Power that was working in Kathleen Norris's life, but that does not diminish the fact that God used her as a mentor and guide.

And who knows? Norris reports that Kray, in her last days while dying of cancer, sat up painfully on her sofa during a last visit and said, "'Those monks are good for you,' adding, 'don't let them forget me.'" Perhaps Norris was not the only one undergoing a transformation.

## THE CHURCH: NOT AS GOOD AS IT SHOULD BE, BUT BETTER THAN IT IS SAID TO BE

It has been fashionable in recent decades, as much or more among believers as among secular skeptics and critics, to bewail the battered institution we call "the church" (or for some, the Church). Norris herself is clear-eyed about the collective church and its shortcomings. She herself lays some of the blame for her early departure from faith on her church's emphasis on abstract doctrine over the concreteness of a story lived. But in telling her own story, she makes clear the crucial role her local church in Lemmon, South Dakota played in her pilgrimage back to belief.

As mentioned previously, Norris did not at first return to her grandmother's church in search of God. To put it colloquially, she checked it out rather than sought it out. She visited the way one might as an adult visit a high school one had attended, a place with memories and maybe still some people you recall, but not a place to return to in any meaningful way. She went to her grandmother's church now and then, not joining it for a decade, but over those years she found it increasingly a place and a people that spoke to who she was and who she was becoming.

As we saw earlier, Norris says, "Believing in God, listening to Bible stories, and especially singing in church on Sunday mornings had been among the greatest joys of my childhood." And she found these same things reasserted themselves. She discovered that "communal worship is something I need," adding elsewhere "the desire to worship is in itself a significant form of belief." And she explains why worship (including singing and prayer) is effective: "it is an experience, not a philosophy or even theology."

This is another recurring theme in Kathleen Norris's narrative of her return to faith. Faith must be experienced in the way any important story is experienced—as a whole person—mind, emotions, body, will, actions. And once again, music does exactly that. Hymns that moved her as a child, move her as an adult, for deeper reasons.

As does Scripture, especially, again, the stories—stories of people trying to live faithfully, often failing, but then finding grace and trying again. As was the case with her. She finds the Bible too profound and wise to be dismissed or demythologized. And she finds settling and meaningful the simple acts associated with the rhythm of the church year—holidays, baptisms, acts of service. Sometimes even the preaching.

She gives the example of once helping out with a funeral. While the service is going on upstairs, the women—who else?—are preparing the simple meal that will follow. "As I put bowls filled with coffee creamer or sugar on the tables, I hear fragments of the Lord's Prayer, a reading from Genesis, a hearty tenor singing Thomas Dorsey's 'Precious Lord, Take My Hand.'" During the meal and the clean-up afterwards, she visits with people she has not seen for years.

So what? How does joining others in putting out sugar bowls, cleaning up afterwards, and chatting with folks one has long not seen and might not soon see again relate to faith or Returning to it? The answer is that for Norris faith in God only began to work again when it permeated her entire life, from putting out sugar bowls at funerals to doing the things one does, week after week, in a worship service. "It was the ordinary events of life itself, coming 'in between' the refrain of the church service, with its familiar creeds, hymns, psalms, and scripture stories, that most developed my religious faith. Worship summed it up and held it together, and it all came to seem like a ballade to me, one that I was living."

Worship for Norris is both an action of faith and an increaser of faith. It is possible because of faith and at the same time makes faith more possible.

We worship because we have faith, and worshipping also strengthens that faith. For Norris, worship is best expressed in liturgy. Not surprisingly, Norris the poet declares "theology is prose . . . but liturgy is poetry." To be meaningful, the liturgy must become part of you, not just something you recite.

Liturgy for Norris is all about symbol and metaphor—not as decorations but as carriers of meaning and spiritual reality. She cites Gail Ramshaw: "If faith is about facts, then we line up the children and make them memorize questions and answers [that is, catechism]. . . . But if we are dealing with poetry instead of prose . . . then . . . [w]e memorize not answers but the chants of the ordinary"—the "ordinary" being a reference to the parts of worship included in every Mass, such as the Kyrie, Sanctus, and Agnus Dei. Make those verbal expressions of faith a part of who you are and what you do and you will learn to worship. As Norris did, especially as modeled by the Benedictines.

Norris was herself surprised to find she was drawn back toward church and toward belief. "It was a shock to realize that, to paraphrase Paul Simon, all the crap I learned in Sunday school was still alive and kicking inside me. I was also astonished to discover how ignorant I was about my own religion."

This raises two important points for many Returners to faith. First, they often find that faith is something deep in their bones, imprinted in their spirit, perhaps even in their brains. It is something easy enough to leave, even to disparage, but they leave faith more readily than faith leaves them. It's sort of like weeding dandelions—you can break off the plant at ground level, but if you don't get the root, it will be back. Norris had no eagerness or even intention to return to faith, but she found it bubbling up around her and within her.

The second point is also a common one: for many years she had rejected a Christianity that was in fact a caricature. When as a late adolescent she severed herself from church and Christian influences, she lost contact with experiences of faith—inside the church and out—that would have deepened her sense of what faith is and could be for a maturing person. Ongoing growth in faith, intellectual and experiential, was cut off, to be replaced by the caricatures of faith from her new influences. She was like someone who knows she doesn't like beets because she tried them unsuccessfully as a child, only to discover as an adult that they taste better than she remembered.

In returning to a community of faith, both parts—community and faith—were necessary and interactive. She is able to return to faith only because she was welcomed into a community. She returned to church before she returned to faith. And the people in the church, without strategy or plan, did the right things. First, they welcomed her without a lot of investigation into what she believed or didn't believe. She says she was thankful to "the congregation for not using . . . heavy-handed tactics on me when I first began attending church. They had respected the mystery of faith—it's like a marriage, in that only the two parties involved really know what's going on—and had pretty much left me alone to work out my relationship with God, and with them."

The second thing they did was to model a simple, everyday, down-to-earth kind of life of faith that seemed both authentic and doable for Norris. "The people in the congregation did evangelize in another sense, by saying and doing things they probably don't remember. . . . [L]ittle things they said or did revealed their faith in healthy and appealing ways." She needed to experience a faith that worked in people's lives before she was willing to risk embracing it again herself. "In retrospect, I can say I joined the church out of basic need; I was becoming a Christian, and as the religion can't be practiced alone, I needed to try to align myself with a community of faith."

The verb "was becoming" is important. Neither as a child nor as an adult did Norris experience a specific, transformational *moment* of being "saved" (she often puts the word in fright quotes, indicating her own discomfort with that way of verifying salvation). She left faith quickly, but came back only slowly over many years. She seems to believe that she is always "becoming a Christian"—something others might call sanctification. She cites Karl Rahner's claim, "I have still to become a Christian," and says monasticism has taught her the need for "continual conversion."

The monks and nuns and the tradition they represented offered Norris not only hospitality but a family. Long after her first encounters, she joins them as an oblate, a lay person dedicated to following the Benedictine rule as much as possible in life outside the monastery. "Once I became an oblate, I found that I had gained an enormous family . . . and like a good family they keep interfering in what I like to pretend is my own life." This family tree includes all the believers of the Bible, and throughout church history, and in her own family tree, and in her little Lemmon church. Not a perfect family, of course, but a needed one.

Norris says she didn't realize she had returned to faith until others told her so. "I first began to think I might have faith, because someone I trust had seen it in me." She describes being invited to teach at a monastic conference and being interrogated by a bishop who questioned whether her theological understandings qualified her to do so (the ghost of childhood confirmation, one could say). The monk who had issued the invitation defended her, calling her "a woman of faith." "I was stunned; never in my life had I thought of myself that way, and here was a monk saying it about me." (Jesus identified faith, or the potential for it, in some of his followers in similar ways.)

And Norris warns against the trap of thinking that a person can be "a church of one." Faith occurs within community and for the benefit of the community. She cites the question Jesus asks in the first chapter of John of some men who approach him, "What is it you seek?" The question is also asked of new monks when seeking acceptance to a monastic community. A traditional answer is, "The mercy of God and fellowship in this community." The church would do well to ask this same question of new members today, and they would do well to give this answer.

Norris offers a bit of hermeneutical analysis of a passage in Luke to make a point about the role of community in faith. She says the oft-cited words of Jesus, "the Kingdom of God is within you" (Luke 17:20–21, NRSV) is more accurately translated "the kingdom of God is *among* you" (a direction various contemporary translation take). That is, no one person hosts the kingdom of God. It only exists where two or three—or many more—are gathered together. Norris found the kingdom again in Lemmon, South Dakota (and in the Dakota monasteries) and became part of it.

## GIVING BELIEVERS AND RETURNERS SOMETHING TO DO

A common idea among folks devoted to building the church is that faith must be made easier for people, especially for moderns. Others say it should be made harder—or at least challenging. The former view gives us seeker churches and progressive churches, where as many obstacles as possible are removed, critics say too often including the scandal of the incarnation and the cross and any notions of sin or self-sacrifice. The latter view embraces those scandals and would seem to agree with the Marine recruiting strategy of seeking only the fit and the few.

Norris's example appears to fall somewhere in between. She is against testing for theological purity, but also seems to be in favor of expecting more from believers than mere church attendance and social awareness. In her own case, the church asking things of her was a key part of her return to faith.

Shocking to Norris, one of the things they asked was for her to preach. She suspects it arose from her grandmother's reputation as an excellent Bible teacher, and the assumption that the writer-granddaughter would be effective as well. The church was looking for a new pastor and they asked her to help fill the pulpit while they searched.

The woman inviting her said, "You're a writer, you can do it." She wasn't sure she could. "I had to contend with my own uncertain Christian faith."

Could one proclaim the faith without even being sure what kind or amount of faith one had? (Of course one could, preachers do it all the time.) She says, "the need was there, and I was able to answer it." Norris says answering this call to preach "helped my faith to mature. The writing and delivering of sermons was an agent of my conversion."

There's a lesson here. Churches flourish when they expect things from their members—even difficult things. The early church made it difficult to join—requiring evidence that people knew what the faith entailed and what they were getting into. Once members, they were expected to serve—each other as well as God. Volunteering—in service to the church and to the larger community—is not merely "doing good"; it is working out one's salvation.

Norris says that in her preaching she tried to think of herself as a translator more than an evangelist, someone to help people better understand the sometimes strange vocabulary of faith as it has been traditionally expressed (later writing *Amazing Grace: A Vocabulary of Faith* with this goal). She was honest with them about her own crooked path back. "I reminded the congregation that people making their way back to church, as I had done, often felt helpless, at the center of a storm." Elsewhere in her writing, she cites the plea of the early church theologian Philo of Alexandria to always "be kind, for everyone you meet is fighting a great battle."

Throughout her returning, Kathleen Norris was, indeed, fighting a great battle. She was able to win it only because she returned to a community that approximated what the church should be: ordinary folks trying to be faithful to a great, all-encompassing story. After one sermon counseling patience with and kindness to returners, a young woman approached her and said, "'I've just begun finding my way back to all this, and I think you can help me.' I was stunned: *me, of all people?*"

Things had come full circle. The woman guided by many others was now herself a guide.

And she continues to be a guide—in her relationships and in her writing. Norris hears often from "people who are exiled from their religious traditions," who have "an enormous hunger for spiritual grounding." She describes one woman who wrote to her expressing a struggle that mirrors in many ways Norris's own pilgrimage. In the process she cites themes that arise in the life of many Returners.

"One woman wrote to me to say she felt a great longing for ritual and community; she said she wanted to mark the year with more than watching the trees change. She'd joined some political organizations and a women's service club but found that it wasn't enough. She was afraid of even thinking of joining a church—the Bible makes her angry, more often than not—but she thought she might have to."

Here it is in one person: the need for something more, for community, for a foundation—for meaning, really—that can't be satisfied by even worthy secular activities, and yet a fear of religion, perhaps with wounding past experiences. A woman who needs some guides, some hospitality, and a community that will let her take her time in finding her way to faith—whether for the first time or once again. True for the letter writer, true for Kathleen Norris.

## RETURNING TO A DIFFERENT FAITH AS A DIFFERENT YOU

Norris's path back to faith reveals something crucial to all such stories. One does not necessarily return to the same expression or understanding of faith as one left, and one certainly does not return as the same person. "I'm not denying the past, or trying to bring it back, but I am seeking in my inheritance what theologian Letty Russell terms a 'useable past.'"

Norris sees herself as navigating between equally unappealing poles, a kind of Scylla and Charybdis of dangers. She points out that the root meaning of the word "religion" is the Latin word for ligament and continues, "For me, religion is the ligament that connects me to my grandmothers, who, representing so clearly the negative and positive aspects of the Christian tradition, made it impossible for me either to reject or accept the religion wholesale. They made it unlikely that I would settle for either the easy answers of fundamentalism or the overintellectualized banalities of a conventionally liberal faith. Instead, the more deeply I've reclaimed what was good in their faith, the more they have set me free to find my own way."

Though she does not dismiss the faith of her fundamentalist grandmother Norris, even acknowledging that some of her seeds are still within her, it is not one she can return to. Neither is their enough sustenance in a rationalistic version that equates faith with simply being a good, spiritual person. Her best option is to explore the path trod by her grandmother Totten. It is not that Norris's faith will be identical, but that it will express itself in a similar spirit of quiet love and kindness, united with service to the church and her neighbors.

"Growing up doesn't necessarily mean rejecting the religion of our ancestors, but it does entail sorting out the good from the bad in order to reclaim what has remained viable." Norris has spent the years since returning to South Dakota seeking to define and reclaim what is viable—to find a "useable past." The main thing her grandmother gave her is "livable faith and a tolerance that allowed her to be open to the world."

A livable faith included a graceful balance between tangible experience and truthful theology. She credits the Benedictine monks and the stories of the desert with teaching her "how easily and even beautifully theology converts into experience, and vice versa." Let people experience love and acceptance and forgiveness and, in time, they will be open to the theological truths that attempt to explain it.

And Norris's use of "open" does not signal a relativistic shrug about human behavior. It is more the openness that made Jesus comfortable hanging out with tax collectors, prostitutes, and a wide variety of sinners. It accepts the biblical claim that "all have sinned" and realizes that, as someone once taught me, if you are wounded in the left leg, then I am wounded in the right. So let's seek healing together.

If Kathleen Norris does not return to the same expression of faith that she left, she also doesn't return as the same person. And then again she does. "I am the same person who departed, so long ago, and not the same at all."

I think she means the same in the sense that she is still a human being with all the needs and desires of every human being. And she has the same temperament, same basic personality, many of the same abilities and core values.

But she left faith in her late teens, and more than twenty years passed to the time she acknowledged a return. She cannot be the same woman, just as she can't step in the same river twice. She has had too many powerful experiences, for good and for bad. She has thought too much, loved and lost too much, even suffered too much to be what she was when she left.

Which is just as well. Because the person she was is not adequate for the kind of faith to which she must return. She left as an adolescent, she is returning as a mature woman. She is ready "to put away childish things" (1 Cor 13:11, NLT).

## HER LIFE OF FAITH AFTER RETURNING

Norris has spent the years since "believing again" in a continuing process of trying to understand what "believing again" means for her and of trying, not always successfully, to live it out. She places the incarnation—God becoming one of us—at the center of both her theology and her daily practice of faith. Theologically she believes it to be "the perfect union of the human and the divine," and believes that fusion of the transcendent and the immanent, of spirit and matter—in time and space—provides the model for how she also sees the daily life of faith. "I look to the local, the particular, the specific, to determine how to express my Christian faith." And at the heart of the local and particular are people and relationships.

But so is art. She says, "I still value music and story over systematic theology." Music lives at the borderline between the spiritual and the physical—more accurately, it fuses the two (another incarnation). And story lives in the particulars of human experience—these named people having this detailed experience in this physical setting with these consequences and implications. So the stories of the New Testament—so the stories of Kathleen Norris's life. And so of yours and mine.

But it hasn't all been a stroll in the park. She has had "to rebuild my religious vocabulary," not with a result that would please everyone, including her legalistic paternal grandmother, but in a way that made a return to faith in God possible for her.

Having once, like many, criticized Christians for their hypocrisies, she responded with the following to the sneering question of a college student about how she could stand to go to church when Christians are such hypocrites: "The only hypocrite I have to worry about on Sunday morning is myself." The hint, probably missed, is that the student should do the same.

She goes so far as to say, "I am reluctant to speak of myself as a 'Christian'; I know how deficient I am in practice." When asked in a radio interview if she identifies as a Christian, she found herself answering, "My problem with that is that so many people who publicly identify themselves as Christians are such jerks about it." But she is wise enough to understand that if she is often a hypocrite, she is also sometimes a jerk, so she stays part of the community anyway.

Returning to the Dakotas and to faith has not eliminated all that has troubled her in the past. She admits, "I'm tempted to despair at times," a recurring affliction throughout her life. But she finds that faith ameliorates it. In New York and before "I leaned on despondency like a crutch and flirted with madness." (See her book *Acedia and Me* for more.) She thanks both God and her mentor Betty Kray that "I tend more to gladness now."

The Christian concept of blessing is particularly meaningful to her. "No matter what one believes in, there is something wonderful about blessing things." Part of Norris's return to faith is a heightened sense of having been blessed and of ongoing blessings in the world around her, including the blessing of her own return to faith. On a long Greyhound bus ride that she was dreading, she sees a fellow passenger and her baby—a poor woman, asleep, with a small child asleep on her breast—"a perfect picture of peace. Welcome to the world, I told myself; I hope I know a blessing when I see one."

These are the kind of incarnational "particulars" that characterize the "lived faith" to which she returned.

As mentioned earlier, Kathleen Norris often speaks of returning to faith as returning to an "inheritance"—something of value passed from one generation to the next. At one point she describes attending, after an extended time away, an evening service in a little country church that she "loves very much." It's situated in a pasture, and as the people arrive in pickup trucks, she hugs as many as she can, for she hasn't seen most of them in many months. They watch a spectacular sunset together and when the mosquitoes come out, they go inside and sing "with gusto the hymns of our childhoods: "Amazing Grace," "I Would Be True," "I Love to Tell the Story."

She finishes the account with simple but profound words, "Welcome home."

## Chapter 3

## LECRAE MOORE: REFORMATION RAPPER

> "Life on earth has sharp teeth."
> —Lecrae, *Unashamed*

> "What should have been a people wound became a God wound."
> Lecrae, interview

> "Faith is starting to crumble, these critics starting to mumble
> Oh my God, I feel dead inside, I feel like suicide."
> Lecrae, "Just Like You"

How many famous, Black hip-hop entertainers have been identified with a fatherless, troubled childhood, with entanglements with drugs, violence, random sexual promiscuity, and gangs? How many famous, Black rappers have been identified at one time as Neo-Reformed Evangelical Christians known to cite John Wesley, Charles Spurgeon, Francis Schaeffer, Tim Keller, John Piper, and the apostle Paul? How many have been associated with both? Only one that I know of—Lecrae.

Lecrae Moore's life has had more ups and downs than a basketball. And it started with a down. Having no relationship with his father, and no wisdom from the replacement male authority figures in his life, being sexually abused by a relative as a child, pushed toward violence as a way of establishing his manhood, and spending his adolescence and youth searching for acceptance and escape through alcohol, drugs, crime, and sex, he had no reason to expect anything from life but pain—and he got plenty of it. But he also had a grandmother who prayed and modeled faith for him.

Eventually he found God and fame and riches and praise. But that wasn't the happy ending one might expect. Instead he also found that fame and praise were fleeting, that wealth couldn't buy meaning for his life, and that his Christian fans were both fickle and relatively unconcerned about Black suffering. For a time he equated fellow Christians with God, many of his old demons returned, and he abandoned his faith—exhausted and confused.

There are, among others, two themes in Lecrae Moore's story that are relevant to why people leave faith—the first is the ongoing effect of toxic personal life circumstances, and the second is the failure of the church and of individual Christians to model the fruits of the spirit toward a hurting fellow believer. And there is also an important theme in Lecrae's eventual return to believing again—an unquenchable thirst for meaning and significance, which he found neither in fame and fortune, nor in the quicksand of human praise.

It's all in his story. It's all in his music.

## LOOKING FOR A FATHER

Perhaps the single most significant fact of Lecrae's early life—a fact that will reassert itself repeatedly thereafter—is a father wound. Or more accurately, the wound of a missing father. His father was gone near the time of Lecrae's birth in October of 1979 in Houston. And he never came back. "I became a fatherless child before I could even pronounce the word *daddy*." His total contact with his father in his life: one card, one phone call, a few random drop-in visits.

The result: a decades-long search for proof that he was valuable, and the conviction that he had to earn that valuing. Lecrae says, "the hole left by my father's absence throbbed constantly, like an open wound that refused to scab over." Not having a father in his life, he imagined one. He would "daydream about what it would be like to have a dad around. My imagination filled the hole my father left with romanticized versions of what I thought he would be like." He fantasized that his dad was likely some kind of superhero. The reality was that his father was a drug addict who ended up in prison.

The lack of a father did not mean a lack of males in Lecrae's life. Sadly, they often deepened the wound. Lecrae describes a typical scene from his adolescence. He got into an argument with his mother. A boyfriend at the time stepped in to tell Lecrae off. "Rage and sadness mixed until tears ran down my face and I erupted like a volcano of emotion: 'I want my daddy.'"

The drunk boyfriend threw his can of beer, just missing Lecrae's face, and yelled a devastating and confirming response. "Your daddy had you, then left you. He doesn't care about you."

It made perfect sense to an already wounded boy.

"*'That's right,'* I thought. *'My dad* did *leave me. And probably for good reason. Who would want a punk like me anyway?'*"

He called himself a punk, and many other derogatory names, because that's what the men in his life repeatedly called him. They considered him weak and took it on themselves to toughen him up for his own good—for his own survival.

A key figure in this was his Uncle Chris—himself only just out of his teens. Uncle Chris arranged fights for Lecrae, on which other men would bet and which he would always lose. He also introduced him to drugs, crime, and gang life. But Lecrae speaks favorably of him now, because at least Uncle Chris cared about him and only acted out of his own brokenness.

In a song entitled "Just Like You," Lecrae later captured the degree to which—always looking for someone to model manhood for him—he idolized Uncle Chris and his other uncles.

> I just wanna be like you,
> Walk like, talk like, even think like you
> The only one I could look to
> You're teaching me to be just like you

Wanting to be just like the men and boys around him, because he had no better models, took him to places a kid shouldn't go.

> You showed me stuff I probably shouldn't have seen,
> But you had barely made it out your teens,
> Took me under your wings
> I wanted hats, I wanted clothes just like you,
> Lean to the side when I rolled just like you
> Didn't care if people didn't like you,
> You wanna bang, I wanna bang too.

So what does this culture tell him is success in life? What does it offer for an identity?

> Now all I see is money, cars, jewels,
> Stars
> Womanizers, tough guys, guns, knives, and scars,
> Drug pushers, thugs, strippers, fast girls, fast life
> Everything I wanted and everything I could ask life
> . . . .
> This is the only way they ever showed
> I got this emptiness inside that got me fighting for approval
> because I missed out on my daddy saying, way to go.

A good life? No. But a life that offered him a place, a place where he knew how to be, where perhaps he could be valued. He says elsewhere that he "just wanted to belong," a devout wish that is clear in this song.

> Whoever wants to lead me
> Even though they lie they still tell me that they love me,
> They say I'm good at bad things at least they proud of me.

In the song, he says to his uncles, "Teach me to do the things that men do." It was a job for his father, but his father wasn't there. Lecrae says Chris and the others taught him what they had themselves been taught— be tough, take what you want, grab for pleasure when it's available, never show weakness. None of that gave him what he needed. "Every one of them seemed to challenge my manhood, but no one helped me find it."

And neither did some of the women in his life. He speaks gratefully of his mother who sacrificed for him, and his grandmother who personified faith for him, and of aunts who loved him. But he also speaks of a female cousin who, when he was around six or seven years old, sexually abused him while babysitting. He was introduced to sexuality much too early and much too perversely and says it shaped unhealthy sexual attitudes and experiences with women for years after.

## GOD AND GRANDMOTHERS

So where was God and church in these early years?

They were around, but he didn't believe them particularly relevant. The one who most clearly kept the possibility for God in Lecrae's young life was his grandmother. (The social scientists need to study *that*: how often and how is it that grandmothers throughout time have been the ones to keep faith fires lit in a family? See 2 Timothy 1:5–7.)

His grandmother's name was Georgia, but everyone called her Big Momma. She was one of sixteen children and raised twelve children herself, not all of them biologically her own. She herself was raised by and she continued to be what Lecrae describes as "the on-fire, Pentecostal, tongues-speaking, Holy-Ghost-baptized kind of Christians." Strict and moralistic, she was a legendary philanthropist, taking food to people living under bridges, making endless missionary trips to orphanages across the border in Mexico from her San Diego home, and making her own home an oasis for those in need and in pain. Lecrae, who spent summers at that home, eventually realized she was simply modeling loving Jesus with her whole heart and her neighbor as herself.

But the young Lecrae understood little of it. Even though she had him baptized in the ocean on the way back from one of their mission trips to Mexico, he says, "I didn't fully understand what all this faith stuff meant at the time." Asked at church when he was twelve to give his testimony, he drew a blank. He thought church was for "older people"—"it wasn't for me." He saw faith at work in his grandmother's service to others, but he went to church only at Christmas and Easter and had trouble staying awake even then.

His mother's efforts at making faith relevant to him were even less successful. Once, while he was arguing with his mother, she handed him a Bible and encouraged him to read it. It only made him angrier. "I remember ripping the pages out of the Bible and throwing it on the floor. 'I don't want this Bible.'"

Lecrae sums up the place of God and faith in his adolescence and youth this way: "In a trauma-filled world like mine, God was an afterthought. God was irrelevant. If God did exist, and I had my doubts, He wasn't looking out for people like me. So why would I waste my time looking for God?"

## FINDING MUSIC, FINDING GOD

The young Lecrae did not want God or the Bible. What he did want, he discovered early on, was to make music. At the age of eleven, having no idea who he was or what his future could be, he won a talent contest at the local Boys and Girls Club with a rap performance. He saw the contest as "an opportunity to prove I was good at something," and the robust response of the audience verified it. While he wasn't a good fighter, he excelled at hip-hop.

Hip-hop became the most important thing in his life—and the most positive—not only because he loved the music, but because it "filled the vacuous cavern left by my father's absence." It "told me my pain was valid" and "at a time when I didn't feel heard or seen, hip-hop made me feel significant."

Hip-hop artists such as Tupac and Ice Cube became his heroes, his models for living, as gang members would also become soon enough. The young Lecrae looked to hip-hop to fill all the voids in his life: "Music was my everything. It was my escape . . . my medicine . . . my therapy . . . my identity . . . my companion . . . my sanity. In the face of so many problems, music was my salvation."

But he adds a caveat: "Some of life's struggles are so severe that even music is powerless to overcome them." This is a truth that will be proved repeatedly in his life to the present day.

Due to the sacrificial efforts of his mother, Lecrae went to college (at North Texas State), bringing both his talents and his disabilities with him. Whereas losing one's religion in college is a common story, it was while at college that Lecrae embraced God and religion. It didn't happen because of anything that occurred in the classroom or in the dorms. It happened at a Christian conference in Atlanta. And it overwhelmed and transformed him.

Lecrae says he had been on a quest for answers to life's big questions starting in high school. "I began doing some soul searching, asking questions about the existence of God and life after death." He started searching world religions, even trying on Islam for a short time. He continued studying world religions in college and decided to look more closely into the Christianity of his grandmother.

He began attending church and Bible studies, hearing and learning things that intrigued him. He decided to throw in his lot with these people. "Even though I was not a Christian, I had experienced enough church that I figured I could fake it."

His experience at the Atlanta conference, which he says he attended in order to meet girls and see the city, was the end of faking it. In one sense, his whole life prepared the ground for his conversion, but an immediate factor was the stereotype-breaking performance at the conference of the Christian hip-hop group The Cross Movement. Lecrae says, I saw "guys who had been shot from being in gangs, girls who were extremely promiscuous in the past; I see rappers, dancers and singers; I see people who came from the same background I came from, and they still embodied who they were culturally, but they were all in love with Jesus and I had never seen that before."

Also instrumental was a talk by James White centering on the biblical assertion "we are bought with a price" and emphasizing how strong Jesus was in taking on the world's sin and accepting the pain of the cross, something that appealed more to Lecrae's machismo upbringing than his previous picture of a meek, soft, sheep-loving Jesus. The conviction later that God had protected his life in a roll-over traffic accident added to his urgent sense that he needed to look to Jesus as God-with-us, not to music or the world's pleasures for his salvation.

Lecrae's sums up this pilgrimage in his song "Zombie."

> I was like a zombie
> Till I was awakened
> Chasin' all the Barbies
> Tryna get the bacon
> Pull up in a new toy
> Feelin' like a rude boy
> Always acting brazy but my heart feel like a chew toy
> . . . .
> In the dark, yeah, I was in the dark, I swear you couldn't tell me nothing
> I was after flesh, I guess I was some type of zombie
> Demons used to haunt me
> Then I heard the voice of God, I'm grateful Jesus called me.

## LEGALIST LECRAE THE PHARISEE

Lecrae's conversion was dramatic, and so was the change in behavior, at least for a while. He became, by his own description, a button-holing, holier-than-thou, I'm-right-and-you're-wrong, come-to-Jesus-or-burn-in-hell evangelist. In his own words, the "Life of the Party Lecrae" now competed with the "Legalistic Lecrae." He became obsessed with theology and theological correctness. He read voraciously in order to know more about God, but also to gather ammunition for intellectual contests. "Rather than focusing on winning people, I was trying to win arguments."

Only later did he realize the extent to which his upbringing was shaping his new faith. "I was taking the machismo of the gangsta mentality and wrapping it in Christianity."

Worse yet, he was allowing his long-standing father wound to influence his relationship with God the Father. "As a child and teenager, I wondered if my biological father abandoned me because I wasn't good enough or worthy of love. I felt like one day maybe I could earn his respect, affection, and presence. This distorted view of what a father is like bled into the way I related to God."

All his life he had believed he had to earn acceptance by performance. If he did the expected things in the approved way—whether good things or bad things—people would like and respect him. Win fights, win talent contests, impress the gang and the girls, even fake faith. So it was instinctive that he had to earn God's favor by being a super Christian. Know the Bible, know theology, go on mission trips (like his godly grandmother), tell everyone about Jesus. "Every day turned into a quest to earn God's approval." He says he saw his relationship with God as "contractual" rather than "covenantal."

By definition, human beings come down from every high, and Lecrae was no exception. He says of the time of his conversion, "I had finally been set free, but I was about to find out if I could live free." He found that he couldn't, at least not completely. He returned to old lifestyle habits at the same time that he tried to live for Christ. He impregnated a young woman and coerced her into an abortion, something he says he deeply regrets. He added cocaine to the drug use he began as an adolescent.

As a result, God often felt distant. In the song "Prayin' for You," the speaker claims to be talking to God on behalf of a friend who isn't feeling God's presence in his life.

> he ain't hearin' You
> And he ain't feelin' me and God I know it's killin' You
> Because it's killin' me
> And matter of fact there's somethin' else he's concealin' see
> The person that I've been prayin' about is really me.

If his relationship with God was unhealthy, his relationship with his Blackness was even worse. He read only white theologians because he believed their theology and thinking were "true" theology and superior to anything arising from his own culture. And he equated the Black church with emotionalism and prosperity preaching, both of which he disrespected. "A year into my faith, I developed a deep disdain for the Black church." He didn't understand the diversity within the Black church, assuming they were all like the few he had experienced. "I was blinded by my own arrogance and ignorance of Black church practices."

He also didn't understand the link between Black church theology and social activism, and that theology could and should be an agent for needed change—in the past and in the present. "I completely missed the theological rootedness of the Black church. I was addicted to being intellectually 'right.'" In rejecting the Black church, Lecrae eventually recognized he was rejecting part of who he was—his own identity that he had been seeking his entire life.

## SINGING TO THE CHOIR

It was not long after his conversion that Lecrae's formal hip-hop career began. Because his faith in God was everything to him at that point, his focus was on putting that career in service of what he believed most important. He became what was at the time still something of an anomaly: a Christian hip-hop artist. And he was enormously successful—perhaps too successful for his own good.

Eventually Lecrae wrestled with the term "Christian hip-hop artist," preferring to describe himself as a hip-hop artist who is also a Christian. "I think Christian is a wonderful noun, but a terrible adjective. Are there Christian shoes, Christian clothes, Christian plumbers, Christian pipes?" He thinks using Christian as an adjective makes people expect his songs to be stealth sermons. "My music is not Christian, Lecrae is."

But a look at the lyrics of his early songs, as well as the audiences for which he performed, suggests why he got the label. An early hit was "Souled Out."

> We Souled Out
> Seeking God's face till we fold out
> You want it, we got it
> We ain't tryin' to hold out
> Break me, shake me, mold me
> I rather die like Christ than live unholy.

And there was "We Don't," in which we find the following:

I'm not the standard at all and wouldn't claim to be
But since Christ snatched me up there's been a lot of change in me
I got my world view corrected; I see things eternal
Yeah I've got a whole new perspective

And consider "Take Me As I Am," in which we hear:

Even though they say You loved the world so much You shed Your blood
God, I feel I'm too messed up for love
. . . .
I thought that first I had to clean up my life
Now I'm here and I just need to cling to the light
I'm ready to do it, but Lord I pray you understand
My life is a mess, will you take me as I am?

Songs like these and his inherent talent made him hugely successful with Christian audiences. He sold out arenas, filled up megachurch auditoriums, fans bought albums in the millions. He earned more money than he could count. He won endless awards, including Grammys from the secular music industry (though in the less respected categories associated with Christian music).

At this time Lecrae didn't think it enough to talk only about Jesus and lifestyle and salvation. He wanted to share his theological sophistication with the unsophisticated, something to impress his mostly white theological mentors and upgrade his followers in the Black church. "I needed to infiltrate my community with sound doctrine and good theology, not that foolish Black church stuff they were receiving every weekend." His raps were sometimes less street evangelism and more like classroom lectures. "My lyrics were almost like a cheat code for Reformed theology."

He later indicates that he is not apologetic about the truth of those lyrics, but realizes the unhealthy impulses behind them—"the theology of the lyrics wasn't an issue, but my motivation for using them was. Inwardly, I was being consumed with the desperate desire to be affirmed by other men"—about "how special I was." The old father wounds had resurfaced in a new expression.

## SEEKING A BIGGER AUDIENCE AND LOSING THE ONE HE HAD

Lecrae's career as a Christian hip-hop artist seemed to give him everything he had long wanted—fame, wealth, respect (even adoration). But it didn't give him peace, and, almost overnight, it fell apart. In terms of career, he made two fateful decisions, both of them growing out of naïveté about the subculture in which he was deemed a great success and model. First, he sought to broaden his audience beyond Christians, and, second, he started opening up about his feelings regarding being a Black man in a culture that seemed not to value Black lives.

Lecrae had long been bothered that rap and hip-hop often centered on violence, misogyny, and life-destroying ways of living. Although he lived out those things himself in his youth, he wanted his own songs to give people hope and something worth living for. The lyrics of his explicitly Christian songs did that. But why not do the same for a larger audience? Why live exclusively in the Christian ghetto? "I had a heart for reaching people who were far from God."

And though many Christian leaders considered their world a haven, not a ghetto, Lecrae learned firsthand what the wider world thought of Christians, especially the wider musical world. He writes of his reception at the 2015 Grammy Awards in Los Angeles. Although he had won two Grammys previously, those were in the "Christian" category, seen in the industry as kind of consolation prizes for the less significant. If recognized at all behind the scenes in Los Angeles, he was introduced with "He's a *Christian* rapper." Sort of like being introduced at the Academy Awards with "He makes cartoons."

He knew he was an outsider and he knew what the word "Christian"—whether adjective or noun—meant for most of the people in the industry: "obnoxious . . . irrelevant . . . hypocritical . . . judgmental . . . ignorant . . . bigoted." He decided that being an outsider was simply part of being a Christian, and reiterated his defining assertion at the time that he was "unashamed" of Christ and the gospel.

But Lecrae thought he could be both "unashamed" and also write honest and hopeful songs that would be listened to in the wider culture. He moved toward being more "mainstream." He soon found out this was heresy to many in his Christian audience.

During this time he was also undergoing something of a revolution as a socially aware Black man. He was increasingly in pain at the highly public deaths of Black men and women, especially during confrontations with police. And he increasingly referred to these things in his lyrics and social media postings. He was shocked to learn that many white Christians did not share that pain. He thought the pain of these deaths should be universal, not controversial, no matter how one judged the causes. "*See, to me these young men/boys represented my cousins, my nephews, my neighbors, my family. My heart broke for them and their families.*"

He thought that Christians were his new family and that they would feel the pain too. Instead, they started calling him ugly names. When he began going mainstream, they called him a "sellout" and a "fake" Christian. Now they added liberal, Marxist, social justice warrior, and race baiter. "They dismissed us as heretics and liberation theologians without ever speaking to us or listening to our pain."

Lecrae lost fans—thirty thousand social media followers canceling him in one day—he lost friends, he lost the approval of mentors and leaders, he lost opportunities for work. More important, he lost his sense of place in the world. He lost his late-discovered answer to the question, "Who am I?" He says, "I was unprepared for the chaotic behavior from fellow Christians—betrayal, backbiting, marginalization, embarrassment, shame, even spiritual abuse—and the church hurt that followed."

Worst of all, his fall from grace in the conservative Christian subculture caused him to doubt the character and the grace of God—and eventually even God's existence. More vital than the question of white Evangelical attitudes about Black lives and bodies, was *"Does God care about Black bodies? Does God see this evil, and does he recognize the sound of our cries?"* Abstractly—"in my mind"—he knew the answer was "yes." That was theology's answer. But he didn't know if it was true experientially. Was God a God "who was close to the oppressed, who advocated for them—God the defender"?

Lecrae says he we was "politically apathetic" before 2016. He was bothered that white Evangelicals seemed as a group, and almost instinctively, to oppose Barak Obama during his time as president. But he was genuinely shocked when they largely embraced Donald Trump. Like many Christians, he thought Trump had no chance to be nominated, much less elected. When both happened, and when he started seeing MAGA shirts at his concerts, he felt even more keenly his alienation from those he had once considered kindred spirits.

And Lecrae was not only receiving darts from conservative, white Christians. A Black academic said dismissively, "Lecrae is a mascot for white evangelicalism," a version of the old "Uncle Tom" slur. While painful, Lecrae took it to heart. He realized that part of his acceptance among Christians was that he was considered "safe . . . for white suburban Christian kids." He invokes Malcolm X's distinction between the "field Negro" and the "house Negro" and decides he had become the latter—someone considered safe by the master. The Christian music industry as a whole was open to Black hip-hop artists, but Christian "followers wanted our theology, our rhymes, our concert experiences, but not our Blackness."

There is a third force in Lecrae's life at this time that combines with his rejection by many Christians and leads him out of Christianity and contributes to a major collapse in his life. And that is the reopening of old wounds and old behaviors connected to those wounds. As his career is under threat, and the enormous pressures of celebrity and staying on top and crazy busyness take their toll, threatening even his marriage, he returns, as he has in the past, to destructive habits to numb the pain. He starts binge drinking, self-medicating with pills of all sorts, spending hours with pornography, and the like.

Eventually he falls into clinical depression. When he shares this with fellow believers he gets mostly Christian clichés—"just pray about it," "take it to the Lord," "let go and let God." He discovers that Christians generally are okay with terms like "trials" and "struggles," but have little understanding or even sympathy for genuine "depression" or other types of mental illness. Real Christians shouldn't have those problems, and if they do, God will fix you up if you ask.

Eventually, Lecrae came to realize that he wasn't just having "trials," he was suffering from a lifetime of trauma, and that the attacks of Christians were just the latest. Collectively, all these things—the abandonment by Christians, the return of his self-destructive habits, the cumulative effect of a lifetime of trauma—led Lecrae away from the church and away from God.

"When I started speaking out about issues of justice, God's people did not love me. They did not embrace me. And what should have been a people wound became a God wound. People had turned their backs on me, but I lumped them in with God and said, 'God has turned his back on me, because his people did.'"

He adds, "I became embittered . . . with all of it." He says he broke all his own rules he had set for himself. "I turned my back on the God I said I would never turn my back on. I was Peter. I was in full denial."

He sums up this part of his life's journey in "Restore Me":

> I lost everything I had inside a couple years
> Lost my faith, I lost my mind, I lost a lot of tears
> I spoke up about these problems that I saw outside
> People turned they back on me, you woulda swore I died
> Molested, abused, abandoned, arrested, accused, and stranded
> I grew up with all this trauma, it's nothing, forget it happened
> Ten years later it show up, life is starting to blow up
> Faith is starting to crumble, these critics starting to mumble
> Oh my God, I feel dead inside, I feel like suicide.

Lecrae is honest about his own contributions to the collapse of his life at this point, as is seen in many of his lyrics, including these from "Drown":

> I'm drowning
> I'm drowning
> Lost in this world with these waves all around me
> Deep in the darkness
> Where it's heartless

Even at his lowest, Lecrae becomes only a half-hearted atheist, expressing uncertainty about God's existence, but not deciding the issue conclusively. But he does doubt greatly the goodness of God, the relevance of God, and the presence of God in his life. He does leave the church, and when explicitly asked if he left Christianity, he says "yes."

## A BIGGER CHURCH:
## FINDING A BLACK ST. MARK IN AFRICA

So how did he find his way back?

Essentially through three pathways. First, he expanded his understanding of Christianity and of the world church, making it possible to return to an expression of faith that he felt more had more integrity and was more inclusive than the one he left. Second, he sought and received skillful, professional help for his clinical depression that, along with renewed spiritual strength, allowed him to come to terms with his lifelong traumas. And third, he found friends—old and new—who came alongside and helped him find his way back to God. Together, they allowed him to find again a meaning for his life that he found nowhere else.

God became real to him once more. Lecrae had been on a quest for truth and meaning and significance from early on; he finally decided that only God was big enough to satisfy that quest.

A central factor in Lecrae's departure from faith was his church wound, the abandonment he felt from believers when he no longer satisfied their expectations. As he says, he allowed that church wound to become a God wound. God the Father seemed to have abandoned him, just as did his earthly father. For Lecrae to be healed, he needed a wider, healthier understanding of the church and of God. He began to get that on a trip to Egypt.

A significant contribution to Lecrae's psychological and spiritual collapse was simple exhaustion. This exhaustion was linked to his habitual need to earn and maintain approval by fulfilling people's expectations. If it was stressful to get to the top of his profession, it was even more stressful to stay there.

His therapists told him to schedule significant breaks from the incessant demands of his life. So he and Darragh, his wife, took a long trip to Egypt—about as far away as he could get. What he found there contributed to the recovery of his health and his faith.

He found, for instance, a history of Christian faith among people of color that was older than anything he had known of before. Coptic Christianity was not only ancient, it had survived centuries of persecution. He was "moved" and "inspired" by stories of faithfulness while under oppression. "They were an example of faithfulness in exile and under extreme duress and persecution," and learning about them "exploded the limitations of what I expected from followers of Jesus."

He was startled by an icon of St. Mark. "One of the foundational pillars of the church was depicted as a dark-skinned man, just like me, in the entirety of his humanity." The experience led him to an important question: "*Why haven't I heard of these people before?*"

Always a reader and explorer, Lecrae widened his search beyond the white theologians he had thought defined faith most accurately and exhaustively. He discovered Black theologians, thinkers, and Christian activists, from Tom Skinner to James Baldwin to Cornel West to James Cone. He sought "to craft a more holistic version of the faith."

This search led him to discard his previous disdain for the Black church, and he no longer thought Black culture inferior to white culture. He came to recognize "the beauty of the African tradition." And he came to realize that he could only be a believer as a Black man, because a Black man was what he was and is. His Blackness was not something that needed to be erased or ignored: "I was created to be my fully embodied Black self in my walk with Jesus."

And what is true on the individual level, he realized, is also true on the collective level. No one tradition, no one expression of the Christian faith exhausts what it means to be a Christian or how one ought to live for God. No one group or tradition is able "to fully display the fullness of who God is." He decides he can be evangelical in the biblical sense without being an Evangelical in the contemporary American sense.

Lecrae builds on the historical breadth of Christianity in his advice to those who are disillusioned with faith because they find themselves disillusioned with "the church," or any particular expression of the church. He says we are free (and responsible) to choose our faith community. The Christian faith is a river with many tributaries; search out one that is healthy for you. He himself came back to a wider expression than he left.

### TAKING TRAUMA SERIOUSLY: SAVED AND HEALED

But Lecrae needed more than increased historical knowledge and a bigger community in his return to God. He also needed healing from his traumas. At the time of his initial conversion, he made the mistake of thinking that "saved" automatically meant "healed." The repercussions from those traumas went underground for a season, like locusts or plague bacilli, but they eventually came back stronger than ever.

Lecrae frequently uses the word "chaos" in describing his life at this time (and earlier). He identifies three primary sources of chaos in our lives: "the consequences of our own chaotic decisions," "the broken nature of the world," and "the sin of others." All contributed to his sense of the collapse in his own life. He felt overwhelmed. He tried to minimize his pain by consigning his trauma to a distant past and repeating the mantra, "It doesn't bother me." And he tried to numb that pain in familiar ways—addiction and self-medication.

It only created chaos, but, according to Kierkegaard, chaos can be a preparation for healing. Kierkegaard says we have to understand that we are lost before we will accept being found: "And this is the simple truth—that to live is to feel oneself lost. He who accepts it has already begun to find himself, to be on firm ground. Instinctively, as do the shipwrecked, he will look around for something to which to cling, and that tragic, ruthless glance, absolutely sincere, because it is a question of his salvation, will cause him to bring order into the chaos of his life. These are the only genuine ideas; the ideas of the shipwrecked. All the rest is rhetoric, posturing, farce."

A person satisfied with his or her life is unlikely to change it, even if it greatly needs changing. Failure, unhappiness, trauma—that is, chaos—can be the starting point for healing, for being what one was created to be, not just what one is satisfied to be.

In the midst of his chaos, Lecrae says, "I felt a constant, annoying hum of anxiety." That leads him to ask another important question: "*What is wrong with me?*" One answer? Nothing that can be cured by the pills the doctor prescribed, the alcohol he himself prescribed, or the Christian clichés many fellow believers prescribed.

His church community of the time had little faith in mental health professionals. It saw them, not entirely without reason, as primarily secularists trying to substitute the psychological for the spiritual—more an enemy than ally in healing wounds. But after an extended period of floundering, Lecrae realized "that what I needed most was a therapist, not a theologian."

But not just any therapist. "I wanted someone who could see me as the Black man, the believer, and the artist I was, and respect all these parts of me." It took him a while, but eventually he found a trained professional who he believed God had given the necessary tools to treat him as a whole person and help him back to health and to God, the ultimate source of all health.

## FRIENDS WHO HAD NOT BEEN FOOLED

Lecrae made his way back from trauma and to the church because he got help for the former and a broader understanding of the latter. But he might not have made it back without friendships. "During my darkest days of recovery and restoration, God sent friends who were willing to surround me with love."

He admits he had consistently lied to these men. He lied about his relationship with God and he lied about the kind of life he was living. He had famously declared himself "unashamed" of the gospel to the world, but he was, at the time, desperately ashamed to admit his brokenness even to himself. He got praise from fans for revealing the pain of his upbringing, including the sexual abuse, but that just made him "the hero of my own songs." He hid, even from friends, the fact that he was still broken and living it out.

He discovered his closest friends had discerned that brokenness all along and loved him anyway, as does God. "I really just wanted them to be my 'yes men' for a season. The truth is, they had been seeing everything I had been doing all along and still loved me."

This is perhaps the most common element in stories of Return to faith. People make it back because of other people—other people God works through to reveal himself to the Returner. "When I came clean, they showered me with grace and mercy I hadn't realized was possible. I was rediscovering community with these men and, in doing so, I was also rediscovering God through them."

Grace, mercy, and love are attributes of God. So says the Bible. So says theology. But they can seem like abstractions. How do we know what these things look and feel like in our everyday lives? Lecrae discovered they are most clearly experienced in the way God's people show these things to us.

Lecrae says he feels an affinity with David—a man devoted to God, but with deep wounds and deep flaws. He was a king. He wanted to be godly. But he was also weak and broken, and a man beset with enemies and chaos. When near despair, David cries out to God, as did Lecrae. And both can say, as Lecrae claims for himself, "I sought the Lord, and he answered me" (Ps 34:4).

Lecrae tells his story in prose and in interviews, but he tells it most authentically in his music, because through it he expresses who he is: a sinner saved by grace. As in "Restored."

> I tried living apart from God
> At times I was feeling so far from God
> My faith in His people done left me scarred
> The hatred and hurt was so bizarre
> I thought that they would always ride for me
> I cried, but nobody replied to me
> I questioned the truth inside of me
> And right about then is when the Devil had lied to me
> Like, hold up, God got you? He don't ever show up
> All His people acting like they know you

Tell you that you do it for the money, fame, power, tryna blow up
Why you playin' games? Time to grow up
. . . .
So what's the point of tryna keep it loyal?
Said you had fake faith, you're starting to race bait
Can't even take dates, you hoping to save faith
Tryna to go mainstream in order to reach folk
Ain't nobody rockin' with you, especially these folks
I lost it while I'm drinking liquor in my closet
I used to pray in here, but now I'm saucy
I'm losing money, I'm a lost prophet
I'm making bad decisions every time I get exhausted
Lord, I don't even really know the real me now (Now)
. . . .
Evil, you ain't got no control of me
I'm never too far from the Blood that flow for me
I lost a lot, but got too much to gain, I'll probably never be the same
But I ain't worried 'cause I know He restoring me.

# Chapter 4

# CHRISTIAN WIMAN: REVENANT BELIEVER AND POET

> "I basically do a little linguistic dance around Christianity, as if I were hedging my bets."
>
> "I felt almost as if God had been telling me, as if *Christ* were telling me (in church no less): get off your mystified ass and *do* something."
>
> —CHRISTIAN WIMAN, *MY BRIGHT ABYSS*

CHRISTIAN WIMAN, BORN IN West Texas in 1966, was for ten years the editor of the prestigious *Poetry* magazine. He is the author of a more than a dozen books of poetry and prose. He addresses his spiritual journey most directly and fully in *My Bright Abyss: Meditations of a Modern Believer*. It's quite the ride.

He opens that book with the beginning of an uncompleted poem that he started a few years earlier:

> My God my bright abyss
> into which all my longings will not go
> once more I come to the edge of what I know
> and believing nothing believe in this:

That's is as far as he got. What comes after the colon? Nothing. To that point in his life, he did not know. He wrote many of his poems to try to find out.

## ANXIOUS AMBIVALENCE AS A PERSISTENT STATE OF MIND AND SPIRIT

There is something you need to know about Christian Wiman from the beginning, even though talking about it will get us ahead of ourselves in telling his story. It's this: he is ambivalent about most everything, including the things he considers most valuable. Ambivalence itself often works just fine for a poet, but coupled with it is his conviction that neither logic nor language is up to the task of describing, much less settling, life-defining issues. It bothers him.

You need to know this in advance because it colors every part of his life and every assertion he makes. That colon at the end of his "bright abyss" poem fragment, and his inability at that point to know what follows, is indicative of one of Christian Wiman's defining intellectual, psychological, and spiritual characteristics: ambivalent truth-seeking, accompanied by a significant degree of anxiety. It is the product of a subtle mind and psyche, hypersensitive to nuance and gradations, linked with an overriding desire to affirm only what is true in a quest for ultimate reality, this combined with the intuition that reality is, foundationally, an infusion of the material by the spiritual. (The complexity of that sentence is a consequence of the complexity of Christian Wiman—poet, thinker, and anxious believer.)

Wiman freely admits that anxiety has been a defining quality of his life—in youth, during years away from religious faith, and in the years since returning. Anxiety is a natural psychological companion of struggle and uncertainty—intellectual, psychological, and spiritual. Struggle and anxiety shake hands in agreement that life is difficult.

This anxious ambivalence is also a feature of Wiman's writing style. Over and over he makes an assertion and then—within the same sentence or in the next one or next paragraph or page or chapter—takes it back or highly qualifies it. We see it in his conversion story—"I faked it," "it was real." He says he can live with all the uncertainties of theology if he can take Christ's resurrection as "indestructible fact." But the next thing following the word "fact" is "(*fact?!*)."

Word and phrases of qualification or contradiction are a recurring stylistic feature. After a paragraph in *My Bright Abyss* linking doubt with simply "dullness of mind and spirit," he starts the next paragraph with "Yes, but . . ."—the ellipsis being his—and then launches off on a qualification. And in that same paragraph he answers his own "either-or" type question with "Both. Neither." And follows on the next page with "And now I doubt the premise with which I began." A passing glance at his prose from various places reveals constructions such as the following: "or no, not even that,"

"Or is it?," "And yet, and yet . . . ," "Or maybe," "no, that is not quite right," "Or, more accurately."

Does this indicate an admirable awareness of the complexity and paradoxes within reality and our lives, or is it simply wishy-washiness?

Both. Neither.

Wiman's is a searching kind of ambivalence, not to be confused with indifference or a lazy "whatever" shrug of the shoulders. He is searching for a position on many things, including faith, that is not simply a vanilla averaging of opposing positions, but a simultaneous holding to the truth inherent in opposing views. The majority of even extreme positions have *some* truth in them. Their error, as discussed earlier, is in taking a partial truth as a whole truth. Wiman wants to hold balancing, even seemingly contradictory, truths in tension, not watering them down to a muddled middle, rather letting each contribute to the fullest possible understanding of what is true and good and beautiful.

It's just that he doesn't think human beings, including himself, are very good at doing this. Wiman, as we will see, is jumpy about many traditional theological formulations and their usefulness, but he does seem to believe in some version of the doctrine of the fall. He sees a seemingly unerasable bent or wound in each of us, and collectively in our institutions and common practices, that keeps us from fully knowing and properly valuing the truth, or reality, or God. And, as a poet, he worries about the ability of language to capture any of this. He says of his audience that he writes for others "at once as confused and certain about the source of life and consciousness as I am."

Essentially, Wiman is a questing skeptic—doubtful about many things, doubtful of his own ability to adequately understand and express, but questing, nonetheless, to know and understand more fully, seeking to commit to something bigger than himself and a flatly atomic world—and to live out that commitment. An industrial-strength Yearner.

His reflections on his prayer life are typical. "I have never felt comfortable praying," adding, "I'm never quite sure that what I do deserves the name." He admits that he prays without complete confidence that God even exists—"I address God *as if*"—and describes his common experience of "praying while wondering how and why and to whom I prayed," while at the same time identifying prayer as a time when many meet the (embodied) transcendent. Wiman then chastises himself for such wavering.

It is a great oversimplification to call Wiman a doubter—as in the tired-out faith versus doubt paradigm. He is frequently dismissive of a lifelong *commitment* to doubt, seeing it as a lazy pose more often than a sincere inquiry. He says such doubt asks nothing of us, allowing us to passively stagnate. This is especially true for the tenuously committed, waiting for certainty, neither fully in nor fully out regarding faith: "O my easy, hazy God—one more little riff on the Ineffable." Wiman is relatively impatient with such stances because he sees it within himself and doesn't like it.

He also doesn't like, but is trying to accept, the reality that, as the Welsh poet R. S. Thomas writes, "God will never be plain," and that faith, for him at least, will never be free of struggle and anxiety, an anxiety that results, in part, from the somewhat desperate hope that things will someday, somehow be otherwise. "I always have this sense that something is going to resolve my spiritual anxieties once and for all, that one day I'll relax and be a believer." In Greek tragedy, this hoped for outcome is called "deus ex machina," God in the machine—a reference to the end of a Greek play where an actor representing one of the gods is lowered from aloft and makes pronouncements and settles the issues raised in the play, resolving all tensions and saving the day. It is thought a weak device in the arts and the expectation of it is equally weak in matters of faith.

Wiman has had his share of transcendent moments—in books, in art, in nature, in writing poetry, in relationships with others, and with God. "But always the anxiety comes back." It's the ancient, defining epistemological question—"How can I be sure?" The answer towards which he is journeying in his writing is, "You can't be—and that's all right" (my words). In matters of religious faith—as in art, as in love, as in friendship, as in politics, as in the possibilities for justice—the expectation of certainty is what philosophy calls a category mistake. It's like asking of a great race horse why it can't fly.

Wiman's pilgrimage suggests that it is far more reasonable—and effective—to accept unsettledness as something that can be part of faith rather than something that must be eliminated from faith. It's what any number of people in the Bible do. And it seems to be where Wiman is heading in his writing, hoping that his unsettledness might even be useful. "I should never pray to be at peace in my belief. I should only pray that my anxiety be given peaceful outlets, that I might be a means to a peace that I myself do not feel." It's one reason he writes.

## UPBRINGING AND EARLY FAITH—"FOR ALL / THE PAIN / PASSED DOWN / THE GENES"

Three words reveal much about Christian Wiman's upbringing and initial Christian faith: fundamentalist, Baptist, Texas. Throw in small town and West Texas and you know even more. Wiman has, as one would expect, complex and conflicting attitudes toward this background. He describes his hometown—Snyder—in three words as well: "tiny, parched, purgatorial."

Both before and after his return to faith in his late thirties and forties, he writes some poems and essays about the people of faith he knew that are scathing and edged with scorn. At the same time, he professes appreciation for the intensity and holistic nature of the faith of those who surrounded him. They were "all in" in a way that he admires, though he finds difficult if not impossible for himself.

Wiman comes from a family with an intergenerational history of violence—to others and to themselves. He tells the story of his grandparents when his mother was fourteen. She is sitting with her brothers at the kitchen table, her own mother at the stove. Her estranged father—Wiman's grandfather—walks in with a gun. Her mother says, "Oh, Fred, no." The father shoots her, the kids run out the back door, and the father lays down beside his dead wife and shoots himself. The kids survived, "but not psychologically intact." It was a reality that Wiman's mother brought with her, never talked about, but always present.

Wiman says of himself regarding his childhood and youth, "I was prone to sudden destructive angers and what my grandmother called 'the sulls.'" He describes his father striking him as the teenage Wiman cursed him and he then retaliating, beating his father with blow after blow which his father, likely feeling guilty for hitting his son, makes no attempt to fend off. That event, he says, "was the end of my childhood."

And there was the shadow of suicide in the family—his grandfather, Aunt Opal, two attempts by his sister, and his own repeated personal ritual of placing a shotgun on the floor, the barrel balanced against his chin, and stretching for the trigger that his arms were too short to quite reach. He adds that he never actually wanted to kill himself, but was, perhaps, simply thinking about "a way of avoiding the more mundane failures of my life."

Does violence run genetically through the generations in families, like cheekbones or hair color?

Add to this that his father would hide away in his room "for months at a time," severely depressed, and that his parents put the whole family through "a nasty, protracted, ruinous divorce in which their children will be used as weapons," and you can see why Wiman says he chose which college to attend "entirely on the basis of its distance from Texas." In college he took up reading poetry, for its form, its music, and "the fact that, as far as I could tell, it had absolutely nothing to do with the world I was from."

All this and more, and yet Wiman, ever the one to see all sides of everything, also says, "my family's very chaotic, but I would not say that I had had a difficult childhood, compared to a lot of people I've seen since then, because I was loved by my family. And a lot of people grow up without love."

Despite everything, he felt loved, and feeling love, as we will see, it central to why Wiman eventually found his way back to God.

But how and in what sense did he find God (or vice versa) in the first place? That is a strange story that Wiman claims never to have understood, then or now.

But first some context: "we went to church three times a week, recited Bible verses over breakfast, and described ourselves as 'charismatic evangelicals.'" (An aside: if they were comfortable with the term "charismatic," they weren't like the Texas Baptists I grew up with.) He says "even in my most pious times I detested church, would often have to be disciplined for my insubordination during the sermons." The only time he paid attention was during testimony time in Wednesday evening services. Think story time, which is what testimonies are, not the theology or judgment time of many Sunday mornings. "I was riveted by those trials of fire," including the testimony of a woman who bore the scars from cutting her own wrists and of the drug-addicted man whose friends strapped him to a bull in a bizarre effort to break his habit.

Wiman's was an extremely monocultural world. "To call the place predominately Christian is like calling the Sahara predominately sand: I never met anybody who didn't believe, until I went off to college. Never met a soul." He says he was raised in "that flat world of work and blunt fundamentalism."

And that world was clear on what it meant to be saved—a word Wiman now says, like Norris, he no longer considers "accurate or helpful." "I grew up with a notion of radical conversion, as sudden, sometimes ravaging call for which the only answer was your life. You must be born again." Wiman's boyhood conversion didn't quite follow that script, but it was close enough.

It happened in one service when he was twelve or so. An altar call was given—the opportunity for anyone in the pews to come forward and publicly declare their acceptance of God's forgiveness and imprint on their life. Wiman jumped out of his pew, but instead of "going forward," as expected, he fled to the church basement. He claims to only vaguely remember the experience, but says he was "filled with Spirit, I was saved." Wiman's father found him in the basement, "muttering incoherently, weeping—ecstatic. . . . I had been called, claimed."

But what did it mean? Wiman says he didn't know then and doesn't know now. He says he barely remembers it. In fact, he claims "the moment means nothing to me now, and I am inclined to rationalize it away." He says the West Texas Baptist culture, leavened with charismaticism, primed him to have such an experience and his "imagination and primordial boredom conspired to answer that expectation with an outright rapture. In short, I faked it."

Which is exactly how the intellectual culture of his college and adulthood would have him see it—a conditioned, emotional response to manipulative pressure. A negative interpretation, also "conditioned."

But then Wiman considers another possibility. "There are problems with this explanation." The theatricality and attention-generating quality of the experience was totally contrary to his personality, and therefore not likely self-manufactured. "There's another option, of course: it was real." Can't prove it, but can't prove otherwise either. "Maybe it happened—and goes on happening.... Maybe ... I don't remember it, but it remembers me."

## LEAVING GOD—WHO PERSISTS IN HANGING AROUND

Unlike many, Christian Wiman did not leave God and his own fundamentalist upbringing with anger, accusations, and bitterness. He simply left. He had been raised in a context that expected, even demanded, belief. When that context changed, the beliefs it supported left with it. As did any love he had for God. "Love does not die without our assent, though often (usually) that assent has been given unconsciously long before we give it consciously." People begin leaving faith, as they leave marriages, long before they consciously acknowledge even to themselves that they are leaving.

Wiman says he had a "bookless ... childhood." He also says that in college and afterward he picked up a "bookish atheism." His movement away from God was not sudden or dramatic, but it was relentless and, eventually, complete. "If some tear truly occurred in the membrane between my existence and existence itself, my mind and God's, it seems to have sealed utterly." He simply stopped thinking about God. God was no longer part of his mental furniture—neither as antagonist or comforter—sort of like a long-forgotten adolescent girlfriend.

Wiman didn't replace God with some other identifiable creed. Similarly to Kathleen Norris, he replaced God with poetry. The reading and writing of poetry became the center of his life. He writes of "falling away from my childhood faith and transferring that entire searching intensity into literature." This is what Matthew Arnold in the nineteenth century, and many others since, have assumed will happen with all intelligent men and women. Faith will wither everywhere as reason, science, and aesthetic experience take its place. Wiman now describes such a view as "not simply quaint but dangerous," but does acknowledge that "poetry is how religious feeling has survived in me."

Wiman also says he had an "unacknowledged belief or need for belief," but that it was "crucified on the crosses of science, humanism, art, or (to name the thing that poisons all these gifts of God) the overweening self." At the age of twenty, he made being a poet his life aim and also believed that he had to be "all in" in that pursuit, just as so many in his youth were "all in" on living as Christians.

That life commitment led him all over the world—from Prague to Paris to many places in America. But in an essay written a few years before he returned to God, he observes, "I've just made my fortieth move in fifteen years," adding, "There is something missing from all this motion, some hunger that all this seeing never sates." It was a hunger that he could not satisfy with poetry. "I have had addresses in all these places, homes in none." It is a common theme in Leavers and Returners—a search for home.

During all those moves, Wiman says, "I did not think of God" except as "an ultimate synonym for ultimate absence, some vague and almost purely rhetorical gesture that signaled little more than a failure of both words and intellect." The only important thing about God was that he wasn't there and couldn't even be talked about usefully.

He describes himself during these years as "drifting through the days on a tide of tiny vanities—a publication, a flirtation, a strong case made for some weak nihilism—nights all adagios and alcohol as my mind tore luxuriously into itself." He describes himself as one of those "who have gone to war with our own minds," a condition he has still not fully escaped.

That war includes internal battles with his upbringing—sometimes affectionate, sometimes mocking. In an essay written when he was thirty-five (and prior to his Return), "A Mile from Hell," he sketches a condescending view of the people in the church of his youth. Roped into a mission trip to Africa in his mid-twenties with those folks and his father, he resorts to crude stereotyping in describing one man as follows: "Blunt, boyish, with one of those edgeless and preternaturally pink faces I associate with middle-American Protestantism." He imagines in derisive tones how these people would likely view favorably the basement conversion experience that he himself no longer values. He pictures how they would, at the time, wonder "what I'd be when I grew up, a preacher, like as not, for hadn't I wept and trembled in the church that day, and look how I had burned with His fire, when the Lord, praise be, had taken hold of my heart."

At that point in his life, Wiman was having none of it. He wonders during the mission trip what his father, a psychiatrist at a state hospital for the criminally insane, might himself believe or not believe about God. He says he doesn't have the kind of relationship with his father to ask him, so he imagines how his father might answer a question about his religious convictions: "What might he say? *I believe in a literal Heaven and Hell, that God sent his son Jesus to die on the cross for my sins and the sins of all humanity.* Too simplistic. *It's a metaphor, a story, a way of organizing and giving meaning to your life.* Too mild. *All religions are one religion, which is to urge toward transcendence; it is not the tale that saves us, but the telling.* Too intellectual. *I'm not religious, but I'm spiritual.* Too squishy."

He is imagining what his father might say, but he might well be describing how he would answer the question for himself at that time. For Wiman, no description of God and faith has ever been adequate. Our minds, our hearts, and language itself are not up to the task.

Wiman doesn't leave his critique of fundamentalism solely to prose. Two poems, written in the midst of his return to faith, are especially harsh. In one, "The Preacher Addresses the Seminarians," the speaker, a preacher, is advising future preachers. (Wiman himself now teaches divinity students.)

> I tell you it's a bitch existence some Sundays
> and it's no good pretending you don't have to pretend
>
> don't have to hitch up those gluefutured nags Hope and Help
> and whip the sorry chariot of yourself
>
> to whatever hell your heaven is on days like these . . . .

And then there's his picture of his childhood church in "We Lived."

> We lived in the long intolerable called God.
> We seemed happy.
>
> I don't mean content, I mean heroin happy,
> donkey dentures . . .

He concludes his description this way:

> I mean
> to be mean.

Well, he succeeds at being mean. One wonders if he includes his mother and grandmother and aunt in these portraits. He seems not to, saying of the latter two, "God was almost instinctive in them, so woven into the textures of their lives that even their daily chores, accompanied by hymns hummed under their breath, had an air of easy devotion." He contrasts their "unanguished faith" with "my own vertiginous intensities" and declares that their "quiet constancy is a disposition to which I aspire."

It was not something to which he aspired in his away years. He aspired then to be a poet and thought that was goal enough. But then he found he was likely, soon, to die.

## RETURNING—TO A DIFFERENT PLACE THAN HE LEFT

Wiman returns to something ultimate (though experienced through the finite), something that can be called God (though the word puzzles him), something that can be called faith (which he sometimes distinguishes from belief), something that even can be called Christian (though he remains jumpy about fellow Christians and the church)—but he returns to something very different from what he left, and, true to his cast of mind and spirit, is never fully confident that he can adequately explain what has happened to him.

If that seems like too many qualifiers for one sentence, welcome to the world of Christian Wiman.

Wiman gives a kind of deceptive clarity to the story of his return to God by identifying three events in his life that are central: ceasing to write poetry, finding human love, and receiving a diagnosis for incurable cancer and the intense pain that eventuated. (It appears to me that Wiman is most comfortable with referring to his pilgrimage as a Return to God [and more specifically Christ] rather than a return to faith, but he also uses the terms faith and belief, and so I will use all three terms—return to God, faith, and belief—interchangeably.)

I call the three events "deceptive clarity" not because each is not central, but because there are so many other factors, twists and turns, speculations (on his part), and resurfacing of dormant influences that no simplified telling of the story does it justice.

I am going to begin, therefore, with something that's hard to put one's finger on.

## SOMETHING MORE

In oversimplified terms, what leads Wiman back to God is his growing conviction, consistent with his life experience and vocation as a poet, that there is "something more" (my phrase) to reality than meets the eye, or any of the other senses, including our sense of calculating reason. The purely secular, purely materialistic accounts of reality increasingly fail to match his experience. In searching for something that does, he finds old stories reasserting themselves in his life—ancient stories even, that must be retold in fresh ways, but which move him closer to the heart of what is true and real ("closer" being as much as Wiman will ever admit is possible).

This sense of something more is not new for Wiman. "I have always believed in that 'beyond,' even during the long years when I would not acknowledge God." He invokes the theoretical physicists when arguing that "what we call reality is conditioned by the limitations of our senses, and there is some other reality much larger and more complex than we are able to perceive." He says this deeper reality is not some mystical world that is entirely separate from the sensory, but rather is a deeper reality within the physical, "multiple dimensions within a single perception." Wiman is less interested in trying to understand pure transcendence, than in perceiving the transcendent *within* the immanent, created world and within his own life.

And this transcendent-within-the-immanent is something that Wiman believes art is especially suited to explore. "I *believe* in visionary feeling and experience, and in the capacity of art to realize those things." Some poets, he says, deal only with what the senses can perceive (William Carlos Williams), while others (T. S. Eliot) find a deeper reality within what the senses perceive, "some mysterious resonance between thing and language, mind and matter, that reveals—and it does feel like revelation—a reality beyond the one we ordinarily see."

Wiman discovers the same going on in his own poetry, including, surprisingly to him in retrospect, the poems he wrote when his interests were entirely this-worldly. "From a Window," a poem Wiman says he wrote a couple of months after his cancer diagnosis, begins this way:

> Incurable and unbelieving
> in any truth but grieving,
>
> I saw a tree inside a tree
> rise kaleidoscopically
>
> as if the leaves had livelier ghosts.

He realizes that the tree within the tree is actually birds, creating with their bodies dispersed in the branches a second reality within the reality of the tree alone, making it "seem fuller now," creating a "strange cohesion / beyond the limits of my vision" that suggests "some excess / of life" which it is his blessing to witness.

There's nothing directly in this poem about God—or even directly about transcendence—but it's an example of Wiman's observation that he finds God everywhere in the poetry he wrote during his away years. He finds in the poem now "a weave of meaning I never meant to make."

In another cancer poem, he explicitly rejects God as relevant:

> It is good to sit even in a rotting body
> in sunlight, uncompromised
> by God, or lack of God . . .

The poem continues as the speaker watches a bee land on his leg, savoring this bit of contact with another creature. He says of this poem, "the very possibility" of God "is pushed roughly to the side," but adds "And yet I felt some saving otherness everywhere in me and around me when I wrote it," wondering if there is "such a thing as an anti-devotional devotional poem."

And these "something more" moments are not limited to art. He speaks of times in our lives when we are "overwhelmed by reality spilling its boundaries," including, in his own life, falling in love, in marriage, having and caring for children, while experiencing pain and praying, and so on. Such things "propel one forward into time and connections," including connections with God.

Wiman believes he is not the only one who experiences this sense of "something more." Many thoughtful people (think Yearners?), though discontent with American religion, "feel the burn of being that drives us out of ourselves, that insistent, persistent gravity of the ghost called God." The metaphors are revealing: "burn" suggests fire, which one can feel either as pain or as warmth (both of which Wiman experiences with God), "gravity" is something one can neither see nor touch nor smell, but is no less real for not being directly sensory. Gravity draws you, whether you wish it or not, like the tractor beam of God's love.

Wiman's sense of "something more" co-exists with his belief that God inheres within his creation: "one aspect of God's nature, the infinite inhering in the specific atomic . . . insights that disclose our beings and situate us in something larger than ourselves."

All of these phrases—"visionary feeling and experience," "the beyond," "a reality beyond the one we ordinarily see," "livelier ghosts," "fuller now," "some excess of life," "meaning I never meant to make," "saving otherness," "reality spilling its boundaries," "the burn of being," "insistent, persistent gravity of the ghost called God"—point to Wiman's lifelong sense that there is something more to life than what we can measure and prove, a sense that persisted in his away years and made more possible his return.

## THE DEPARTURE OF THE MUSE

And now to the three life experiences which Wiman identifies as central to his return to God. The first was a drying up of the poetic springs. The sources of those springs stretch back to his childhood. He tells the endearing story of his first poem publication. When he was six or seven, his family visited First Baptist Church in Dallas, the biggest Baptist church in the world at the time. When the pastor gave the altar call, young Wiman ran down the aisle to the front. His parents "thought I was going to get saved." But instead he handed the pastor a poem he had written.

> I love the Lord, and the Lord loves me.
> I will not forget, and neither will He.

The pastor saw to it that the poem was published in the Southern Baptist newsletter, "my biggest publication," Wiman now says with a laugh.

More seriously, Wiman says that his childhood was "the very forge and working-house of poetry," as it is for many writers of all genres. But it wasn't until college and after that poetry became his god.

Having made the writing of poetry the paramount goal of his life, it was no small thing when, in his mid-thirties, he found himself no longer writing poetry. It was less a matter of writer's block than a crisis of belief. Poetry, and the ways he made sense of the world after abandoning faith, could no longer provide the sense of meaning and significance that his soul demanded. They were idols who no longer earned his worship.

Wiman describes his turn away from writing poetry this way: "after making poetry the central purpose of my life for almost two decades, I stopped writing. Partly this was a conscious decision. I told myself that I had exhausted one way of writing, and I do think there was truth in that. The deeper truth, though, is that I myself was exhausted. To believe that being conscious means primarily being conscious of loss, to find life authentic only in the apprehension of death, is to pitch your tent at the edge of an abyss, 'and when you gaze long into the abyss,' Nietzsche says, 'the abyss also gazes into you.' I blinked."

Essentially, Wiman's cessation from poetry was the result of a crisis of faith—the various secular faiths with which he had replaced religious faith, but especially his faith that poetry alone could bear the weight of giving his life the meaning and significance that he required. To again oversimplify, if extinction is the final end of all life, what good is accomplished by writing poems? Human beings have always looked high and low for ultimate meaning, and if there is anything that contemporary secular intellectuals agree on, it is that there is no such thing.

Ironically, making poetry the ultimate thing was bad for his poetry. "I felt that I was giving everything to poetry, and you had to give everything to poetry; and yet, at the same time, I felt some sort of essential energy missing from some of my poems." By limiting himself to engaging only physical reality—which pure secularism claims is all there is—he was robbing his poems of depth.

Poetry had become his religion and it did not provide what he needed to live. "I had to eventually give up that notion that you could give your whole life to poetry, that poetry could be this abstract thing that you could devote your life to. I'd made a god. You talk about idolatry, I'd made a god out of it. And I had to have that shattered in order to come to write some of the poems that are in *Every Riven Thing*. I had to really have that notion tested severely." Moving away from making poetry for a time actually helped him later write better poems. And it left open a place in his life for another center.

Wiman wonders, in fact, whether his decision was entirely his own. "On another level, though, the decision to stop writing wasn't mine. Whatever connection I had long experienced between word and world, whatever charge in the former I had relied on to let me feel the latter, went dead. Did I give up poetry, or was it taken from me? . . . I'm not sure." "Taken from" suggests he thinks it possible that God removed writing poetry from his life as a preparation for his Return to him.

In the early stages of his Return to faith, Wiman returned to poetry, now a vehicle for exploring more than surface reality. "God doesn't give a gift without giving an obligation to use it. *How* one uses it, though—that's when things get complicated." His gift of language and perception is both a blessing and a threat. They can lead him deeper into life and into spiritual reality, but they can also make him only a detached observer of life—and of things of the spirit.

Wiman doesn't return to writing with conventionally religious poems. His anxiety about so many things, including God, continues. He is not at ease about exactly what he believes or how to express it or how he is supposed to live it out. He continues to reject many aspects of traditional American Christianity. But he does call himself a Christian and he writes incisive poems of what that means and doesn't mean for him. An example, entitled "When the Time's Toxins":

> When the time's toxins
> have seeped into every cell
>
> and like a salted plot
> from which all rain, all green, are gone

I and life are leached
of meaning

somehow a seed
of belief

sprouts the instant
I acknowledge it:

little weedy hardy would-be
greenness

tugged upward
by light

while deep within
roots like talons

are taking hold again
of this our only earth.

## THE DISCOVERY OF LOVE—HUMAN AND DIVINE

A poet falling in love doesn't, in itself, seem either unusual or likely to spark a spiritual renaissance resulting in a radical change in how one perceives reality. In Christian Wiman's case, however, the experience initiated a larger quest to discover an adequate grounding for the existence of human love, which contributed to his return to God and to an understanding of God's love for his creation.

It began when Wiman was thirty-seven years old, approximately two years before his cancer diagnosis, at Albert's Café on Elm Street in Chicago. Wiman was at the beginning of his ten-year run as editor of *Poetry*, one of the world's most famous literary magazines. Up to this time, his was a "life deflected by art." If there was not room for God in a life dominated by his omnivorous commitment to poetry, there was also not much room for energy-absorbing relationships. "I thought for years that any love had to be limiting, that it was a zero-sum game: what you gave with one part of yourself had to be taken from another."

In his new love for Danielle Chapman, he discovers otherwise. Just prior to this time, in the midst of not writing poetry, he says "the world went gray for me, and I couldn't accomplish even the simplest actions without great difficulty, the very air viscous and inhibiting." Finding love changed all that. "The sense I have is of color slowly aching into things, the world coming brilliantly, abradingly alive."

Because of love, the world becomes, literally, more real to him. Wiman uses the word "being" to describe fundamental reality—and in time to equate it with God. "It . . . felt, for the first time in my life, like I was being fully possessed by being itself." He cites Simone Weil: "Joy is the overflowing consciousness of reality" and, Wiman says, "that's what I had, a joy that was at once so overflowing that it enlarged existence, and yet so rooted in actual things that, again for the first time, that's what I began to feel: rootedness."

This man who wandered the world, addresses in many places but a home in none, finds in love something that begins rooting him to what is truly real. And this human love, in making the world come alive, pushes him toward the source of all love. "The closer I came to reality, the more I longed for divinity—or, more accurately perhaps, the more divinity seemed so obviously a part of reality."

Wiman explores the link between human love and divine love, dismissing the "I only have eyes for you" clichés of purely romantic love. "We tend to think of love as closing out the world, and we can only see the face of the beloved, and that everything else goes quiet or goes numb. But actually, what I experienced . . . is that the love demanded to be something else. It demanded to be expressed beyond the expression of the participants. It kept demanding more. And that excess energy, I think, is God. And I think it's God in us, trying to return to its source."

The experience of both human love and the longing for the divine source of love led Wiman and Danielle to begin, haltingly, doing some of the acts of faith, including prayer. "We began to say a kind of prayer before our evening meals—jokingly at first, awkwardly, but then with intensifying seriousness and deliberation, trying to name each thing that we were thankful for, and in so doing, praise the thing we could not name." Doing some of the acts of faith before one has faith is, perhaps, like stretching before running.

It got worse. "On most Sundays we would even briefly entertain—again, half-jokingly—the idea of going to church." Church—the place of services he said he "detested" as a child. The place he associated with a "bouncy brand of American optimism" and whose services had been torturous for him in the handful of times he had attended as an adult. At first it was a bridge too far. "The very morning after we got engaged, in fact, we paused for a long time outside a church on Michigan Avenue. The service was just about to start, organ music pouring out of the wide open doors into the late May sun, and we stood there holding each other and debating whether or not to walk inside. In the end it was I who resisted."

Eventually, together, they did find a church—one that made faith in God seem more possible rather than less.

"God's love creates and sustains human love." That God is the source and sustainer of love and that love is a means to explore the mystery of immanent transcendence are ideas that Wiman says he would have "actively denigrated" before he actually experienced it. He and Danielle needed a way of expressing gratitude for the joy and sense of being fully alive that their love gave them—and they found it in a person and in a method. They were "searching for some form in which to put, mostly, our praise, some sense of a being—or Being itself—to receive it." The person was God and the method was prayer and worship.

They were to discover that prayer was necessary for more than praise. It would provide a "beacon and bulwark . . . when the devastation came."

## THE CANCER WARD—NOT ONLY FOR RUSSIAN NOVELISTS

That "devastation" Wiman refers to began with a diagnosis. It came on his thirty-ninth birthday. It told him he had a rare and incurable form of cancer of the blood. It didn't apprise him fully of how much he was going to suffer. And it didn't mention that cancer would be a major factor in his return to God.

Looking back, Wiman sees the timing of his diagnosis as providential (though he doesn't use the word). If he had gotten it earlier in life—before he found love and what it had awakened—he would have taken it as a confirmation of his fatalistic and constricted view of life. "It would have been the bearable oblivion of despair, not the unbearable, and therefore galvanizing, pain of particular grief." The particular grief, which he and Danielle shared, crying together on the couch, "was not my death, exactly, but the death of the life we had imagined with each other." Just when love had entered his life, and made him consider the possibilities again of God's love, the door seemed to be slamming shut on his even having a life.

But not before torturing him first.

As we have seen, Wiman shares in the modern skepticism about the ability of language to adequately describe reality (though, unlike some, he thinks it profitable to keep trying). Nonetheless, he is quite articulate—at times distressingly so—in finding words and metaphors for the intense physical pain he felt for years. Here are some scattered lines from the poem "Darkcharms": "Radiated, palliated, sheened gray like infected meat," "Needle of knowledge, needle of nothingness, / Grinding through my spine to sip at the marrow of me," "up crawls / my cockroach hope, lone survivor of the fire I am." The poem ends with a sound washing over him in the cancer ward: "Now, near me, not me, a girl, shameless, veinless, screams."

Wiman describes an excruciating pressure in his bones as though the marrow in them is trying to explode the bone that encases it. Both the disease and the drugs that combat it eat away at his body: "my inner skin was skinned mouth to bowels." It is not difficult to understand the opening line to that untitled poem: "I don't want to be alive anymore."

He tries again and again to convey what he despairs of conveying. "It's hard to describe extreme pain, and the pain of cancer has an otherworldly intimacy that makes it almost impervious to words. It feels like existence itself is eating you."

Intense suffering—physical and mental—can turn one toward God or away from God. With Christian Wiman, it seems, at different times and even at the same time, to do both. Consider the "I don't want to be alive anymore" poem.

> One is not meant to turn on one's creator
> with ferocity expendable only in one way.
>
> Or is that exactly how one is meant to turn
> to burn
>
> beyond the love that from beyond being
> has come to us.

Elsewhere he says, "Some days fury courses through me with the chemicals and all I want to do is desecrate." And those are the days in which he is able to think at all. Even when disposed to look for God, the pain can be so great that all thought is obliterated. "How does one remember God, reach for God, realize God in the midst of one's life if one is constantly being overwhelmed by that life?" Intense and unceasing physical pain blots out his ability to think about other things. And in moments when one can think, God is likely to be low on the list of things one must think about—including one's spouse.

So how did cancer and suffering turn him toward God? Answer: haltingly but steadily. First, it jolted him out of any complacency about life and death and the meaning of both. Wiman says one effect of his diagnosis was "to startle the heart out of its ruts and ruins." If life can never be the same, the question is raised, "What should it be instead?" At the heart of his answer was a return to ultimate things, to reality at its fullest, to the source of the love he was now experiencing—despite the pain that sometimes silenced him even with his wife who cared for him.

Church helped.

"Then one morning we found ourselves going to church. Found ourselves. That's exactly what it felt like, in both senses of the phrase, as if some impulse in each of us had finally been catalyzed into action, so that we were casting aside the Sunday paper and moving toward the door with barely a word between us; and as if, once inside the church, we were discovering exactly where and who we were meant to be." Here are two senses of "found ourselves": as opposed to consciously acting, and in finding who we really were, our true identity—as creatures of God.

It wasn't an easy return, but it was a healing one. "That first service was excruciating, in that it seemed to tear all wounds wide open, and it was profoundly comforting, in that it seemed to offer the only possible balm."

Christ helped too.

It would be harder for Christian Wiman to believe in God if one expression of God (yes, language is not adequate to explain the Trinity) were not in the person of Christ. One of the things that turns Wiman toward rather than away from God in this time is the growing realization that Christ knows—physically, empirically—what he is going through, having given up the prerogatives of divinity in order to suffer with us—most graphically on the cross, though not only there. To the degree that Wiman has a theology, the incarnation—God with us—is at its center.

Eventually, Wiman links his discovery of love with cancer's discovery of him, and sees both as pointing him toward God. "I was led to God by joy, but led to words, you might say, by grief. It was meeting my wife that first made me—made us—want to acknowledge the love that our own seemed to imply and include. It was the threat of death that made me want to give my inchoate feelings of faith some definite form. I knew that I believed, but I didn't really know what I believed." Writing poems returned to him, and he has explored all these things in both poetry and prose ever since.

This linking of his experience of love and of pain is suggested in "One Time":

> I have listened
> to the breathing of the woman I love beyond
> my ability to love. Praise to the pain
> scalding us toward each other.

Suffering has intensified their love and their shared spiritual quest.

The weeks and months of pain after his diagnosis, says Wiman, created "an excess of meaning for which I had no context." It's an interesting phrase, "excess of meaning" (and reminiscent of "some excess / of life" in his previously cited "From a Window" poem). It suggests that his experience demanded an explanation that nothing in his then secular, materialistic belief system could adequately supply. It literally could not satisfactorily account for the reality he was encountering. "My old ideas simply were not adequate for the extremes of joy and grief that I experienced." And that lack further awakened his lifelong sense that there is "something more."

Human minds have been wrestling with the meaning of suffering, if any, since Job and before. Wiman puts his toe in those waters, admitting that, "One considers the meaning of suffering only when one is not actually suffering." He suggests a link between suffering and soul, and that perhaps one implies and necessarily includes the other. He notes "the ancient intuition that suffering and soul are mysterious cognates" and applies it to his own pilgrimage.

"I have passed through pain I could never have imagined, pain that seemed to incinerate all my thoughts of God and live sitting there in ashes, alone. I have been isolated even from my wife, though her love was constant, as was mine. I have come back, for now, even hungrier for God, for *Christ*, for all the difficult bliss of this life I have been given. But there is great weariness too. And fear. And fury."

He understands that "to suggest a connection between suffering and soul can be an obscenity to someone in the midst of it. And not simply an obscenity, but a lie." But he insists, "I was not wrong all those years to believe that suffering is at the very center of our existence, and that there can be no untranquilized life that does not fully confront this fact. The mistake lay in thinking grief the means of confrontation, rather than love. To come to this realization is not to be suddenly 'at ease in the world.' I don't really think it's possible for humans to be at the same time conscious and comfortable."

How is "love" a "confrontation" with suffering? He explains elsewhere: "Life tears us apart, but through those wounds, if we have tended them, love may enter us . . . ." The love may be of others, or others for you, or of you for yourself, but "in all these . . . there burns the abiding love of God."

Wiman writes, "Every day I feel a little more the impress of eternity." A terminal medical diagnosis will have that effect. When Christian Wiman got his, and when his bodily pain proved the diagnosis true, he, like Jacob, wrestled. Often he wanted only to "desecrate," but ultimately he interpreted the story he was living in a way that pointed him back to his Creator. In "And I Said to My Soul, Be Loud," he shouts,

> For I am come a whirlwind of wasted things
> and I will ride this tantrum back to God.

## DID HE EVER LEAVE? LATENT VERSUS DORMANT FAITH

Wiman says many times and in many ways that he may never have left faith in God at all. He claims he was "always religious," even "obsessed" with religion and with the possibility of God, and that much of what he wrote in poetry and prose in his away years testify to that. He was God-haunted even when running full-speed after poetry instead.

Wiman claims "faith was latent within me." Elsewhere he uses the word "dormant." There's a significant difference between these two words. Latent suggests something possible but not yet realized. Dormant suggests something that once was and is no longer, but with the possibility of returning. The possibility of being a scholar or athlete is latent within a small child, as yet unrealized. A daffodil in winter is dormant—once flowering and with the potential of flowering again.

For conservative theologians, this raises the debate over "eternal security," the question of whether when one has a salvation experience, that salvation can ever be reversed or lost. (I thought about it a lot as a child.) Some say yes—if one consciously and consistently repudiates that experience. Others say no, not even the person in question can undo what God has once done for them.

This is the kind of theological question for which Wiman himself has little respect or interest. But it arises in a different form in his writing when he himself declared himself far removed from anything resembling faith. In his mid-thirties, before he found love and before his diagnosis and before he began a turn back toward God, Wiman refers to his church basement conversion and speculates that it is less a memory than a "latent, living sensation, buried in the body, waiting to break out and be life again."

This is a common feeling among Returners. They speak of returning to something that, even though they wandered or fled from or even openly repudiated God, they couldn't escape—something that's in their bones, that called them back home.

At the time of writing the essay that mocks the mission trip to Africa, Wiman asks himself, "Do I want that charge again, or the time that it enlivened?" And follows it immediately with another question: "Is God merely a synonym of gone?" Essentially his answer to the first question was "no," and his answer to the second was "yes." Later he would reverse the answer to the first, while remaining ambivalent about the answer to the second. ("Gone," for Wiman, not being the same as "not existing.")

Less than five years after asking those questions, Wiman writes, "I begin to feel faith's latency echoing back down the days through which I walked—I thought—faithlessly." Whether thinking one is "faithless" makes it so or not, whether one is "once saved, always saved" or not, whether the distinction between latent and dormant is useful, the fact is that Christian Wiman was drawn again to God and the things of God. He wondered in his mid-thirties essay "if my brain were a bell that God, running out of options, sometimes strikes." By the end of his thirties, the bell starts ringing overtime—loud, if not always clear.

## RETURNING YES—BUT TO WHAT?

Wiman insists, correctly, that it is not possible to return to the faith of your childhood. "If you believe at fifty what you believed at fifteen, then you have not lived—or have denied the reality of your life." This should be true of most every significant belief, secular or religious. Even if the core tenet is still believed, it should be deepened and reshaped and tested and made more realistic by one's life experiences. A fifteen-year-old's "I believe in God" ought not to mean exactly the same thing when affirmed again many years later.

And Wiman definitely does not return to the faith of his Texas Baptist youth. What he does return to is unclear even to him—and seems likely always to be so. There are any number of contributing reasons for this.

One is the general influence of the modernity and postmodernity that we all breathe. Ours is an age of skepticism about essentially everything—especially among the hyper-reflective, a club of which Wiman is a card-carrying member. Science and the humanities alike tell us that doubt is the only path to truth (the latter never with a capital letter). For science, doubt leads to testing and measurement. For the current humanities, it simply leads to more doubt.

Wiman lived and lives among folks who have made doubt and absence a mark of sophistication and even courage. "How comfortable we become with our own intellectual and spiritual discomfort." He remarks on "the fierceness with which we cling to beliefs that have made us miserable, or beliefs that prove to be so obviously inadequate," an observation that applies to secularists and believers alike. He finds that people actually need, even enjoy, their anxieties and doubts, and writers and artists more than most, needing them as subject matter and, ironically, inspiration for their art.

This phenomenon is common among the most intense spiritual seekers: "Lacking intensity in our lives, we say that we are distant from God and then seek to make that distance into an intense experience." Their doubts are the most interesting thing in their lives and they are loathe to part with them. "Pain has its pleasures, not the least of which are its reliability, immediacy, and even, in a strange way, companionability." He cites the poet Marianne Moore: "Without loneliness I should be more lonely, so I keep it."

Wiman sees this danger in himself and speaks against it. "God is not absent. He is everywhere in the world we are too dispirited to love." Notice that he does not criticize here a failure to love God, but a failure to love the world, in which Wiman characteristically includes both the natural world and human relationships. "All too often the task to which we are called is simply to show a kindness to the irritating person in the cubicle next to us, say, or to touch the face of a spouse from whom we ourselves have been long absent, letting grace wake love from our intense, self-enclosed sleep." Love of life echoes and will further awaken love of God and a sense of God's love for you.

Wiman speaks against making a fetish or idol of doubt—or despair, writing, "Sometimes we want despair to be ultimate because it absolves us of action." But he does endorse and practice what he calls "devotional doubt." He contrasts doubt as a means of escape from commitment with doubt as a necessary expression of faith. (If one has certainty, one does not need faith, because faith lives in spaces where certainty does not.) He identifies three characteristics of devotional doubt: humility, insufficiency, and mystery.

Humility—not to be confused with radical skepticism—protects healthy faith from both "the seductive assurance and instant contempt of secularism" and "the hive-like certainties of churches." There are fundamentalist versions of both the secular and the religious, and Wiman wants to avoid both.

Humility leads one to realize one's insufficiency. Not the "low self-esteem" that American culture abhors, but the simple acknowledgment of the severe limitations both of our knowledge—especially of ultimate things—and of our ability to live by our own strength in light of those ultimate things.

A prime example of insufficiency, ironically for someone gifted with words, is language. Wiman loves words and uses them incessantly to probe reality, but, like many today, he feels they are not up to the job. "Every word . . . begins to leak meaning the minute you turn your attention to it." This is especially true of words about God. "I have tried to learn the language of Christianity but often feel that I have made no progress at all."

The third element of "devotional doubt"—mystery—is clearly compatible with the other two. In fact, it's pretty much all we have left. The less we can know for certain, the more that will be a mystery. But Wiman's idea of mystery is not simply lack of knowledge. Mystery is not a lack of something for him, it is a rich store of something—something we can experience, though often indirectly.

Wiman can be categorical and absolutist in affirming how little we can be sure of when it comes to doctrine and dogma. Doctrines and theologies are *human thinking* about divine revelation, and so, by definition, something less than the revelation they describe—sometimes much less. In fact, sometimes wrong. Doctrine must recognize itself as provisional if it is to be useful. "One must learn to be in unknowingness without being proud of it."

In the end, Wiman believes it is a mistake to overemphasize what we don't know. He admits that he "all too often forgets that it is much more important to assert and lay claim to the God that you believe in rather than forever drawing the line at the doctrines you don't." Wiman, as we have seen, believe that words and doctrines often fail us. But, unlike some, he also believes we should never give up trying to make ourselves and reality understandable. It's what humans do.

Like many Returners (including Kathleen Norris), Wiman is much more open to faith expressed in story than faith expressed in doctrine. He points to Jesus' use of parables. "Christ speaks in stories as a way of preparing his followers to stake their lives on a story, because existence is not a puzzle to be solved, but a narrative to be inherited and undergone and transformed person by person." This approach works because human beings naturally understand the language and strategy of stories.

In fact our brains are so constructed as to process reality narratively, always looking for a plot, always seeking out characters and meaning. The Bible is essentially telling a grand story, with an overarching plot, a central character, and a meaningful ending. It invites us to be characters in the story, and Christian Wiman, after a time away, accepted again the invitation.

But not without hesitations, ambivalences, and second guesses. "I basically do a little linguistic dance around Christianity, as if I were hedging my bets." That is not an admission that will endear him to the strictly orthodox, but it's a dance that many who read him have engaged in and will understand. It is not whether his approach to God can work for everyone, it is only a question of whether it works for Christian Wiman and God.

## WHAT HE AFFIRMS WITHOUT BLINKING

There are common patterns in the theology and practice of Returners. For all his skittishness about orthodox theology and Returning to church, there are a few things that Wiman proclaims without hesitation. These include the conviction that God must be met within this world and not in a world beyond, the vital role of relationships in the life of faith, the centrality of the person and work of Christ, and the necessity of faith manifesting itself in a life of active engagement.

The common denominator in each of these is relevance. Many people leave faith not because they are offended or intellectually disappointed, but simply because the whole world of faith seems less and less relevant to their lives—especially when those lives are crowded with busyness. Leaving home for college; starting and maintaining a career; negotiating relationships of all kinds; meeting the needs of children, spouses, and extended family; allotting time for recreation and self-care; and on and on. Western culture discourages spiritual health as much by its packed calendar as by its secularism.

The whole life of the soul and one's relationship with God becomes distant, hypothetical, and estranged. It's one more thing "to do." And many find it's one more thing too many. One is only likely to find one's way back to faith if, as happens with Wiman and with most all Returners, they rediscover that faith is first relevant and then essential to how they live.

## FINDING GOD WITHIN THE WORLD

Wiman has little interest in God sitting on a throne in heaven. He does not deny the transcendence of God, but insists that we can only experience him in this world. God has to come to us—and, most clearly in the person of Christ, Wiman believes that God has.

God's immanence in his creation is apparent in different interrelated ways. He is present in physical nature. He is present in individual human beings. He is present in human relationships of all kinds. There is nowhere, essentially, where God is not present. "Faith in God is, in the deepest sense, faith in life."

He compares this view with that of his childhood culture. His fundamentalist upbringing warned him to beware of the world and its false pleasures. Wiman still believes that many of the pleasures of the world *are* false, but in his Return he looks to the created world and our daily lives as the place to meet God.

So if God is everywhere present in this life, why does Wiman speak so frequently of God's absence, even seeing it as a defining experience for modern men and women? Why is an intense relationship with God not a common and continuous experience?

Since it is not so with Wiman, and many others, there is a tendency to wonder if past experiences with God even happened—as Wiman wondered about his childhood conversion experience. As Kathleen Norris discovered, secular friends will tend, Wiman says, to psychologize one's return to faith and suggest hidden motivations, something Wiman himself is prone to do. Doing so "eats away at the intensity of the experience that made you proclaim, however quietly, your recovered faith, and soon you find yourself getting stalled in arguments between religion and science, theology and history, trying to nail down doctrine like some huge and much-torn tent in the wind."

Wiman does not know why God does not make himself more plain, but his act of writing about his experiences with God within the details of his life—in both poetry and prose—is itself an important way of verifying to himself the authenticity of those experiences. "To experience grace is one thing; to integrate it into your life is quite another. What I crave now is that integration, some speech that is true to the transcendent nature of grace yet adequate to the hard reality in which daily faith operates. I crave, I suppose, the poetry *and* prose of knowing."

A God who is seen to be close and concrete rather than distant and abstract is a relevant God. Wiman explores this in his poetry, but also recognizes that it is also necessary to find confirmation of it in his life: "it means nothing to make a space for the miraculous in one's work if one can't recognize some true intrusion in one's life."

## CHRIST, CANCER, AND THE CROSS: THE GOD WHO KNOWS OUR SUFFERING

The ultimate expression of transcendence merging with immanence in the Christian understanding is called incarnation. It asserts that God, in the person of Christ, chose to become one with his creation and to share in its joys, temptations, and pain. Though Wiman knows he can't prove that it happened, it is the one doctrine about which he shows little ambivalence.

This is ironic in the sense that the incarnation, depending as it does on that most mysterious of concepts—God as three-in-one—is perhaps the most mysterious of all theological concepts. It defeats rational analysis. Yet Wiman rejects the common ways of taming this mystery: Jesus was a good man but only a man; the resurrection is a symbol not a fact, encouraging us to seek symbolic resurrections in our own life; or the ancient heresy, the opposite of Jesus as only man: Jesus was God, but his humanity was an illusion.

Wiman contrasts "the fog" of our understanding of God with "the clarity of Christ." That clarity, for Wiman, centers on two things—both concretely demonstrated by Christ's life—his love and his suffering. Both reinforce Wiman's conviction that God is met in the details of this world. "If nature abhors a vacuum, Christ abhors a vagueness. If God is love, Christ is love for this one person, this one place, this one time-bound and time-ravaged self." Wiman, ambivalent about many things, is not vague about the love of Christ, which he reciprocates.

And that love showed itself most powerfully on the cross. Following Jürgen Moltmann and others, Wiman believes Christian theology, especially after the Holocaust and other moderns horrors, must be formed, in Moltmann's words, "in earshot of the dying Christ." Having suffered excruciating pain himself, Wiman hears and identifies with Christ's full humanity in his cry on the cross, "My God, my God, why has thou forsaken me?" This is someone he can believe—and it is something that makes Christ believable.

Wiman acknowledges that without resurrection there is no Christ, only a long-dead Jesus. "Sometimes it seems that I can happily hold all Christian tenets in an active abeyance, a fusion of faith and skepticism that includes and transcends literal and figurative truths, if I can hold fast to one indestructible fact (*fact?!*): Christ's resurrection."

He questions his word "fact" because, of course, he can't prove the resurrection to have happened—he must rely on testimonies, that is, on story. And he dithers for a few paragraphs on how his belief in this fact waxes and wanes. But then he writes words his childhood pastors would have affirmed. "Christ. He won't go away." He rejects the "Jeffersonian Christ" stripped of the miraculous, and says, "No, to be a Christian has to mean believing in the resurrected Christ"—though he feels less and less inclined to argue about it or seek proofs.

Ultimately, Wiman can accept Christ's resurrection because he has experienced his own resurrection from the death sentence of cancer—and he believes Christ played a role. "Christ's life is not simply a model for how to live, but the living truth of my own existence. Christ is not alive because he rose from the dead two thousand years ago. He arose from the dead two thousand years ago because he is alive right now."

A faith infused with the living Christ is a relevant faith.

## FAITH AND RELATIONSHIPS: IT'S WHO YOU KNOW

A disruption in human relationships often contributes to a person leaving the church and faith. A healthy, meaningful human relationship often contributes to that same person coming back. For Christian Wiman, relationships are a primary way in which God makes himself known to us. Faith not only involves community, it is itself communally held.

We read of Christ in Scripture, we can address Christ in worship and in prayer, but, Wiman says, "Christ comes alive in the communion between people." There is endless talk in religious and other circles about love. But what is it? How does one experience it? What content can one assign to the assertion "God is love"? Wiman's answer is that we can best (only?) experience God's love in Christ, and we can best (only?) experience Christ's love through another human being.

"Human love catalyzes the love of Christ." A catalyst is a chemical agent that makes possible an interaction between two other chemicals that would not otherwise interact. Receiving love from another human being is both evidence of Christ's love for you (Christ being the ultimate source of that and all love) and opens the door for your love of Christ (because it gives you experience in loving).

Someone who feels human love is more likely to be open to God's love than someone who doesn't. Hence the role of acceptance and love in helping people return to faith. "What one craves is supernatural love, but one finds it only within human love. That is why I am, such as I am, a Christian, because I can feel God only through physical existence, can feel his love only in the love of other people."

Wiman's life is his own best example. He identifies falling in love with Danielle as a crucial part of his return to faith. It wasn't that she was already a person of faith and evangelized him. It was more simply that she loved him, and the shared joy of that started them both on a shared quest for an understanding of reality that explained it.

Love was soon followed by suffering. Like love, suffering posed a question: what is the meaning, if any, of suffering? Wiman says that question for him was not answered by theology, nor by his attempts to evade theology, but "by the depth and integrity and essential innocence of the communion occurring between two individuals." Love is the only response to unrelieved suffering that does any good.

And that love should grow exponentially among believers. Wiman asserts, "we depend on others for our faith." Of course each one has an individual relationship with God, but if it is only individual, it is a stunted faith. Wiman recognizes the need for solitude and silence in matters of the spirit, "but spiritual experience that is *solely* solitude inevitably leads to despair."

Love exists to be given away—"the love of Christ is not something you can ever hoard." One's own share of love grows in direct proportion to one's passing it freely and lavishly to others. Hence the importance of living out one's faith in the company of others. Hence the inescapable command of Christian mothers: "go to church."

Church is not a suggestion in the Bible; it is both a command and an assumption. Every returner to faith has to confront, at some point, the question of what to do about church. The failures of church often contributes to their leaving. The prospect of returning is comforting to some, terrifying to others. Wiman describes an attempt to return to church, not necessarily to faith, during his away years. These were not fundamentalist churches. He says he "mumbled along with the hymns" and tried to listen to the sermons, but "became the same hive of nerves I was in childhood, wanting it only to be over."

But in the earliest stages of his slow return to faith, Wiman and Danielle crossed paths with a pastor who had the wisdom to meet Wiman where he was, rather than where the pastor was. They dropped in on a church at the end of their block that he had walked past countless times without ever bothering to identify its denomination. The service was far from full, and the pastor bravely and effectively addressed "how the void of God and the love of God come together in the mystery of the cross." Wiman was impressed, but nonetheless ducked out the side door to avoid speaking with him.

But a week or so later, as God would have it, he ran into the pastor on the street. Wiman was not pleased. "I was in no mood to chat, especially not to an enthusiastic preacher, and all my thoughts were hostile." The pastor, however, was wise enough to do three things—two were matters of avoidance and one was a gesture of compassion.

The first thing he avoided was enthusiastic, glad-handing proselytizing (the kind of "bouncy" faith that Wiman despises). The second thing he avoided was churchy language, words and slogans that, as with Kathleen Norris, Wiman thinks are badly in need of refreshment. And the gesture came when they were about to part and "the severity of my [medical] situation and our unfamiliarity with each other left us with no words." The pastor unconsciously placed his hand over his heart and "a flicker of empathetic anguish crossed his face."

That human gesture melted Wiman's hostility and, perhaps, began a restoration of hope in the possibilities of church as a place where human love and divine love could intermingle. "It sliced right through me. It cut through the cloud I was living in and let the plain day pour its balm upon me. It was, I am sure, one of those moments when we enact and reflect a mercy and mystery that are greater than we are, when the void of God and the love God, incomprehensible pain and the peace that passeth understanding, come together in a single human act."

The interaction with this wise pastor sparked hope. Wiman does not hope easily. It does not come naturally to him, nor does he find abundant evidence in the world to support it. He cites the Irish poet Seamus Heaney's assertion that hope "is a state of the soul rather than a response to the evidence." Ultimately, Wiman decides "hope, in the end, is like joy—not willed but given." Given by God, sometimes directly and sometimes indirectly.

Since returning to faith, Wiman and Danielle have not had an easy time finding a church with a quorum of kindred spirits. The church in general is still more a challenge for him than a haven. And yet, he says, "I feel a strong need—an imperative, really—to believe something in common; indeed, I feel that any belief I have that is not in some way shared is probably just the workings of my own ego, a common form of modern idolatry."

Wiman needs to believe something in common, worship in common, love in common, serve in common, and generally live life in common. It is the only way to more fully know and experience God. It makes faith relevant again.

## BE YE DOERS OF THE WORD, AND NOT HEARERS ONLY

A sore spot with many leavers is their common claim that the church is more often a part of the world's problems than a part of the solution. This complaint is often voiced by folks who know little of what the church actually does to help repair the world and who often have done little or nothing themselves, but it ranks high in the reasons people give for rejecting faith.

Wiman does not dismiss the charge. He returned to faith with the conviction that his own faith had to make a difference in the world, not just in his own life. At one point he feels that God is telling him to cut back on the mental churning: "as if *Christ* were telling me (in church no less): get off your mystified ass and *do* something." He believes faith is often experienced in silence, but that it must result in being an agent for change in the world, not just in one's own life. "Silence is the language of faith. Action—be it church or charity, politics or poetry—is the translation." Silence refers to one's "meditative communion with God" and action to that which flows out of that communion into the life you are living.

Action, yes, but Wiman rejects "virtuous busyness." Exhausting oneself with "service" of all kinds can actually diminish one's intimate relationship with God (found more directly in prayer and worship). And, perhaps with his own experience with the nonchurchy pastor in mind, he warns against "an overeager urge to proselytize, or a too-avid grasp of 'the truth.'" Citing St. Francis's famous dictum, "Preach the gospel at all times and, if necessary, use words," he says, "To be sure, the injunction to evangelize is upon every believer, but there is a strict hierarchy of effective methods."

One more of Wiman's relationships is significant: kids. And one more responsibility. A Return is sometimes influenced by realizing when raising children that one has a responsibility to ground them in something bigger than the world's definitions of significance and success. "I've got little kids now, and I do think about what I should teach them and how I should teach them, in terms of their spiritual lives." When children first appeared in his life, it made Wiman inspect both his responsibility and his own grounding.

## SUMMING UP

Christian Wiman's life, as we have seen, displays many of the recurring characteristics of a Returner to faith. He has an allergy to dogma, though he admits, within limits, its necessity. He cuts slack for those who believe differently than he does, including people following other religions. He is wary of the church, and at the same time is deeply grateful for the opportunity to be in a community of seekers.

Wiman is also profoundly aware that he has been a recipient of grace. "I waste too much time in the little lightless caverns of my own mind. So much of faith has so little to do with belief, and so much to with acceptance. . . . Acceptance of grace." Grace is one of those transcendent realities which can only be experienced within the immanent, within this world, within a life, and within shared lives. He doesn't have the words or images or metaphors to adequately describe it, but, as a poet and recipient, he tries.

Wiman ends *My Bright Abyss* with the same fragment of a poem with which he started, but with an important difference.

> My God my bright abyss
> into which all my longings will not go
> once more I come to the edge of what I know
> and believing nothing believe in this.

Do you see the difference? I am happy to say that I did—happy because poetry readers like to participate in the making of meaning in a poem—a difference he points out himself in an interview I read later. The first fragment ends in a colon, putting the emphasis on "this" and frustrating the reader (and the poet) who expects something important to follow, but which does not. The second version ends in a period, putting the emphasis on "believe" and suggesting that "this" is everything he has explored and affirmed in the entire book and in his poems and in his life. In effect, he is saying I believe in the things which I have experienced and affirmed: love, grace, God—especially in Christ as Emmanuel, God with us.

He says that for a long time he was not been able to say what should come after the colon of the original fragment. He also says at the beginning of the book, "what I crave at this point in my life is to speak more plainly what it is I believe." He doesn't entirely succeed, because he is speaking of things that are not plain, things that are beyond words (and certainly beyond proof), but things that are no less real for that.

A return to faith for Wiman is larger than a return to "*the* Faith" because the latter is likely to be too narrow and sectarian for him. His faith is and will always be a work in progress—and he wouldn't have it any other way. And his relationship to the church, and to orthodox theology, will always be fraught—a source of comfort but also of anxiety and strain. But he willingly calls himself a Christian and is full of gratitude for what God in Christ has done for him (including, I am happy to say, his cancer being in remission at the time of this writing). And Christian Wiman has spoken "more plainly" about that—in poetry and prose that not only sketch his own journey away from and back to faith, but also makes it more possible for others to do the same.

## Chapter 5

## DAN WAKEFIELD: WAKING UP SCREAMING

> "One balmy spring morning in Hollywood, a month or so before my forty-eight birthday, I woke up screaming."
>
> —DAN WAKEFIELD, *RETURNING*

IF SEARCHING FOR A life that makes every stop on the Leaving and Returning trail, look no further than Dan Wakefield—novelist, journalist, screen writer, memoirist, and teacher. Raised Baptist, awash in Bible stories and hymns and rousing youth groups, he began leaving faith, ironically, at the moment of his official entry—baptism—and continued leaving through college, only returning because important guides and experiences kept alive the possibility of taking Jesus seriously even when Wakefield had no intention of returning to the faith of his youth. He left faith progressively and returned to it only slowly, after a long period marked by alcoholism, drug abuse, and chasing illusions.

### SONGS, STORIES, AND WATER-FOUNTAIN MIRACLES

In Wakefield's early years in the church, he was presented with an appealing expression of Christianity that emphasized the love of Jesus for everyone and conveyed faith through story and song. His recounting will likely bring a smile to anyone raised in a similar church environment. His Sunday school class was taught "with genuine joy" by the young pastor and his wife who made the Bible and the Christian life seem fun:

... they taught by telling stories. They made the Bible stories come alive with their spirited recounting, sometimes by acting out parts, sometimes with home-made "visual aids" like crayon-drawn pictures and maps, sometimes with ingenious recreations of miracles. I remember still the thrill of Mrs. McCarthy demonstrating how the rod of Moses brought water from a stone as she tapped a brown paper bag (arranged to look just like a rock) covering a drinking fountain that Reverend McCarthy hid behind and turned on to spout a tremendous jet of miraculous water!

And the songs and hymns they sang were "not the solemn, stately songs of the Presbyterians but rousing Baptist hymns like 'Life is Like a Mountain Railroad' and 'Throw Out the Lifeline'"—the latter accompanied by everyone simulating throwing out a life preserver to a drowning soul.

Peppy songs and body motions too! Who wouldn't want to follow Jesus?

And strangely enough for a Baptist church of that era, "We didn't hear a word about hell-fire or damnation but rather were told of the love of Jesus, who seemed in this Baptist view to be a strong, wise, understanding fellow—a kind of divine lifeguard."

The young Dan experienced the traditional altar call of such churches and says, "I was among those who heeded the call to come forward and declare that I believed in this Christ as my savior."

He not only had fun, he also had guides and mentors, one of the most important being Amy at the Presbyterian church his family attended before they went Baptist. "I remember her in red, a large, round shining apple of a woman, brown hair pulled back in a bun, face scrubbed and glowing, eyes lively and glinting, mouth in a smile that seemed a genuine expression of delight at being a believer in and bearer of the 'good news' of Christianity."

Amy radiated warmth, safety, and love—and that was the heart of her message about faith. "One of the main lessons I remember from Amy's Sunday school was that God loved everyone regardless of race, creed, or color," an assertion that was verified by a picture outside their class that showed Jesus surrounded by little children of every color. Proof positive, even though Dan remembers no children of color actually being in his class.

This teacher, these lessons, and that picture stayed with Wakefield long after he had left faith and the church, including when he went to the South as a "practicing intellectual atheist" to cover the civil rights movement for *The Nation*. He says he believed Amy as a boy when she said Jesus loved everyone, and "even when I no longer 'believed in' Jesus, I believed in Amy and the lesson she had taught us."

Amy also helped counsel Dan's parents during a difficult time in their marriage and in the household. Wakefield says many in the church thought her a bit "off," but he honors her as an early guide who planted seeds that would germinate years later.

## CHRIST AS A WHITE LIGHT

Dan Wakefield had a mystical, "white light" boyhood experience that confirmed his faith. He was a child who thought believing in God was simply "part of being a good American, appropriate and even necessary for a Cub Scout working his way up to being a Boy Scout." He considered himself "a regular person," not someone especially holy.

But then something very irregular happened to him at the age of nine. He had gone to bed, said his prayers, and was waiting for sleep—but still wide awake—"when I had the sensation that my whole body was filled with light. It was a white light of such brightness and intensity that it seemed almost silver . . . filling every part of my body from my head to my feet."

He continues, "I did not hear any voice, or any sound at all for that matter, but with the light came the understanding that it was Christ. The light was the presence of Christ, and I was not simply in his presence, his presence was in me . . . infusing my whole being."

He says, "The experience was not frightening, but reassuring, like a blessing, a gift, and a confirmation all at once." He didn't tell anyone about it for years, because he didn't need to. He says he didn't need it explained because he knew exactly what it was and what it meant. Christ had come to him. He went on with his life as he had before, the only real change being that he decided that instead of a football coach when he grew up, he would be a minister.

## LEAVING WHILE IN THE BAPTISTRY: DOING IT MY WAY

So what happened? He had a positive experience of church and faith as a child, had loving guides and mentors, and even a direct, mystical experience with Christ. Sounds like the makings of a lifer, someone who would think back on that direct experience if ever doubts or obstacles arose.

What happened, to oversimplify, is late adolescence.

A primary conviction of that life stage—especially in American culture—is the heart cry, "You're not the boss of me!" Late adolescence (lasting well into adulthood for some) is the time of declaring one's self free of all external restraints—one wants to live one's own life, make one's own decisions, and even create one's own reality, with nobody else telling you what to think or what to do. Not exactly compatible with the call to place one's trust instead in a Creator God who made everything, including you and your life, and telling you both what to think and what to do.

Religion increasingly seemed antiquated and unmodern to Wakefield. Concepts like sin, guilt, and on-your-knees confession "were the kind of thing that gave God a bad name in our enlightened psychological era."

While he still believed in God, he increasingly looked to nature for sustenance and meaning. He came to define the divine—and God—as a "sense of feeling in tune with the universe"—and he still does. Rightly understood, this can be a sense compatible with orthodox Christianity, but it can also lend itself to a generic vagueness that expresses itself in, as we've seen in the other stories, the common refrain, "I'm spiritual, but not religious," a direction in which the young Dan Wakefield was headed.

Ironically, the general direction of his life away from faith and toward making himself accountable to no one and no thing began earlier with his baptism (delayed for Baptists until he was old enough to know what he was choosing). He was given the opportunity to pick a hymn that would be played as he walked up to the big tank for his total-immersion, formal entry into the body of believers. Thinking his old favorite, "Throw Out the Lifeline," might not be appropriate for a fellow about to be dunked, he wavered between "What a Friend I Have in Jesus" and "Leaning on the Everlasting Arms."

Unfortunately, he forgot to tell the organist either one. So as he approached the tank, he heard her playing a hymn that he "really hated," whose lyrics expressed the antithesis of what he wanted for his life:

> Have thine own way, Lord,
> Have thine own way,
> Thou are the potter,
> I am the clay. . . .

Nothing could be further from the desires of his adolescent mind, and it was enough to propel him out of churchgoing and on his way out of faith. "It asked God to 'mold me' into whatever He wanted, and that didn't seem fair. To hell with it. I stopped going to Sunday school and gave up the idea of being a minister," deciding to return to his earlier plan of being the head football coach at Notre Dame, "whether God liked it or not." Adding, "Firmly in charge of my own fate, I entered the fury of adolescence."

## READING ONE'S WAY OUT OF FAITH

This was a seminal event, but not a conclusive one. It actually took Wakefield quite a while to complete his exit from faith. Another factor was that long before this his family had stopped going to church. His parents were still believers, but going to church no longer seemed important to them. It cut the children off from positive role models like Amy and gave them the impression that faith was only marginally important, if at all.

And as seems so often the case in these stories, Wakefield's departure from faith was completed, with an exclamation point, in college. He started college elsewhere, but ended up at Columbia in New York.

He says the completion of his exit from faith was based largely on reading, skeptical professors, artsiness, and Freud. Like Kathleen Norris at Bennington, Wakefield discovered Columbia to be a place of "thoughts and ideas, books and poems and paintings, music and art." All of it intoxicating. All of it exciting. All of which replaced for the most part any lingering interest in God or church.

He recalls one professor who condescendingly dismissed the religious conviction of a student who had timorously expressed his belief in Christ's divinity. Wakefield said he felt "embarrassed for the guy" and realized that only a year earlier it might have been him. Lesson learned. It was the moment he first became aware that he was longer a Christian.

Wakefield indicates, "I had finished my high school career in a blaze of teenage glory" that swept across a wide range of activities and honors. He continued that success in college, reinforcing his long-standing conviction that "I could mold my own fate (without troublesome intervention from God)." His adolescent determination to run his own life was coming true.

Wakefield inhaled the religious skepticism as well as the secular humanist celebrations of university intellectual life, saying, "It was another kind of baptism." He continues, "Reading seemed the most 'real' part of my life." And he read widely—from Hemingway and Fitzgerald to Marx, Nietzsche, and Freud—all the big names, his new mentors and guides, none of whom took God seriously. (One of his professors did take Jesus seriously, which we'll get to in a bit.)

He read the seminal work of William James, an intellectual giant "who did not share Freud's acrimonious view of religion," but whose universalism about and psychologizing of spiritual things was even more devastating to a specific commitment to Christianity than was outright ridicule. James said that the kind of "white light" experience that Wakefield had as a boy was simply a "photism," a "hallucinatory . . . experience" that was purely psychological and quite common.

Wakefield applied this to his own life and ran with it. "With my Jesus-as-light experience 'explained away,' then, the last obstacle to my full embrace of atheism was removed, and I was free to form my own personal view of a universe without a God." That word again—appearing so often in the stories of Leavers—"free."

Wakefield makes it clear that he doesn't "blame" Columbia for his loss of faith (though his family did). He says that was accomplished even more completely by the popular ministers of the day. He had particular disdain for people like Norman Vincent Peale: "the greatest and most disturbing assault on my feeling for Jesus (and my connection with Christianity) was not coming from the atheistic Columbia professors but from popular Christian ministers of the day who were trying to make Jesus relevant to the spirit of the fifties by turning him into a glad-handing kind of Rotarian businessman, a spiritual version of the current symbol of conformity, the Man in the Gray Flannel Suit." Making Jesus relevant by making him conform to the spirit of any age is the surest way to make him irrelevant instead.

All in all, Wakefield summarizes his time in college as one of "angry intellectual dismissal of God and church." It was an exciting time. The future looked bright. He was free. At the same time, he says "I was often depressed." Freed from outdated ideas, in charge of one's life, enjoying the life of the mind and the body among like-minded peers—and yet "often depressed." It's not every Leaver's story by any means, but it's also not uncommon.

## WAKING UP SCREAMING

Career success for Dan Wakefield came early and often, first as a journalist in the late 1950's and sixties, then as a novelist beginning in 1970, and later as a screen writer, film producer, and teacher. He published early on in major periodicals such as *The Atlantic Monthly*, *Harper's*, *Esquire*, and *The New York Times Magazine*. He was a staff writer for *The Nation*, which took him from covering civil rights in the South to crises in Israel. He collected various awards and honors along the way.

At the same time that his professional career was ascending, his personal life was cratering. Wakefield opens his groundbreaking memoir *Returning* with this sentence (which demonstrates that he knows how to start any writing with a hook): "One balmy spring morning in Hollywood, a month or so before my forty-eighth birthday, I woke up screaming."

He says this did not happen because he was waking up from a nightmare. "It was, rather, a response to the reality that another morning had broken in a life I could only deal with sedated by wine, loud noise, moving images, and wired to electronic games that further distracted my fragmented attention from a growing sense of blank, nameless pain in the pit of my very being, my most essential self."

This event and others like it were the culmination of years of abusing drugs and alcohol, coupled with a frustrating and fruitless search for healing and meaning in places that didn't provide either. "I was drinking to numb myself, to blank out the psychic or existential pain or whatever is the name we give to a feeling of emptiness of soul and the resulting anxiety and lurking terror of it." Similarly, he says he used drugs not primarily for the high, "but for blotting out pain, the pain of that interior or psychic void that I think is the absence of spiritual substance, the hole that is left by the lack of any power higher than the human."

He also found that he had difficulty even being a good atheist. On the day he woke up screaming, he found an old Bible—one "I hadn't opened for nearly a quarter of a century"—and turned to the Twenty-Third Psalm ("The Lord is my shepherd"). It calmed him, as it always had in his youth, though it engendered no thoughts of returning to faith.

At other times he discovered himself, almost against his will, praying. In the heady excitement of realizing his calling as a writer—in the writer's mecca New York City nonetheless—"Without any other thought I got down on my knees and gave thanks to God, in prayer."

Later, he worried that taking a work trip to Israel might threaten his highly defended secularism. He was alarmed when at the Sea of Galilee an old hymn started running through his head, "I Walked Today Where Jesus Walked." In his letters home to a friend, "I was constantly proving to her (and myself) that my sojourn in the Holy Land and visits to religious sites was in no way corrupting the purity or zeal of my unbelief."

Finding sustenance in the Bible, thanking in prayer a God he did not even believe existed, old hymns running through his head—what was this? William James, of course, would have a psychological explanation, as would the therapists Wakefield was seeing. But whatever the explanation, these break-ins into his life made him feel like a traitor, maybe even one of Holden Caulfield's phonies. "Even if it was only force of habit, it bothered me and made me feel guilty for not being true to my atheism (not only religion had the power to produce guilt, I discovered)."

He was especially bothered that the Lord's Prayer—"the most annoyingly persistent prayer of all"—invaded repeatedly. "I fought it, but still it kept penetrating my consciousness, 'saying itself' to me against my will." Wakefield fought back by repeating the famous "nada" parody prayer of unbelief from Hemingway's short story, "A Clean, Well-lighted Place": "Our nada, who art in nada, nada be thy name. Thy kingdom nada. Thy will be nada in nada as it is in nada. . . . Hail nothing full of nothing, nothing is with thee."

No wonder he woke up screaming.

Okay, believing in nothing does not lead everyone to despair. Some people appear to get along fine. And pure naturalistic secularism asserts all kinds of values and things to believe in, even if it doesn't usually supply a believable foundation for them. But in Wakefield's case, the replacement stories felt increasingly thin: "now that I had eliminated God, there was a void. I had filled the ethical holes with snippets of sayings from my literary heroes, but this still left other gaps."

## MAYBE FREUD CAN FIX IT

The gap filler Dan Wakefield relied on most and the longest was psychiatry. If one can no longer believe in God, perhaps one can be believe in and seek healing from Freud and the masters of the psyche. "As with many others like me, I had literally replaced religion with psychiatry, for I was seeking the long-lasting, earthly kind of salvation I hadn't gotten from baptism and church and Jesus."

He felt he was on a noble quest for truth, a common feeling among Leavers in general. "I believed I had started a journey that would guide me to the truth, and I believed that any process involving the pursuit and discovery of the truth was ennobling, if not sacred." And he was flattered when his first analyst said he was a good candidate for this quest through psychoanalysis and was likely to succeed.

Wakefield started analysis when he was twenty-five and estimated then that by the time he was thirty, he would have everything figured out, fixed up, and be ready to shout his healing and his freedom from the rooftops. It didn't quite work out that way. "The time on the couch itself, the famous fifty-minute analytic hour, was not at all what I had imagined. In fact, it was not only disappointing, it was a crashing bore."

He found the sessions "tedious" and was put off by the emotional distance the psychiatrists maintained—with their endless, flat "Yes, go on"—and by their insistence that he was expected to discover for himself the answers to his questions. He describes one traumatic session where he sought help for an alcohol-fueled, terrifying hallucination. The therapist suggested tranquilizers. Wakefield slid off the couch and onto the floor "in agony," crawled to a chair next to the therapist, and started using its leg to smash himself in the face. The psychiatrist, unperturbed, mentioned that the hour was almost up and asked calmly if Wakefield had a friend that could pick him up.

He was further discouraged when he discovered people who have been in psychoanalysis for fifteen years and more without reaching their goal. Finally he gave up. "I poured more thoughts and dreams and memories and time and parental money into the black hole, but there was no sign of light, no glimmer of understanding, much less healing revelation."

Wakefield compares his loss of faith in psychoanalysis with the lost faith in the 1950s of Arthur Koestler and other intellectuals in Communism, as captured in the title of Koestler's book, *The God That Failed*. The same, he said, was true for his "generation who tried to find through Freudian psychoanalysis a substitute for God, a 'scientific' formula for self-gratification, for 'having my own way.'" Wakefield had insisted since adolescence on "having my own way," and it had failed him.

It is important to add (with Lecrae's experience in mind) that Wakefield makes a distinction between psychoanalysis in particular and psychotherapy in general. The first was a failure for him, the second is something he later sought out himself and found helpful, because it "is an aid to understand and cope with the pains of life, rather than provide a meaning for it." Psychotherapy helped him heal from, among other things, psychoanalysis. (And psychoanalysis itself has changed significantly in recent decades, including acknowledging that religious belief isn't necessarily pathological.)

In brief, Wakefield found that the stories he had turned to as replacements for his faith story had failed him. He had put his faith in freedom from faith. He was not wrong to value the life of the mind, or writing and creativity, or work for a fairer world. But he discovered he was wrong to look to them for ultimate meaning, and he concluded that he was certainly wrong to think that Freud could successfully take the place of Jesus.

## USEFUL DISILLUSIONMENT

One could say that the first step in Dan Wakefield's return to faith was disillusionment. It is a common first step for Returners. As we saw with Lecrae, if anyone is happy with their life and their understanding of what is real and true and good, they are unlikely to look for another understanding. If they have replaced a truer understanding with one that is less true—or even false—then it is good to become disillusioned with that replacement.

But disillusionment with his replacement stories did not lead Wakefield immediately to a return to faith or even a desire to return. If one can slowly drift away from faith in God, one can also slowly—very slowly—drift back (as was the case with Kathleen Norris). With steps forward and steps back along the way. This was the case with Dan Wakefield.

## FINDING BELIEVABLE CHRISTIANS

Wakefield says that with the collapse of both his ideology and his health, he felt a sense of "exile" from atheism and the life he had been living. And he had the common exile experience of yearning for a place where he fit, where he could flourish instead of flounder, a place called home.

One step toward home was hanging out with Christians, something he hadn't done since high school. These weren't just any Christians—he didn't yet have the stomach for that—they were the Christians dedicating their lives to social justice and serving the poor at the Catholic Worker "hospitality house" in the Bowery section of New York, an area associated at the time with poverty, addiction, prostitution, homelessness, and despair.

He admired their integrity and was drawn to them "in spite of their being openly and unashamedly religious." They "might be crackpots, but by any God you chose to swear by, they were not phonies." He read Dorothy Day with respect because of her hard-living, atheistic past, and found her referencing the Bible when she talked about their motivation: "This is our job here, to put on Christ, and to put off the old man." Wakefield grudgingly admired that "she did not beat around the bush."

Wakefield also found a Protestant version of the Catholic workers at the East Harlem Protestant Parish. For the first time since childhood, he found "a minister *I* could talk to, even about the religion I had declared myself an enemy of." That minister said that one reason he was drawn to working with those whose lives were decimated by addiction was that such people "come face to face with the deepest questions of existence." The pastor said those were the questions he also was interested in—and Wakefield agreed.

Wakefield says he felt a kinship with these kinds of Christians, and that they "kept me in touch with a reality beyond my own psychic navel." Their lives testified to the possibility of a reality he had dismissed. He now links them to something Jesus said, as recorded in all four Gospels: "For whosoever will save his life shall lose it: but whosoever will lose his life for my sake, the same shall save it." Wakefield says that "for my sake" includes people like those in the Bowery, for Jesus also says, "As ye do it unto the least of these, ye do it unto me."

## MORE GUIDES AND MENTORS—EVEN A PROFESSOR

Wakefield's title for one his chapters in *Returning* is "Guides." He had a lot of them. One of the first—while Wakefield was in the late stages of his flight from faith—was Mark Van Doren, a famous academic and the only professor he can recall at Columbia who took Jesus seriously.

Wakefield says Van Doren "saved Jesus for me," not as an object of faith, but as a character in stories that deserved respect. "As with all books we read, Van Doren honored the story, took it on its own terms, and helped us to absorb and understand it, to look at it fresh, not through the eyes of other interpreters, but with our own vision."

Van Doren said the Gospels painted Jesus as "the sternest of men," not interested in pleasing people nor in being "liked." Nor did he promise success and prosperity for his followers. In other words, the exact opposite of the picture painted by the Norman Vincent Peales of the world. It was a picture of a fiercer Jesus than Wakefield had imagined heretofore, and (as in Lecrae's experience) one more easily believed.

Van Doren was equally important for directing Wakefield's reading. He put him on to Thomas Merton, the Trappist monk and spiritual explorer. It was years after the recommendation before Wakefield actually read Merton, but when he did he found a kindred spirit. He read everything by Merton he could find, starting with *The Seven Storey Mountain*, but was especially taken with his short "meditation" *He is Risen*. In it, Merton said matter-of-factly that Christ "is in history with us, walking ahead of us to where we are going."

As with other Returners we have looked at, many of Wakefield's guides back to faith were writers—from both the past and the present. He engaged their fictional characters, memoirs, philosophical and theological reflections, poetry, and other genres of the written word. He specifically mentions St. Theresa, Dostoevsky, Henry James, and Albert Schweitzer, and contemporaries like J. D. Salinger, Carson McCullers, Chaim Potok, Eudora Welty, Robert Coles, Peter Matthiessen, and Annie Dillard.

During the years he was reading these people he was also a self-described "wanderer" and heavily addicted. "What seem miraculous in retrospect is that any sort of spiritual sensations at all pierced through the heavy armor of my atheism and the fog of my alcoholic/narcotic consumption during that era. And yet they did, as I think they most often do for us, through the guardian-angel 'messengers' or 'guides' whom we meet in the flesh or . . . in writing (and, for some people, in painting and music as well)."

The common thread in these writers for Wakefield is not that they explicitly advocate for God, but that they take the idea of transcendence seriously, and that they explore the possibility of that which is beyond time and space also infusing and giving meaning *to* time and space. (Compare Christian Wiman.) He cites the Catholic novelist Mary Gordon: "Faith requires that you say, 'There is a larger story than this story.'"

He quotes a passage from Salinger's *Catcher in the Rye*, spoken by a teacher to Holden Caulfield, that I suspect speaks also for Wakefield's hopes for his own writing: "Many, many men have been just as troubled morally and spiritually as you are right now. Happily, some of them kept records of their troubles. You'll learn from them—if you want to. Just as some day, if you have something to offer, someone will learn something from you."

## A SURPRISING RETURN TO A SURPRISING CHURCH

And along with a slow move back toward faith was a return to church. He didn't see it coming. It started in a Boston bar at Christmastime. A fellow at the table said "out of the blue" that he'd "like to go to Mass somewhere on Christmas Eve." Having been to church only once in the last twenty-five years, Wakefield had a reaction that surprised himself: "I didn't say anything, but a thought came into my mind, as swift and unexpected as it was unfamiliar: *I'd like to do that too*."

Unexpected and unfamiliar—simple nostalgia? a prompt from God? a whisper from the id? Whatever it was, Wakefield checked the local paper and chose King's Chapel in Boston, which describes itself as a Christian Unitarian church, a contradiction in terms for those in Wakefield's Presbyterian and Baptist past, but perhaps the only kind of place that Wakefield's hesitant return to faith could have survived at the time. And a church which states a goal even a Baptist could affirm (though understand differently): "In the love of truth, and the spirit of Jesus Christ, we unite for the worship of God and the service of all."

He heard a sermon that identified the three wise men as "latecomers" in their worship of the Christ child that made him feel a bit "singled out," but it was a literary and sophisticated sermon (based on a scene from a novel by Evelyn Waugh) and so did not drive him away. It took a few months for him to work up the courage to go again, courage being necessary because he recalled William F. Buckley's comment that "if you mention God more than once at New York dinner parties you aren't invited back." Being known as a churchgoer would not enhance any writer's career in New York. (Something Kathleen Norris also learned.)

At the following Easter he decided to go for it, even though he was nervous about being spotted while "crossing the Boston Commons on a . . .

Sunday morning wearing a suit and tie, a giveaway sign of churchgoing." To his surprise, he found neighbors and even a few friends among those in the congregation.

## AN EXILE FINDS A HOME

Wakefield had just returned to Boston from Hollywood, the latter a place that felt rootless and alien to him. He came back in an attempt to satisfy a deep need for "the pleasure and solace of *place*." Returning to church—and to the rituals of worship enacted in a community—contributed to that sense of finding a place, a home. "Birth and death and resurrection, beginnings and endings and renewals, were observed and celebrated in ceremonies that made me feel I belonged—not just to a neighborhood and a place, but to a larger order of things, a universal sequence of life and death and rebirth."

Wakefield says of this time in his life, "I was exiled for good from the world of atheism," but adds, "it's in exile that we sometimes find a home." Exile, he notes, is a fundamental part of the human experience. Adam and Eve were exiles, as was Abraham, and Mary and Joseph and Jesus, and the first apostles, and on and on. Wakefield decided that the church is "full of exiles" and that it provides a home for them all. So why not for him too?

Wakefield notes a key phrase in the story of the prodigal son. At his lowest, starving among the pigs, we are told the young man "came to himself." Wakefield believes the same thing happened to him—he came to himself. When someone loses consciousness and then returns, we say he or she "came to," back to an awareness of reality, of where and who they are. Wakefield experienced his return to God and to the church as just that.

But he also quickly adds that it did not end all his troubles, nor should it be expected to. "Going to church, even belonging to it, did not solves life's problems—if anything they seemed to escalate around the time—but it gave me a sense of living in a larger context, of being part of something greater than what I could see through the tunnel vision of my personal concerns."

It took him five years after joining the church to finally conquer alcohol and drugs. Having participated in endless secular programs over his life, he found that what finally made it possible was "prayer, meditation, Bible study, and the Church." In time, he felt as though these "life-numbing addictions" were "lifted," and the "only concept that seemed to describe such experience was that of 'grace,' and the accompanying adjective 'amazing' came to mind along with it."

He had not only started reading the Bible again, he was even asked to teach it at King's Chapel (not unlike Kathleen Norris's church asking her to preach). He found that teaching it made it come alive for him, and the book he had once dismissed now "became a source of power" that was "like holding up a mirror to my own life, a mirror in which I sometimes saw things I was trying to keep hidden, even from myself." The first Bible passage he was asked to teach on was the story of the man who "cleans his house of demons," only to have seven worse ones come instead. "I realized, with a shock, how I'd been deceiving myself, how much more 'housecleaning' I had to do."

Wakefield also had one of those quasi-mystical experiences that Returners sometimes recount, not as dramatic as his childhood "white light" experience, but striking nonetheless. He describes walking to church past the Boston cemetery that housed the grave of a seventeenth-century, churchgoing ancestor. Lost in thought, he suddenly felt "stopped by what felt like a gentle but firm blow to my midsection," strong enough to make him gasp for air. He instinctively looked across the street and realized he was parallel to his ancestor's grave, the ancestor who has two children buried in the grounds of King's Chapel, the church to which Wakefield was walking. And he suddenly felt a connection to a family of faith that brought tears to his eyes. "Knowing that the ancestors of my genealogical family were in the very ground of the place to which I had been so naturally drawn seemed part of the whole intricate pattern of my journey and return."

Even with all these developments in his life, Wakefield says, "I cannot pinpoint any particular time when I suddenly believed in God again." He had never liked the word "conversion"; it seemed too melodramatic and he associated its use with the unattractive political beliefs of the people who used it. He says his pastor explained that the underlying word, in both Hebrew and Greek, does not mean "born again," but rather "turning." "That's what my experience felt like—as if I'd been walking in one direction and then, in response to some inner pull, I turned."

It was a profound turning, not just an adjustment or helpful enhancement. He cites an encounter with Henri Nouwen and the priest's stern warning to him that "Christianity is not for getting your life together!" And the old Yiddish proverb states it for him even more forcefully, "God is not an uncle. God is an earthquake."

And faith in God is not a fixed, unchanging thing. "Faith is not static, nor is it in my experience a state or condition you arrive at and settle down in comfortably, having 'found it,' like a hidden Easter egg, or an answer to the meaning of life. Faith is dynamic, changing and challenging, taking on new shapes and forms, fading for a while and then manifesting in ways you least expect, sometimes subtly, sometimes shaking the very foundations of your being."

## A PLAIN CHRISTIAN, PURSUED BY GOD

Throughout his life, including while an atheist, Wakefield returned repeatedly to Psalm 23, not least when he felt he himself was passing through "the valley of the shadow of death." But years after his Return to faith, he decided that Psalm 139 described his long journey:

> Whither shall I go from they spirit? Or whither shall I flee from thy presence.
> If I ascend up into heaven, thou art there: if I make my bed in hell, behold, thou art there.
> If I take the wings of the morning, and dwell in the uttermost parts of the sea;
> Even there shall thy hand lead me, and thy right hand shall hold me.
> If I say, Surely the darkness shall cover me; even the night shall be light about me.
> Yea, the darkness hideth not from thee; but the night shineth as the day: the darkness and the light are both alike to thee.

Dan Wakefield did not return to the same expression of faith that he left. Befitting his church at that time, and his own spiritual convictions, Wakefield echoes the light metaphor of the psalm when he affirms that all religions have light in them. But he declares plainly, "For me, the light is Christ." Trying to avoid labels of all kinds, he says, "I'd like to declare myself a 'plain' Christian—the kind who's forgiven for his sins by the Jesus who forgave the woman at the well . . . ," a Christian "who believes in the crucifixion and Resurrection, and knows the human versions of both experiences."

# SHORTER STORIES OF OTHER PUBLIC FIGURES

IN ORDER TO EXPLORE more widely the diversity of experiences of Leavers and Returners, the following chapters offer vignettes of other public figures who have made the journey out of and back to faith. They are abbreviated versions of much longer and more complex stories, focusing on one or two factors in leaving and returning that highlight the wide variety. As with the previous, fuller chapters, these rely on published accounts from each person, using their own words.

## Chapter 6

## ANNE RICE: FROM JESUS TO VAMPIRES AND BACK AGAIN

"I couldn't believe in God. But the simple fact was: I did. The world of atheism was cracking apart for me, just as once the world of Catholic faith had cracked apart. I was losing my faith in the nonexistence of God."

—Anne Rice, *Called Out of Darkness*

Vampires as spiritual questers—who would think it? Anne Rice would. That's how she saw her characters in her many Vampire Chronicles novels, and it was a quest she followed in her own life. Raised in the totally immersive Catholicism of mid-twentieth-century New Orleans, she abandoned faith and church for almost thirty years, only to return when her faith in the replacement story—atheistic humanism—crumbled. Then, in the last part of her life, she fled the church once again, while retaining her faith in Jesus as the Christ. Jesus—yes, Christianity as religion—no.

The Catholicism of Anne Rice's childhood not only comprised her religious faith, it defined reality for her—not just in terms of what is true, but of the shape and texture and feeling of everyday life. Faith and God for her was sensory, sensuous, and everywhere present.

The faith of her childhood and adolescence was aesthetic and emotional rather than cerebral. She describes the pregnant spaces in churches and chapels and nature in which these spiritual encounters took place. "It is important to stress . . . that my earliest experiences involved beauty"—beauty "evoked such profound feeling in me that I often felt pain."

Architecture, statues, paintings, hymns, chants, smells, the sight of trees radiant in the sun—all this and much more made faith in God and the things of God a whole-person, daily experience for the young Anne Rice. "Everywhere I turned, I was assaulted by the sensuous and the atmospheric, and the beautiful." God made everything and therefore everything Anne knew of was fair game for exploring and enjoying.

Among the things she knew was that God "loved us, made us, and took care of us, that we belonged to Him; and I remember loving Jesus as God." She also knew, as she had been taught, that the bread in the tabernacle box on the altar was the very body of Jesus. Her mother said to her, "'He is on that altar. Get up and go.'" And she did. "I was as certain that Jesus was there as I was that the streetcars passed our house. I was nourished on the complexity of this." At this stage she found complexity nourishing; later in her life, complexity became quite troubling—as it does for many Leavers.

Anne's early faith felt to her completely natural and intimate. She talked endlessly to the people of the Bible and church history, including to their statues in church. "I talked all the time back then to The Little Flower. . . . And I talked to St. Joseph. . . . I talked to the Blessed Mother unendingly, and I talked to Jesus all the time." She could talk to them, unconcerned about time and space, because these were eternal beings and they were her family.

Jesus was especially accessible. "You could talk to the Child Jesus or you could talk to Jesus on the cross, or Jesus in the tabernacle. It was all Jesus. Jesus was beyond time, and Jesus was actually beyond place. . . . Jesus heard you whenever you spoke to Him. And Jesus saw you all the time whether you wanted Him to, or not. The concepts were not puzzling and they were part of life."

Anne was also drawn to the drama of ritual. "Ceremonies of the church were also part of this tapestry." They enacted a story, just as did the stations of the cross on the church walls, and they were beautiful and sensuous and full of meaning, never more so than in the consecration of the host during Eucharist—"a moment of spectacular importance and utter silence."

And then there was the music—sung in pre-Vatican II Latin, and all the better for that. The meaning of the words didn't matter. "The meaning was in the tone and the sound. . . . The sentiment, the sense of the sacred, the sense of the splendid opportunity, were all embodied in the tones and the music. . . . What mattered was that through the singing itself we were connecting with the Divine."

She left these services feeling "intoxicated," filled with "immense gratitude and wonder." Church and worship were the high points of her life. "I don't remember ever not wanting to go to a Mass or a service. I don't remember ever getting bored during one."

Anne's wholly positive experience with faith and church in her early childhood was not matched by her experience in Catholic schools. In brief, she says she hated her eleven years there. It was everything that church experience itself was not: authoritarian, harsh, intolerant, and legalistic.

Nonetheless, faith itself persisted throughout adolescence. When she was twelve she asked her father to build her an oratory—a private place for prayer and worship. "I was trying to be a saint." She "wanted to become a priest. When I was told that was impossible, I couldn't grasp why." It was the first but not the last collision between her feminist sensibilities and the Church.

The single most important person in shaping her early experiences of God was her mother. A highly intelligent woman who would die of alcoholism at age forty-eight when Anne was starting college, her mother "taught me a vital and rich Catholicism, and a very compassionate Catholicism." The compassionate aspect is important, because Anne Rice's later perception that it was no longer part of the church led her away from the church not once, but twice.

Rice sums up her Catholic youth this way: "we lived and breathed our religion and our religion was interesting, and vast, and immensely satisfying."

So when and why did she leave it?

Despite her satisfaction with her faith and the church, she left for perhaps the single most common reason that Leavers leave: the larger world outside of faith seemed more interesting, more inviting, more pleasurable, more ethical (especially with its interest in justice)—in brief, more true. Especially for a young woman becoming more philosophical and attracted to ideas. And it seemed to allow one to escape the often agonizing struggles with notions of sin, transcendence, miracles, heaven and hell, and identifying ultimate meaning. She describes what drew her away in simple terms: "It fell apart for me . . . simply because I was growing up," adding, "I was becoming curious about 'the modern world.'"

Most Leavers do not become atheists. They often live in a suspended state of long-term ambivalence, not exactly denying the possibility of God, but not affirming it either, certainly not with any specificity. They often adopt a form of "live and let live" that expresses itself as "believe what you want and let others do the same." It fits perfectly with Western individualism, relativism, and superficial tolerance.

Not so with Anne Rice. Beginning in college, she stated unequivocally that she was an atheist and that she looked to naturalistic, secular humanism for answers to life's big questions.

The most basic of those had to do with life's ultimate meaning—something Rice explored throughout her life and writing. As a young college student she embraced the conviction of Camus and other thought leaders of the time that it had none. Camus argued human life was absurd (because we yearn for ultimate meaning in a world that does not provide it), but that we should act with ethical integrity anyway, leaving unresolved the problem of convincingly identifying the ethical or moral in a relativistic world.

She saw this stance as courageous and honest, and she uses such terms to describe how she saw her own exit from faith and the church. She describes herself as "hungry for learning" and she discovers thinkers like Kierkegaard, Heidegger, Sartre, Camus, Kant, Huxley, and books such as "Nabokov's *Lolita*, even if it was a scandal"—maybe *especially* because it was a scandal.

Just as Kathleen Norris discovered at Bennington, Anne Rice discovered that her fellow students took sex casually and "weren't tormented by notions of sin." And as with Norris, Rice's own sexual inexperience "became something of a running joke."

She sums up this new world this way: "All around me I saw not only interesting people, but essentially good people, people with ethics, direction, goals, values—and these people weren't Catholic. They negotiated their moral decisions with considerable thought but without the guidance, it seemed, of any established church. I liked them. I was learning from them, learning from fellow classmates as well as teachers."

The result? "My faith began to crack apart."

And seeking guidance from the church merely completed the process. Torn by doubts, she turned to a priest for counsel. When he discovered how completely she had been raised in the church, he said, "For a Catholic like you, there is no life outside the Catholic Church."

As someone who was just beginning to discover how much life there was, in fact, outside the church, she recoiled: "when he said it, something in me revolted. I didn't argue with him. But I was no longer a Catholic when I left the room."

The church, which had been everything to her and almost wholly positive, was now seen as an enemy of her heart's new desires: "I hungered for experience, for risk. And I also believed mightily in the life of the mind, and the life of the artist. . . . The church had become for me anti-art and anti-mind. No longer was there a blending of the aesthetic and the religious as there had been throughout my childhood."

Even more destructive to her faith than her disillusionment with the church was her inability to separate it from her relationship with God. Her Catholicism had always equated God and the church, and she continued with that equation when her view of the church collapsed. She believed that when one went, the other went with it.

And it didn't help that she had long before stopped talking to God. "I hadn't felt entitled to talk to Him in a long while. I'd felt too demoralized to talk to Him. I just wasn't the Catholic girl who had a right to talk to him.... I think I had to stop believing in God in order to quit His church, and the pressure to quit became intolerable."

She found that she couldn't any longer bring to God her doubts and questions, including about God's very existence. "I never put my dilemma before God.... I failed to see Him as a Person of Infinite Compassion. My religious mind was an authoritarian mind, and once I found myself at odds with God, I couldn't speak to Him. I couldn't question Him. Instead I made decision *about* Him" (my emphasis). God became an intellectual question rather than a relationship.

The church, in her view, didn't have an adequate answer for her questions. In fact, the church was evidence *against* the possibility that there was a God: "The church, with all its rules ... had become absolutely proof to me that God didn't exist.... There just couldn't be a God. A God would never have made a church so unnatural and so narrow and so seemingly fragile—vulnerable to information, that is—as the Catholic Church."

She generalized her feelings about Catholicism to all of Christianity, perhaps to all religion: "People who believed in God believed in churches, and churches told you lies. Not only did they tell you lies, they made you tell lies. They taught you how to tell those lies when you were a little child."

She felt the Catholic Church in particular lied about its past and its failures—from the Inquisition to selling indulgences to its unfairness to women: "their goal was always the same—to gloss over the failings or corruption of the church.... As I lost my faith in God and in this church, these many lies seemed proof to me that I was moving away from falsehood and into truth."

So how did this Leaving work out?

Emotionally difficult at first, then feeling brave and honest, then long years of never looking back. "After a few months of dismal grieving for my faith, I began to feel a new relaxation, and a new passion for life." Leavers commonly express a sense of relief and freedom when they first leave faith and the church. Rice says there was also a darker edge: "But I felt a certain bitter darkness too. The world without God was a world in which anything might happen, and there would never be justice" for the poor and oppressed. She is impressed that the secular humanists she knew cared about such people, but she recognizes that in a naturalistic world without God, justice is simply another elusive and subjective concept. And no life hereafter to make things right.

With no guarantor of meaning, "we had to construct meaning in the silence in the wake of the departure of God." That might sound appealing to a young person hungry for experience, risk, and knowledge. But appealing or no, it was where Anne Rice found herself by the age of twenty. "So began my flight from the realm of faith and beauty and harmony which had been my childhood."

That flight included marriage to her high school sweetheart, Stan Rice, a man she loved and admired tremendously, and who, after forty-one years of marriage, died too soon in 2002. He, too, was an atheist—on steroids. He "scoffed at all religion in general. He did more than scoff. He felt it was stupid, vain, false, and possibly he thought it was evil."

Her husband's view was common among their friends when they lived in San Francisco and Berkeley. Rice discovered that secularism, like religion, has its taboos, and thoughts one is not allowed to think, certainly not publicly. "To think that a personal God had made the world was to yield to a demonic and superstitious and destructive belief." Such people were widely tolerant of diverse lifestyles, but less so of diverse beliefs.

Their early marriage included suffering. Their daughter, Michele, died of leukemia before she was six. It was an example of the randomness Rice now believed characterized reality.

Two years later in 1976 she published her first novel, and that changed the direction of her life. She did not expect a great response to *Interview with a Vampire*, and while in hardback it did not have one. But when it was issued in paper it exploded in popularity, not only among a cult following, but in the general reading public.

In hindsight, Rice saw that first novel as "an obvious lament for my lost faith. The vampires roam in a world without God; and Louis, the heartbroken hero, searches for a meaningful context in vain." It was a search that mirrored the author's own search, one that lasted for three decades, and continued even when she found again what she was looking for. She further describes that first novel—a description that more or less fits them all—as "a fusion of the aesthetic and the moral with some tentative connection to the lost harmony of my Catholic girlhood."

As well as receiving fame and riches, Rice also welcomed into the world a son—Christopher, born in 1978 (and now himself a successful novelist). Looking back, she says he was "aptly named, because he brought a saving grace into our lives that was all but miraculous."

Anne Rice wrote thirty-seven books in all, the most famous of which were the more than twenty novels of what came to be called the Vampire Chronicles and related novels. She says they are "experiments in loving and suffering and persevering. . . . I poured out the darkness and despair of an atheist struggling to establish bonds and hopes in a godless world."

Essentially, she did what Camus and many others suggested—she looked for and tried to live out lasting values in a world that didn't have any. It took honesty, they said, to admit there were none; it took bravery to live as though there were.

She summarizes how she eventually came to see the vampire novels: "These books transparently reflect a journey through atheism and back to God. It is impossible not to see this. They reflect an attempt to determine what is good and what is evil in an atheistic world. They are about the struggle of brothers and sisters in a world without credible fathers and mothers. They reflect an obsession with the possibility of a new and enlightened moral order."

She then adds, "Did I know this when I wrote them? No."

This admission that she was heading toward God before she was even desiring, much less looking for, God is not uncommon among Returners. At some point they often express the feeling that God is pursuing them. Rice cites more than once the famous Francis Thompson poem that portrays God as a bloodhound relentlessly pursuing the one who is fleeing his love.

She also says, "I wrote twenty-one books before faith returned to me." It is noteworthy that she implies that faith seeks her out—"returned to me"—rather than she consciously choosing to return to faith. It suggests that people return to faith, when they do, because God never stops pursuing the lost, and eventually they accept that they are found—and loved.

Rice's words above show clearly that she realized that she was on a spiritual quest. But they do not explain why she thought a return to faith was the fulfillment of that quest. What in her life guided her in that direction?

One important factor was studying history. She did so as part of her research for the settings of her novels: "The more I read of history—any history—the more my atheism became shaky. History, as well as Creation, was talking to me about God." She was especially moved by "the survival of the Jews, . . . which was talking to me about God. I was seeing patterns in history that I could not account for according to the theories of history I'd inherited in school. . . . A great love of the Jewish people began to burn in me." How did they survive as a community? "There was no convincing sociological or economic explanation at all."

Not everyone would find this convincing evidence for God, but Rice did. "If any one 'thing' in all my studies led me back to Christ, it was His people, the Jews." God seemed to her to show up in human history over and over.

Another important factor was her acceptance by her Irish Catholic, New Orleans family. When she moved back to New Orleans in 1998, she expected "to be rejected and shunned," the common fate of people who left the church when she was a child. Instead, she was welcomed back home. "To my amazement, these churchgoing people completely embraced Stan and Christopher and me," opening their homes and asking no questions about her leaving the church or her "transgressive" novels.

She not only found that "This acceptance puzzled me and interested me," she also was "intrigued by the way they managed to live in the world as Catholics." Rice had been unable since college to integrate faith and the modern world, believing it was one or the other. She was intrigued that "They had found a way to live faithfully with absolutes, and above all they had found a way to continue day in and day out believing in God."

They became examples of the possibility, even though she still did not see it as a possibility for herself. "Of course I believed that I could never really be one of these people again." She says she remained "doggedly and religiously faithful to an atheism in which I no longer believed."

She realized that atheism was just as much a faith as her previous belief in God. And it dissolved for her just as that first faith had dissolved. "I couldn't believe in God. But the simple fact was: I did. The world of atheism was cracking apart for me, just as once the world of Catholic faith had cracked apart. I was losing my faith in the nonexistence of God."

Losing her faith in atheism, yes, but she was not yet abandoning it. Three earlier trips abroad in the mid-1990s were crucial in loosening atheism's hold (just as Lecrae's trip to Africa was crucial for his Return.) The first was a trip to Israel. She told herself and others (as had Dan Wakefield), "I only wanted to see the geography," not admitting, "I was secretly obsessed with Jesus Christ, but I didn't tell anyone, and I didn't tell myself." She wanted to be where Jesus had been.

A second trip was to Brazil. She wished to see the famous statue of Christ the Redeemer on the mountain outside Rio. When she arrived, the huge statue was shrouded in clouds. As she stood there, the clouds lifted and there was Jesus with arms outstretched. "The moment was beyond any rational description. It didn't matter to me what anyone else felt or wanted from this journey. I had come thousands of miles to stand here. And here was the Lord."

She did not fall to her knees in faith, "But something greater than a creedal formulation took hold of me, a sense that this Lord of Lords belonged to me in all His beauty and grandeur." She wrestled with whether this experience of Jesus was simply of something symbolic or was something more. She decided at that time that it was, at the least, an experience of love. She lacked the courage to say more, but she felt clearly the sense of being pursued by God.

The last was a trip to Rome. As she did in all her travels, she visited churches, spaces that had been so important to the faith of her youth. She found herself sitting in a pew in St. Peter's during a communion service. She wanted desperately to partake in the Eucharist but felt she couldn't. She began to cry. "The pain of this moment was unforgettable. I felt I was not acknowledging something that I knew to be true; God was there. God was everywhere. God was God."

All of the above was preparatory for her actual Return to faith.

Rice wrestled with whether a return to God was an expression of cowardice or of courage. She uses both words in describing the struggle. She finally decided that the Return was simply an expression of who she was and what she now believed to be true.

There were still a number of steps in her full Return. She did not come back without a fight: "There was a storm in my heart and soul that had little to do with other people and their decision. I held out against God and I held out against the church because I thought I was holding out for bitter truth."

And yet the world all around her was testifying to the reality of God. "The creation was talking to me of God. . . . The music of a violin sang to me of God." The great painters and composers "talked to me of God. . . . The world around me was filled to the brim with God. And the person of Jesus Christ . . . weighed on my 'rational' mind." Even Christopher, "our free-thinking son," said he believed in God.

She speaks of "the Jesus who wouldn't go away" and says (like the characters in Flannery O'Connor's work) that she became "Christ haunted." The incarnation "began to obsess me as something unique in the history of the ancient religions I constantly studied." Eventually she proclaims, "the Incarnation has become the central overwhelming and sustaining mystery of my life."

Even the vampire novels she was writing played a role in her Return: "My own writing took me again and again and again to God"—as her characters "obsessed with the tension between kinds of religious fervor."

Despite all this, she says, "Yet I clung to my atheism; I clung with a martyr's determination."

Another of the many turning points in her pilgrimage—she calls them "small miracles"—came in December of 1998. The first occurred after a night of reading Augustine and others that led her to a decision to make peace with the church. Her journal entry for that day reads, "This is a happy day for me—my reconciliation to the Church. . . . I feel peace and quiet in my soul. I feel happiness."

The next day she goes to church and takes communion, the first time in decades. She says she was nervous when given the host, but afterward went to a side chapel to offer "my special prayer of thanks to God for giving me the Gift of Faith and the strength to do this." In her journal that day, she invokes again her favorite theological truth: "My mind was on Mass and Communion. I love the story of the Incarnation so much—the idea of a God becomes a man for love."

Rice says the second "small miracle" of that time was less important but just as unexpected. A week after taking communion, she fell into a diabetic coma—her first indication that she had the disease—and almost died. The doctors saved her. She indicates that the first miracle, returning to the church and faith is much more "complex" than the second, and she investigates it at length.

The key word Rice uses to describe her Return is "surrender"—not an easy thing for a woman who had long seen herself as a quester after hard truths, as one committed to wrestling meaning from a meaningless world. The thing that made it possible was her conviction that God, in the person of Jesus Christ, was deserving of surrendering to: "what I recall most vividly is surrender—a determination to give in to something deeply believed and deeply felt. I loved God. . . . I loved Him in the Person of Jesus Christ, and I wanted to go back to Him."

Rice did not return to God as an ultimate but distant Being, but to God as Emmanuel, living among us, sharing our experience. Jesus is the highest expression of God's love for his creation. And Jesus' living out of that love among us—to the point of death and resurrection—shows that God can be trusted. Both are central for Rice: "It was only in love and trust that belief followed."

And because she could trust God, she no longer had to have all the answers herself. She no longer had to be in total control and have irrefutable knowledge: "In the moment of surrender, I let go of all the theological or social questions which had kept me from Him for countless years. I simply let them go. . . . If He knew everything I did not have to know everything, and . . . in seeking to know everything, I'd been, all of my life, missing the entire point."

Rice uses the language of literature to explain her confidence in God's knowing: "In this great novel that was His creation, He knew every plot, every character, every action, every voice, every syllable, and every jot of ink. And why should I remain apart from Him just because I couldn't grasp all this?" And she adds, once again, "It was love that brought me to this awareness."

Rice returned to faith through an acceptance of love and a resultant trust that expressed itself as belief. But she never expected that her renewed life of faith would be easy—and it wasn't. She told herself at the time, "This will not be easy; this will not bring comfort. This is not going to make you feel good. This is going to be hard! But this is where you must go."

It would be hard, in part, because she had long been estranged from the Catholic Church and didn't know much of what its current stand was on social issues close to her heart (didn't even know the name of the Pope at the time). She said she didn't even care: "It didn't really matter how wretched it was going to be. I had to go! I wasn't going to deny Him any longer. I was going *home*."

In typical fashion, she decided she needed to know more—about Christianity in general, about the Bible in particular, and about the Church to which she is Returning (and which she heard had changed since the 1950s). So she read and studied. In describing her childhood faith earlier in *Called Out of Darkness*, she indicates the Catholic Church of her youth did not forbid reading the Bible for yourself, but also didn't encourage it. Now she found that she had "so little knowledge of Scripture that it was embarrassing." (It's not unusual for Leavers to be quite ignorant of what it is they are Leaving.)

She began studying the Bible intently, making use of scholars, many of them Protestant. Eventually, the Gospel of John, for instance, "stopped being a passel of quotations, and became a living account."

In addition to studying the Bible, she discovered in writing her novels about the life of Christ that the central call God made on her life was to love people. She calls it another "turning point." "I began then to realize what the message of Christ was for me: to love my friends and to love my enemies. And the mystery was that loving my friends was sometimes harder than loving my enemies." In fact, she decided that "Loving our neighbors and our enemies is perhaps the very hardest thing that Christ demands."

Lamentably, Rice discovered that Christ's demand for loving everyone is often unfulfilled within the church itself—and always has been. She says of Christianity in general, "We have been a quarreling religion from the beginning, born out of an earlier quarreling religion."

And she identifies it as the world's greatest argument against faith in God: "what drives people away from Christ is the Christian who does not know how to love." Rice applies it to herself, lamenting all the sins of unkindness and verbal cruelty that she was guilty of over the years.

Rice instinctively shied away from argument and controversy all her life (though she had famous intellectual shouting matches with husband Stan), and she tried to continue that with her return to the church, declaring "I do not want to be tempted by divisions and controversies." She adds, "I see people driven away from churches by these issues."

These words about being "driven away," written in 2008, would prove sadly prophetic—because they come true in Anne Rice's own life.

In time she does learn more about the ongoing stance of the Catholic Church on the social issues that were so important to her. The Church that told her when she was a child that she could not grow up to be a priest was still telling that to women. The church that said abortion was a sin against God was still saying it was a sin. And the church that always opposed same-sex physical relations, now opposed same-sex marriage. Christopher, her much loved son, is gay—and an activist—though she claimed that fact was not relevant to her own support for gay marriage. In addition to this, churches widely—of all kinds—had become deeply political, about which she said "the politics of religion has almost nothing to do with the biblical Christ."

At the end of her 2008 memoir about her return to faith, Rice makes a vow with Peter-like confidence: "I will never leave Him again, no matter what the scandals or the quarrels of His church on earth, and I will not leave His church either." Crucially, she kept the first part of the vow, as far as we know, to the end of her life. But the second part proved too much for her.

Only two years later she announced the following: "Today I quit being a Christian. . . . I remain committed to Christ as always but not to being 'Christian' or to being part of Christianity. It's simply impossible for me to 'belong' to this quarrelsome, hostile, disputatious, and deservedly infamous group. For ten years, I've tried. I've failed. I'm an outsider. My conscience will allow nothing else."

She elaborates: "My faith in Christ is central to my life. My conversion from a pessimistic atheist lost in a world I didn't understand, to an optimistic believer in a universe created and sustained by a loving God is crucial to me. But following Christ does not mean following His followers. Christ is infinitely more important than Christianity and always will be, no matter what Christianity is, has been, or might become."

These are direct, even aggressive words. Whether they are loving, the reader can decide. The positive take is that they reflect the righteous anger of Jesus while chasing the money changers out of the temple. The single most important fact for a person of faith is that she claims she still is one.

Essentially, Anne Rice became, eleven years before her death, a Done—one who, as was discussed in the opening chapter, is Done with church but not necessarily with God. In fact, having left the church twice, she is something of a Super Done. It raises the question of how important it is, or not, that a Returner to God also be a Returner to the church. Christ created the church and calls believers to participate in it. Most who come back to faith also come back to some form of the church, though often, as we have seen, to a different expression than the one they left.

Rice was asked if she had considered joining a progressive Protestant church, which would typically share all of her social convictions. She said she had not considered it. Perhaps that priest who said that raised as she was, she would never be happy outside the Catholic church was not entirely wrong, even though it offended her deeply at the time.

Perhaps it is proper to give the last word to a character in a late novel, *The Wolf Gift*, in which a werewolf prays the following: "Dear God, help me. Do not forget me on this tiny cinder lost in a galaxy that is lost—a heart no bigger than a speck of dust beating, beating against death, against meaninglessness, against guilt, against sorrow."

That was Anne Rice's prayer as she returned to faith in Christ. And she believed that the God of love answered her prayer.

## Chapter 7

## ROSARIA BUTTERFIELD: THE COST OF COMING OUT CHRISTIAN

"If the world hates you, remember that it hated me first. The world would love you as one of its own if you belonged to it, but you are no longer part of the world. I chose you to come out of the world, so it hates you.

—JESUS (JOHN 15:18–19, NLT)

"To my amazement, these churchgoing people completely embraced Stan and Christopher and me. They didn't question my disconnection from Catholicism. They said nothing about the transgressive books I'd written. They simply welcomed us into their homes and into their arms."

—ANNE RICE, *CALLED OUT OF DARKNESS*

LEAVING FAITH AND CHURCH often involves leaving relationships and communities. Sometimes Returning means the same. Rosario Butterfield was deeply involved in the lesbian community—as scholar, activist, and in her personal life with her lesbian partner. Raised a Catholic, she became a Universalist Unitarian. She and her friends mocked Christians as bigoted, intolerant, and stupid (a step beyond merely ignorant). She eventually left lesbianism and came back to faith largely through God's use of a couple who showed her extended kindness and hospitality over a long period. Coming back cost her the love, friendship, and respect of her lesbian and academic community. In finding God again, she found the pearl of great price. It cost her everything she had.

Rosaria was raised Catholic. She calls it "my childhood faith." It was a liberal version of Catholicism—Father Paul said the resurrection was a metaphor. And "Sister Mary Margaret taught me that original sin was like being born with a big bleach spot on my navy skirt." That didn't sound very bad to the young Rosaria, "sort of tie-dyed." The Sister added that if she went to Mass and took the host often enough, the spot would be filled in and her skirt would look fine.

The two words she most often associates with her parents are drunk and angry. Her father was an alcoholic and petty white-collar criminal (unbeknownst to the family at the time). Her mother drank heavily also and was clinically manic—alternating between generosity and rage. "In the presence of my mother, my job was to anticipate her every emotional need, body block all conversations that disobeyed her lordship, and, using any means available, keep her from exploding."

Though they took Rosaria to church and put her in Catholic schools, both parents were essentially hostile to religion. Every day when her father dropped the kids off at school, he said, "Be good, be polite, learn a lot, and don't believe anything the nuns tell you." Her mother was accepting when Rosaria declared herself a lesbian, but when "I came out as a Christian . . . all hell broke loose."

This background raises the question of how real or deep her childhood faith actually was. Did she ever have a faith to leave and return to? This is a question that can be asked of many of us regarding faith when young. God himself only knows. But Rosaria certainly considered herself a Christian in those years and says she loved the church as a child. Answer enough.

Her faith and her Catholicism were not things she consciously chose at a particular time—any more, she says, than she chose her Italian heritage. As with Anne Rice, it was simply the air she breathed as a child—as natural and unquestioned as walking or eating. It came to an abrupt and identifiable end, however, when she, through a friend, experienced a great betrayal. "I didn't ever remember a time when I chose to be Catholic, but I clearly remember the time I choose to walk away from the church—after my best friend confessed to having sex with our parish priest."

Many people report dissatisfaction leading to disaffection with the church—for reasons great and small. None are more devastating to faith than the sexual abuse of children and adolescents by those meant to spiritually nurture them. Such events damage the spirit not only of the victims, but of many who hear the stories of the victims. These violations of trust are among the most common reasons people give today for leaving the church and rejecting faith in God.

The legitimate response that it is a mistake to blame God for the heinous acts of human beings, even of church leaders, does not alleviate the repulsion. "For someone raised Catholic, . . . the church was God himself, so I never thought about separating the two." For many Leavers (compare Lecrae and Ann Rice), this equation is unquestioned—if the church fails me, then God has failed me. Case closed.

In Rosaria's case the crisis was compounded by the fact that the abusive priest, despite having sex with many children, was also the best priest she ever had in terms of teaching about "God's commandments, law, and love." The moral failure of a highly successful religious leader is all the more damaging, because the gap between appearance and reality is all the greater.

With the collapse of her religious faith, Rosaria had a replacement faith readily at hand. "I felt the furious betrayal of a jilted believer. My feminist vocabulary gave me the words to articulate this fury." Feminism became her new religion. Actually her religion was more expansive than that. It included a wholehearted embrace of lesbianism and affirmation of all the proliferating subdivisions of sexual identity.

She not only embraced all this, she became expert in it—a leader, a scholar, an activist, an exemplar. There is no more welcoming home for her adopted creed than the contemporary American university. There is no halfway in these things. She says identity politics in academia requires one to be a member of the group whose experiences you are researching. No one is considered expert in lesbianism, for instance, unless one is one. On her syllabi, she announced that any paper not written from a feminist perspective will receive a grade of "F."

Rosaria taught English and cultural studies at Syracuse University, specializing in "queer theory." She was "a rising star," lecturing on related topics around the country, including at Harvard, and co-writing her university's policy on benefits for partners, as opposed to spouses. This secular religion offered everything she needed: it explained her life, it explained the society she lived in, it explained human history, it gave her meaning and purpose and direction. And, despite the fact that she was heterosexual heretofore, it gave her a lesbian lover with whom she lived for ten years.

It also gave her a community, a replacement for the community that she lost when she left the church. Rosaria makes it clear today that she still values that community and believes it has a lot to teach Christians and the church about how to love and support a wide variety of people. Unfortunately, with her return to faith (and to heterosexuality), she found that particular community no longer valued *her*.

So how to account for her return? Unlike many, she did not experience a lack of meaning in her life after leaving God. Her enthusiasm for her replacement view of the world surpassed any enthusiasm she ever had for Christian faith and the church. "My life was happy, meaningful, and full." Belying a common Christian stereotype of the immoral unbeliever, she passionately "cared about morality, justice, and compassion"—more than most religious folk it seemed.

Along with her friends, she actively disdained American Christianity. "I considered myself an atheist, having rejected my Catholic childhood and what I perceived to be the superstitions and illogic of the historic Christian faith. I found Christians to be difficult, sour, fearful, and intellectually unengaged people."

She went further than disdain. She engaged in research for a book exposing conservative Christianity as a fraud and danger, especially in its political, culture-war forms. Politicized religion was anathema to her. "The surround sound of Christian dogma comingling [sic] with Republican politics" required a response. She thought Christianity well represented by a bumper sticker she agreed with: "Lord, please protect me from Your people!" All in all, "Christians just scared me to death."

Rosaria Butterfield at this point would have consider herself the last person to return to anything like a traditional, orthodox faith in God. So what happened?

Her return started with a letter from a reader of an article she wrote for the local newspaper attacking Promise Keepers—a conservative Christian movement focusing on men's role as husbands. It's title made her thesis clear: "The Promise Keepers' Message is a Threat to Democracy." She got many responses from the article, dividing them in piles on her desk between supporting ones and hate mail. And she got one that she didn't quite know how to categorize.

It was from Ken Smith, a local pastor. Rather than blasting her, or even arguing with her, it simply asked questions—such as how she had arrived at her positions, what were her presuppositions, and the like—the kind of questions an academic could respect. Initially, she threw the letter away, but then fished it out of the recycling and put it on her desk, "where it stared at me for a week."

Eventually there was a phone call and then an invitation to her to come to dinner. She accepted, not because she was interested in a return to faith, but for the good of her book. "My motives at the time were straightforward: Surely this will be good for my research."

Butterfield was used to seeing Christians at gay pride parades—holding placards with Bible verses promising they all were going to hell. She hadn't met any Christians exactly like the Smiths. "He did not mock. He engaged."

That dinner began a two-year process of returning to the church and to faith. Her description of her relationship with them should be studied by anyone trying to influence someone toward Christ and the church:

> Ken and his wife, Floy, and I became friends. They entered my world. They met my friends. We did book exchanges. We talked openly about sexuality and politics. They did not act as if such conversations were polluting them. They did not treat me like a blank slate. When we ate together, Ken prayed in a way I had never heard before. His prayers were intimate. Vulnerable. He repented of his sin in front of me. He thanked God for all things. Ken's God was holy and firm, yet full of mercy. And because Ken and Floy did not invite me to church, I knew it was safe to be friends.

A lot of key themes and words here: friends, "entered my world," exchanges, talked openly, intimate, vulnerable, mercy. And the wisdom to know that in Rosaria's case, at least, a quick invitation to church was not a high priority.

Nor was firing Bible verses at her. She says doing so would have simply ended conversations. At the time, she considered the Bible toxic, so hitting her with "the Bible says" would have been worse than counterproductive. On the other hand, as part of her research to understand the enemy, she read the Bible herself voraciously. Her community noticed. One of her transgender friends pulled her aside and warned, "This Bible reading is changing you, Rosaria." And it was.

So was singing the Psalter, something they did every Sunday evening at the Smith's house. The four-part harmony moved her, but the words of the Psalms at first were "startling, disarming, offensive, even vile." Offensive to her secular, ideological mind, but calling to her at the same time. "The music of the Psalms called something out from me, something that ranged between bitter rage and secret consent."

Rosaria kept going back to the Smith house, especially on Sunday evenings when they would often have many people over. She kept her guard up for a long time, openly scornful of these people and referring to it with her lesbian partner as "the cult house." "I despised them, I mocked them, I made sport of our Bible reading and Psalm singing, and they loved me, and included me, and prayed for me."

Rosaria would come to believe that the thing that began her Return to faith was what she calls "radical ordinary hospitality"—people simply opening their homes and hearts and seeing everyone, without exception, as neighbors needing God's love, as people made, each one, in the image of God and therefore valuable. The Smiths invited her to dinner, over and over. They treated her and her views with respect. They didn't pressure her, simply loved her. Their love made God's love more believable.

Rosaria's relationship with Ken and Floy demonstrates an almost universal factor in the story of Returners coming back to faith. There is nearly always a key person or persons who point the way back. They not only point, they model. Their lives become for the Returner one of the best arguments for Returning. They show that faith actually works, that it is real. By so doing, they make *God* real for the Returner.

Rosaria was not drawn back to faith by hospitality alone. (It was more than just the bean soup.) Ken helped her see that the seeds of faith, dormant though they might be, were still present in her life. He probed her with quiet questions about her past faith, about her attitudes toward the church, about her conception of God.

He asked about her experience as a Catholic. Had she been baptized? She wondered why an infant baptism could even be relevant. Ken suggested it meant, among other things, that she is a member of a family—God's family, a family she found it was not so easy to escape, and which eventually she came to embrace.

Had she ever repudiated the Apostles' Creed that she had memorized (and which, strangely, she found had been coming back into her head, irritatingly so)? Seeds planted earlier in her life started to flower.

She did not return to faith as abruptly as she left it. She returned to church before she returned to faith, beginning with the Presbyterian church that Ken Smith pastored. She found numerous models and mentors there in addition to the Smiths. She decided she needed to know more about godliness as it applied to women and she "went through the church directory and picked out the three women whose godliness, sense of self, personal strength, and integrity really stood out to me."

She meditated on powerful sermons by other members of the staff, learned from a Black woman educator, and while away from home experienced "real Christian living" through extended hospitality from Jerry and Ann and others. She calls them "teachers and role models" and gives this overview: "Pastor Bruce taught me to apply the means of grace that God provides to repent and to grow in sanctification. Jerry and Ann taught me to pray even when I didn't feel like it. Karla taught me to sacrifice and take risks. And Dean modeled for me how one grafts 'Christian' and 'professor' into one."

It was a long process of discovering, at a deeper level than she had ever experienced before, what was real and true and beautiful. "God slowly and powerfully changed me. I don't mean here that God changed me from gay to straight. The blood of Christ is too powerful to merely reflect status-shifts in identity or sexuality. God made me to see myself in the context of his love, his design, his authority, his sovereignty, his salvation, and in his holiness. I saw that in my pride I was persecuting Jesus himself, the one and only source of atoning love."

All of this did not come quickly or easily. She knew that returning to faith would not be simply an addition to her life, but a cataclysmic overthrow of it. Like C. S. Lewis, who famously described himself as "the most dejected and reluctant convert in all England," Rosaria says, "I fought with everything I had. I did not want this. I did not ask for this. I counted the costs. And I did not like the math on the other side of the equal sign." She understood that it was going to cost her everything—except the dog. And it did.

In the company of the Smiths and her church community, which had been praying for her for a long time, "Jesus triumphed. And I was a broken mess. Conversion was a train wreck. I did not want to lose everything that I loved. But the voice of God sang a sanguine love song in the rubble of my world."

Rosaria came to understand that her primary sin was not anything to do with garden variety sin or sexual sin. "My sin was that I was persecuting Jesus by failing to love him best. All the other issues were shadows and types of that sin. I lost my friends and my community. But he preserved my soul, renewed my hope, and restored my meaning and purpose, even in the midst of great turmoil and grief. Because God made me see that if I was set apart from before the foundations of the world to love and obey him, resistance was impossible."

Her sin was the one that Augustine had seen as foundational—inordinate love: the failure to love and value things at their true worth, loving too much things that did not deserve that degree of love, and loving too little the things that did, most centrally God in Jesus, her Creator and lover of her soul.

She needed not only to love Jesus but to love his church. Not every individual expression of it—not every congregation, every Christian leader, every movement—but to love and serve and be loved by the institution Jesus himself created.

She says Ken taught her that she "was not 'joining' a church, but rather was making a covenant with God." And that covenant would be lived out within "a church body." She found her church to be a healthy expression of such a community, with services that had "no show, no comedian pastors, no rock bands, no skits, no videos, no interpretive dancing." No cutting edge, just community and solid teaching.

One reason given for young people leaving the church is its failure to instruct them robustly in the faith—intellectually and theologically as well as emotionally. She says, "I'm grateful that the Lord brought me to a church that was as strong on teaching as it is on compassion." Not teaching instead of compassion, but the two intertwined.

Rosaria identifies pride as one of her besetting sins. It showed itself in her reluctance to make her return to faith known in her academic and lesbian community. Having long laughed along with her friends at Christians, having built her life around sexual and political identity, having embraced her calling as a leader in a progressive vision of the future, how could she explain that she was now back in church and pursuing God?

When some people have an experience with God, they want the whole world to know about it. Rosaria Butterfield says, "I wanted to go back to bed and draw the covers over my head." Initially she takes her return not as a "blessing" but as "a train wreck." And she has reason to be worried.

She describes her public 'coming out' moment" as a Christian as follows: "I saw my ex-girl friend and my lesbian- and gay-supporting graduate students go stone cold in disgust and disappointment." She was and is seen as a "laughingstock" and "traitor" by many in her former community. She was "out" as a follower of Christ. She had been an "outsider" as a lesbian, and was now an outsider for being a Christian. "This was my conversion in a nutshell: I lost everything but the dog."

Rosaria would have liked for her former and her present community to learn from each other and from her experience. She states it as a goal: "My lesbian friends had to learn that not all Christians are bigots. My Christian friends had to learn that Christians have a lot to learn from gay and lesbian folks about mercy work." But she says, "I didn't know how to bridge the two groups." Maybe they are bridgeable only by God.

She also says, "When I became a Christian, I had to change everything—my life, my friends, my writing, my teaching, my advising, my clothes, my speech, my thoughts." She had to ask herself a painful question, "Was I willing to suffer like Christ? Was I willing to be considered stupid . . . ?" Unlike some Christians in the world, she did not face the pain of torture or death; she faced the pain of being thought a fool by people she cared about. She decided to accept that.

Today, Rosaria Butterfield is a spokesperson for a specific kind of evangelism—the evangelism of hospitality. It calls people to "see strangers as neighbors and neighbors as family of God. . . . They open doors; they seek out the underprivileged. They know that the gospel comes with a house key." She is married to husband Kent, has adopted children, has taken in many in fostering and makes lots and lots of soup, often for strangers.

The actions of a perverse shepherd led Rosaria Butterfield out of the church and away from God. The actions of two faithful shepherds helped lead her back. They made faith winsome again. They made it believable. She is trying now to do the same. The church can learn from all three examples.

## Chapter 8

## A. N. WILSON: THE FAILURE OF ALTERNATE EXPLANATIONS

"But, my child, let me give you some further advice: Be careful, for writing books is endless, and much study wears you out."

—(Ecclesiastes 12:12, NLT)

The British writer and thinker (the two don't always go together) A. N. Wilson is in many ways a classic intellectual. He is unusually intelligent, curious, widely learned, verbally gifted (especially useful for slicing and dicing his intellectual opponents), and prolific. He processes reality primarily through words and ideas, and is intimately familiar with the history of both in the Western world over the centuries. He was also a man of faith until the middle of his career who then suddenly, loudly, and aggressively abandoned that faith, mocking as foolish those who continued in it, and relishing being in the company of the popular intellectual atheists of the day. He then slowly made—and is continuing to make—his way back to faith as he found that the secular replacement stories didn't live up to their promises.

Born in 1950 in the English midlands, Wilson had an elite education, including Rugby and Oxford. He was raised in the Anglican Church and initially entered Oxford at St Stephen's House, a Church of England seminary, with the goal of becoming an Anglican priest. He stayed only a year, transferring to New College, Oxford, at which, among other places, he would later teach.

Since the late 1970s Wilson has written more than twenty novels and about thirty books of nonfiction, many of them critical biographies of important figures from political and intellectual history, such as Dante, Darwin, Tolstoy, Queen Victoria, and the apostle Paul. At the same time, as if he needed more to do, Wilson has been a very active journalist, churning out articles, reviews, and essays at a furious rate. If Wilson has opinions about something or someone—and he has lots of them—they are likely to find their way into print.

And they are likely to be witty, confident, and iconoclastic. And sometimes smug, condescending, intellectually snobbish, and not necessarily backed up by the facts. All of which make him interesting to read.

Wilson has not written extensively, that I can find, about the nature of his initial faith. Having spent his childhood and youth in the church, however, and having studied for the purpose of serving in it, and having maintained that faith into this thirties, I think it is fair to assume that it was serious and an significant part of his life.

His faith, however, did not make it to his forties. In the late 1980s, a well-known figure in the literary and intellectual world, Wilson made what he himself later described as a sudden and very public decision to abandon his faith. In typical Wilson fashion, he not only left it, he trashed it as he departed.

At risk of oversimplification, and apart from any investigation of deep psychological forces at work, it appears the major stated reason Wilson left faith is that he no longer found it believable. The whole Christian story—from the Bible to church history to belief in a transcendent, spiritual reality beyond the physical—was simply no longer credible for him. It was an offense to reason, to science, to the direction of history, and to progress—that is, an offense to modernity.

Some people leave religious faith quietly, not even fully announcing it to themselves. Wilson doesn't do anything quietly. One of his first publications, in 1991, after his departure was the short work *Against Religion: Why We Should Live Without It*, a work whose title makes its contents self-evident. Even more telling, perhaps, was a biography he published near the same time on the great modern saint for some—especially American Evangelicals—C. S. Lewis.

In this book, which one reviewer called "sweetly poisonous," Wilson is as much interested in what he sees as the cultish veneration of Lewis as he is in Lewis himself. He works hard to deflate them both, providing a psychoanalytic picture of Lewis as trapped in childlike arrested development due to the death of his mother when Lewis was only nine.

Wilson is irritated in this book that Lewis is considered a brilliant thinker by many, diminishing the significance of Lewis earning three firsts in three different disciplines at Oxford and making a great deal out of a single debate later in Lewis's life that most acknowledge him losing, and which Wilson argues made him, in humiliation, give up apologetics and start writing imaginative children's stories.

Wilson says that writing this biography of Lewis was not only a product of his lost faith, but a cause and confirmation of it. "I can remember almost yelling that reading C. S. Lewis's *Mere Christianity* made me a non-believer—not just in Lewis's version of Christianity, but in Christianity itself. On that occasion, I realised that after a lifetime of churchgoing, the whole house of cards had collapsed for me—the sense of God's presence in life, and the notion that there was any kind of God, let alone a merciful God, in this brutal, nasty world. . . . It was a nonsense, together with the idea of a personal God, or a loving God in a suffering universe. Nonsense, nonsense, nonsense."

It is ironic that a book by Lewis that has led so many people into faith is the same book that helped lead someone else out of it. During the rest of the 1990s, Wilson writes, among other books, similarly skeptical biographies of Jesus and Paul and one entitled *God's Funeral: The Decline of Faith in Western Civilization*.

He testified, as many Leavers have, to the almost giddy relief he felt when he no longer had to believe in God and in the Christian understanding of reality. "It was such a relief to discard it all that, for months, I walked on air." He felt, for the first time perhaps, that he fit in with the intellectual world around him. "At last! I could join in the creed shared by so many (most?) of my intelligent contemporaries in the western world—that men and women are purely material beings (whatever that is supposed to mean), that 'this is all there is' (ditto), that God, Jesus and religion are a load of baloney: and worse than that, the cause of much (no, come on, let yourself go), most (why stint yourself—go for it, man), all the trouble in the world, from Jerusalem to Belfast, from Washington to Islamabad."

Wilson's books after his "road to Dawkins" experience (my dubious wordplay), and his enthusiastic journalistic attacks on religion (including a snarky description of Billy Graham—"the old matinee idol"), made him suddenly very popular among a growing breed of what was soon to be called the New Atheists, a popularity he very much relished. He delighted in social interactions with name atheists such as Christopher Hitchens and Richard Dawkins. He recounts a kind of atheist catechism that Hitchens put him through while sipping wine together after dinner:

"So—absolutely no God?"

"Nope," I was able to say with Moonie-zeal.

"No future life, nothing 'out there'?"

"No," I obediently replied.

Wilson felt he finally fit in. "As a hesitant, doubting, religious man I'd never known how they felt. But, as a born-again atheist, I now knew exactly what satisfactions were on offer. For the first time in my 38 years I was at one with my own generation. I had become like one of the Billy Grahamites, only in reverse."

Like people walking down the aisle at a Billy Graham meeting, he had experienced a conversion. He felt elated. He was in step with his times. He believed only what it was reasonable to believe—no embarrassing virgin births or resurrections from the dead or promises involving eternity, no indefensible Crusades, or abuse of women, ethnicities, and the sexually diverse. Fully modern. Fully rational. Fully believable.

Until, that is, he could no longer believe his new beliefs.

Everyone lives by a story or stories, whether consciously or not. No important story can be abandoned without another story eventually taking its place. Some people who leave faith are less aware than others that they have replaced one set of beliefs with another. They think, if they think at all, that they can keep the good parts of their former belief, and ditch the unpleasing parts, oblivious to the reality that they have abandoned the foundational beliefs that make those "good parts" credible.

Wilson is not one of those people. He was very aware that he was moving from a belief in spiritual transcendence to an embracing of materialistic immanence. The world is flat, as that great intellectual John Lennon crooned:

> Imagine there's no heaven
> It's easy if you try
> No hell below us
> Above us, only sky.

Because the world is flat, human culture is self-made. There are no values, no beauty, no goodness, no truth (most of all, no Truth) that we have not ourselves made. Nature knows nothing of justice, of compassion, of art, of faith. We have made—made up—all these things—*imagined* them says Lennon—and we can change them anytime we wish, to suit ourselves, individually or corporately.

Ironically enough, given the common clichés about skepticism leading to loss of religious faith, Wilson attributes his conversion to atheism, in part, to a lapse in his lifelong habit of skepticism. "By nature a doubting Thomas, I should have distrusted the symptoms when I underwent a 'conversion experience' 20 years ago. Something was happening which was out of character—the inner glow of complete certainty, the heady sense of being at one with the great tide of fellow non-believers."

People of faith are often chastised for their certainty, a possibility that has supposedly evaporated in our relativistic world, but Wilson found that there was more a sense of comforting certainty among his new atheist friends than he ever had as a believer. And he found that certainty—actually certitude—is as brittle for fundamentalist atheists as it is for fundamentalistic Christians. Once it cracks, it is likely to splinter.

Among the things that caused his own atheistic certainty to crack was the example of faith in so many people, throughout history and still today, who he greatly admired and whose lives he would wish to emulate. "I was drawn, over and over again, to the disconcerting recognition that so very many of the people I had most admired and loved, either in life or in books, had been believers." He contrasts what he calls the "ephemeral pundits" of nonbelief today with those who have embraced faith over the centuries and opts to be part of the latter community. "I have as my companions in belief such Christians as Dostoevsky, T. S. Eliot, Samuel Johnson and all the saints, known and unknown, throughout the ages." He adds Thomas More, Bach, and Bonhoeffer.

This could be called the "kindred spirits argument." Whose lives embody what I most desire for my own? Whose lives make their beliefs and values believable? Who do I want to be like; who do I want to hang out with?

He contrasts, for instance, the ethics that flow from Bonhoeffer's Christian faith—which both resulted in his execution by the Nazis and sustained him in it—with those derived from pure Darwinian materialism. "Read Pastor Bonhoeffer's book *Ethics*, and ask yourself what sort of mad world is created by those who think that ethics are a purely human construct. Think of Bonhoeffer's serenity before he was hanged, even though he was in love and had everything to look forward to." Wilson simply could no longer consider such people stupid or ignorant or somehow out of touch with reality. They struck him instead as in touch with the deepest and truest reality there is.

Wilson also came to realize that the most important things in life involved more than the intellect. Long too much dazzled by his own intelligence, he came to realize that we are more than our minds, and that more than the intellect must be heard from in deciding what is real and worth committing to. He realized that "religion, once the glow of conversion had worn off, was not a matter of argument alone. It involves the whole person." The lives of those Christians he admired taught this, and so did the pain he felt with the death in a short span of family and friends. "Watching a whole cluster of friends, and my own mother, die over quite a short space of time convinced me that purely materialist 'explanations' for our mysterious human existence simply won't do."

They "won't do" on an intellectual level for Wilson, but on an ethical, aesthetic, and emotional level as well. The music of Bach comes not simply from the complexities of his brain, but also from the truth and power of his faith. "J. S. Bach believed the story, and set it to music. Most of the greatest writers and thinkers of the past 1,500 years have believed it." So Wilson decides he will risk believing it himself.

Which leads him, after his return to faith, to joining with seventy or eighty people from the two churches near where he lives to walk together around the neighborhood on a Palm Sunday with palm branches, singing "All Glory, Laud and Honor!"—to the smiles of some observers, the bemusement of others, and the honking horns of drivers who are upset with them for sometimes blocking the road. What would Hitchens and Dawkins think of their former disciple now?

Wilson, ever in character, says he is glad that his returned faith to faith irritates and amazes the materialists. If he is being foolish, he likes the company of his fellow fools—from Dante to Dostoevsky to Bonhoeffer. The Easter story does not answer all our questions, especially not our rationalistic ones. "Nor is it irrational. On the contrary, it meets our reason and our hearts together, for it addresses the whole person."

The Easter story "changes people's lives because it helps us understand that we, like Jesus, are born as spiritual beings." Ironically (I find myself using the concept of irony a lot with Wilson, and with Returners generally), Wilson is echoing the C. S. Lewis he once diminished, who claimed, "You don't have a soul. You are a soul. You have a body."

Wilson continues regarding our spiritual essence, "Every inner prompting of conscience, every glimmering sense of beauty, every response we make to music, every experience we have of love—whether of physical love, sexual love, family love or the love of friends—and every experience of bereavement, reminds us of this fact about ourselves."

Wilson says that one of the strongest arguments for faith is simply radically transformed lives. The faith story starts with Creation and reaches its climax in the working out of that story at Christmas and Easter. In walking around his neighborhood with palms and song, Wilson is testifying to his own return to the story and transformation by it.

# HEARING FROM THE COMMON FOLK

To this point, we have heard from public figures who have access to a printing press or microphone or both. They have shared their important stories in print (often scattered through various books and interviews) for anyone interested and, in doing so, have done a great service.

But there are many, many more folks who have taken similar paths whose stories are known only to themselves or to a few. These are people who may be sitting just down the pew from you, or are teaching your Sunday school class, or are cleaning the church building, or perhaps haven't yet worked up the courage to return to church, though they have returned to faith.

If there was no great strategy in choosing the preceding stories from public figures, there is even less in collecting the following stories. I simply asked around and these are responses. Some are friends. Some write and are telling their own stories. I tell the stories of others, including their words in the telling.

Some left faith entirely, some only traveled to the edge, some are not sure which. Since the line dividing stressed belief and unbelief is murky—again, known only to God—these travelers often are not clear themselves whether they ever actually stopped believing in the God of the Bible, or whether they just wrestled with God—Jacob-like—until, exhausted, they decided, for a variety of reasons, to accept the risks and rewards of committed faith.

# Chapter 9

## A LOVE STORY
### by PAULA HUSTON

**I am seven**, lying on my back on a soft bed of forest mulch and gazing up through great gnarled tree branches at the blue Sierra sky. I have always loved trees, but these are more than trees. These are giant sequoias, huge stately Beings older than anything else I know about, and they are so beautiful they make my chest hurt. I stare upward as far as I can see; I am a bird swimming through air. I want to lie on my back in this grove of enormous Beings for the rest of time, but then I hear my mother calling and make myself return to the land of the living.

**I am ten**, all dressed up for my favorite holiday. I am wearing white patent leather shoes, white gloves, and a starched yellow Easter dress. My Easter hat, a white headband covered with pink and yellow plastic daisies, is perched atop my white-blond hair. The front of the church is smothered in white lilies; bars of morning light through the 1950s version of medieval stained-glass windows fracture into blobs-of-many-colors when they strike the deep red carpet. Eldre, the organist, has been swept away in a rapture of bass notes. Three trumpeters are playing their hearts out—blast after joyful blast—and we are shout-singing my favorite hymn: "Jesus Christ is risen today, hallelujah! Our triumphant holy way, hallelujah!"

Easter morning at Christ Lutheran Church in Southern California. My dad, along with the other dads from Minnesota where we are from, helped build this church. We members of Christ Lutheran are all Scandinavian, a fact that makes me proud. I'm proud of Minnesota too, which is full of Scandinavians—in my own family's case, Norwegians. This is what Norwegians from Minnesota do: they find other Minnesota transplants and build yet another upside-down-boat–shaped Scandinavian Lutheran church.

Along with serving on the construction crew, my dad is the church treasurer. He is also in charge of the Memory Work program. The thought here is that Russia may eventually try to annihilate us with nuclear warheads. If we survive the attack, we will all be thrown in prison where—under Communist rule—Bibles will not be allowed. So starting in kindergarten, we are strongly encouraged to memorize important verses from the Bible, for the Communists cannot erase what is embedded in our minds.

Every time we get yet another slice of Scripture under our belts, we Christ Lutheran kids go to my dad and recite it as accurately as possible. The program ends in sixth grade, and if we make it all the way through, we will have memorized a significant chunk of both the Old and New Testaments, not to mention *Luther's Small Catechism.* Plus, won a prize. I've got two years to go. My mom teaches Sunday school. We attend a lot of church potlucks and also bring casseroles to the spring picnic, where Pastor Art plays football with the high school boys.

I love my church. I can't imagine religion being handled any other way than it is right here at Christ Lutheran.

**I am twelve**, recently graduated from the Memory Work program (the prize turns out to be a white Bible with my name on it, emblazoned in gold), and I'll soon be moving on to junior high and confirmation classes. These happen on Saturday mornings and will last for two years. Since I'm already a straight-A student, I'm sure I'll do fine. Meanwhile, Pastor Art's wife has started hiring me to babysit their three little kids. Since I'm the oldest of five, I guess they think I've got the required expertise.

The first time my dad drops me off at their house, I'm nervous. This is our pastor's *private house*, after all. Not that Pastor Art is one to stand on ceremony—look at those church picnic football games—but still. Every Sunday morning when he places his palms on the podium to deliver his sermon, he becomes something more than human, though I really can't put what that is into words. All I know when I go to his house to babysit is that I don't want to see any private things, like his toothbrush or his beer in the fridge, or some fly-fishing magazine lying around. Whether he wants it or not, I need him to be special.

To my horror, his wife, a very pretty woman who is still dressing for their outing, calls me into their bedroom to give me instructions about their kids. She is carefully outlining her lips in front of their bedroom vanity mirror; the bed is not made; the back of her dress is not yet zipped up; I can see a couple of dirty white socks—*men's* socks—balled up in the corner of the room. Please, Pastor Art, I am silently praying. Please, please, don't come out of the bathroom in your sleeveless undershirt. Don't let him do it, God.

Instead, he needs her help with his tie, just like my dad does from my mom, and he has to give his shoes one last swipe of brown polish before they go. And then I am left alone in their house, in charge of their towheaded kids—they could easily pass for Norwegian toddlers—and when I am trying to feed the three of them dinner, I discover something even worse than the balled-up white socks: their silverware drawer is as big a mess as my mom's.

**I am fifteen,** still an A student, the president of our Luther League group, and in charge of our monthly Sunday night meetings at the church. The big news at Christ Lutheran is that we have a new pastor, Reverend George. Another Norwegian from Minnesota, of course, but quite different than Pastor Art. He's got some ideas about "the youth," as he calls us. He wants us to know a lot more about the world than he thinks we probably know. We have already been to Tijuana twice in caravans of cars driven by volunteer parents to deliver canned goods and used clothing to an orphanage he's familiar with there. He has taken a group of us to a halfway house in Hollywood where "ex-cons," as one of the parents calls them, are living in a rehab situation. "Rehab," I'm pretty sure, has something to do with drugs. He thinks that kids our age can handle anything, which excites me because I fervently believe this too, though most of our parents do not.

Tonight we have visitors: a group of kids from Calvary Chapel, a place I've heard of from *Life Magazine*—a place where street people and drug addicts and young runaways are being converted and their lives turned around. This visit by the Calvary kids is a good example of how Pastor George tries to expand our horizons. I am dubious at first—they seem overly enthusiastic, too ready to share their "personal testimonies," too eager to hug us, as though we are long lost friends of theirs from kindergarten days. Some of them are overly thin, their eyelids an irritated rabbity-looking pink. Some look far too old for their ages, and one of the girls tells us that up until she got born again a few months back, she was a prostitute. I don't like the way they keep saying "Jay-sus!" and "Praise the Lord!"

Then we make a "prayer circle," clasping hands with the kids on either side of us. One of them begins to pray, then another takes over, and suddenly I feel myself falling, falling, then caught and held upright by the skinny fingers of a fourteen-year-old ex-addict on one side and the former prostitute on the other. Embarrassed and frightened, I begin to weep. Lights pop and snap in my head. I'm afraid I might pass out.

For the next three months, I lock myself in the bathroom each day after school so I can read the Bible uninterrupted. If God can straighten out those poor Calvary kids, I think, then he can do *any*thing, and my constant urge is to "praise him without ceasing," as one of them so reverently, if incorrectly, put it. Which I do, including at night when I should be sleeping.

My increasing fatigue, however, can't compete with my euphoria. I am swept up in a fiery whirlwind of God, and nothing—not even my quest to become valedictorian—can possibly matter more than this. God has gotten loose from Christ Lutheran Church and into me.

Then I meet a boy from another Luther League group across town: my first date, my first kiss, my first love. In an instant, my focus swings from God to this new miracle in my life: a boy who loves me back. On our first date, I decide I will marry him. All the tremendous energy of devotion I've been so ineptly grappling with for the past three months finally has a human target.

After the shock of losing this spiritual high wears off, I have to admit that replacing God with a boy has been a relief. It feels a lot more normal, at least.

**I am seventeen,** lying on a cot in a lightless adobe clinic in a village in Honduras. Though I tell myself I am miserable—my true love is back home in California, isn't he?—I am supercharged with the adventure of it all. I can't believe my parents let me go on this program, which is called "Amigos de las Americas," and is run by a couple of good-looking guys in their early twenties, the sons of United Fruit Company executives, who drive Honduras's muddy roads in beat-up old pick-ups with broken shock absorbers and assure us that we are making a difference in the world.

Though I have been flirting with the idea of becoming the next Albert Schweitzer since I was ten, I am no longer flirting; thanks to Amigos, I am now 100 percent committed. I *must* go into medicine, if not as a doctor, then as a nurse. I *must* serve the poor and downtrodden. This is why Pastor George asked if I'd be willing to volunteer in this inoculation program in Central America. He clearly recognized this calling in me. This Honduran village called Guinope—along with the orphanage in Tijuana, the halfway house in Hollywood, and the big sister/big brother program for the kids in the Carmelitos Housing Project—is where real life is happening. And even though the God who once set me so embarrassingly on fire has vanished as though he never existed, as far as church is concerned, I'm still all in.

**I am nineteen,** walking down the aisle in a long-sleeved, Empire-style dress and trailing veil. I am not going to be a doctor after all. I'm not even going to college. Instead, I'm marrying that boy of mine and working full-time as a clerk for a chemist who makes concoctions for printed circuit boards so that my young fiancé, a promising baseball pitcher, can finish his degree and get drafted by a great team and go on to the majors.

The music for my wedding is being provided by the "Lord's Joyful," a hootenanny-style Christian guitar group I started several years ago at Christ Lutheran. Though we mostly play at old people's homes, we have gotten pretty good. And now they are all here, cheering me on. The weird thing is, here they all are, singing and clapping for Jesus, but I haven't believed in God for quite some time by now. This faith crisis happened after Honduras. I saw too many innocent people undergoing too much suffering. When I got back to California and went to Pastor George about this faith problem of mine, he didn't have a lot to say. His fifteen-year-old son, two years younger than me, had just been diagnosed with terminal cancer.

So I quietly let God go for good—I hadn't felt a single spark of him for quite awhile, after all—though not the church. Never the church. I believe in the good work the church is doing. Which is why it is okay that the "Lord's Joyful" are singing for my wedding today.

**I am twenty-four**, the mother of a six-week-old baby girl, and she is being baptized today, though not at Christ Lutheran Church. We no longer live in Southern California. My husband is still playing baseball, though not professionally—by the time he finished college, he'd injured his shoulder and that was that. So here we are in a new town in a new part of the state in a new Lutheran church, filled with the same sort of former Midwesterners I grew up with. I am comfortable among them. By now I have been a churchgoing nonbeliever for seven years. Nobody knows. In fact, I'm so good at pretending to be a Christian that I have been put in charge of the youth group.

After the baptism, our new pastor introduces us to several young couples who attend this church. One of these couples lives in our neighborhood. Our pastor says he hopes we can all become friends.

**I am thirty-six,** a living cliché, a divorced and remarried woman in a philosophy classroom, bent on finally getting a degree. My professor is lecturing on Hume, something to do with a great breakthrough he made in the—what was it? The eighteenth century? I'm trying my best to take good notes but I'm yawning. After all, I'm not only a full-time student but a mother of four (I always put it this way, never mentioning that two are my seldom-seen stepdaughters), a wife, a university employee. Not to mention, a serious writer. I'm doing my best, I think defensively. This is something I often do: defend myself to myself, as though I am two people in terrible disagreement. I struggle to pay attention, but so far this business—modern ethics—is dryer than dry. Then, however, my professor says something that makes my head come up. "What Hume was pointing out was a simple thing no one had spelled out quite so explicitly before, and that is the gap between 'is' and 'ought.'"

This arrests me for some reason, though at first I'm not even sure what it means. I look up Hume's own words on the subject and find myself disturbed. What Hume is asking, I finally decide, is how we justify our morality. And I don't have a clue.

I want Hume to be wrong. I want there to be an anchor for goodness that's stronger than, as he puts it, "habit and convention," and I'm surprised at myself for wanting this so badly, considering what I've been up to for the past decade. Oddly enough, however, I would rather believe I've been contravening some venerable, weighty, pure law of goodness than simply flying in the face of arbitrary social mores.

I take more ethics classes, all from the same professor, mostly because I am too embarrassed to trot my ignorance before anybody else in his department. I read bits of Plato, Aristotle, Augustine, each making me more miserably aware of two separate but related problems: the depth of my ignorance and the confusion that reigns in my moral life. When I am not taking a class, I am asking questions. I can't seem to get enough of this business: it is as though I have been thirsty for years and am finally being offered an unlimited supply of fresh water, even though there are times this waters burns going down.

The day arrives when I begin to bring my own life into these discussions, and I realize that I have developed an urgent need to get better, to *be* better. The woman who once wanted to be Albert Schweitzer, I think sadly. What *happened* to her? I confess some of this to my professor, who knows how to listen and what not to say. He assures me that I am not alone, that countless human beings have been down this road before me. I tell him how frightened I am, that I don't believe I have the courage or strength to change myself no matter how I want to. I tell him I wish I *could* believe in God, that this would probably help, but I can't. I gave up on God after Honduras, I explain, when I was only seventeen. When he asks me why, I tell him, a long litany of accusations having to do with God's seemingly insouciant disregard for the suffering of innocents. I'm guessing this will make more sense to him than that bizarre and ultimately anticlimactic Calvary Chapel experience of mine.

My professor says, "There's a way to read the Bible that doesn't make God out to be a fool."

**I am thirty-nine,** still struggling, but in a different way. I've accepted my professor's challenge—I've studied Christ's words—and what they've pointed me toward is something so profound I can hardly bear to think about it. Because thinking about it will require doing something about it, and I'm not yet ready for that.

Though I stopped going to the Lutheran church after my divorce and new marriage to the man I first met on the morning of my daughter's baptism, today I'm sitting in a pew at the local Catholic church, where I sometimes come for a little tranquility. The light is very bright high up where the windows are, softer below. The old white adobe walls, bulging fatly here and there, look soft too, not like the cold gray stone of the big European cathedrals, but homespun. The pews are simple, straight-backed, uncomfortable, green, scarred by a couple of centuries of school kids' surreptitious carvings. One of Father Serra's California mission churches.

This time I have not come for tranquility, however, but to meet my professor's wife. He's told me about her; she sounds different from anybody else I know—*better* is perhaps a more appropriate word, and better is what I need to be. She goes regularly to a monastery up the coast, she has monk friends, she says the rosary, all of which sounds unbelievably medieval but strangely compelling. The truth is I am looking for proof that God, if he actually exists (and I'm starting to think—no, *hope*—that he does), is not anything like the charismatic fantasy I fell for at fifteen, and that sane people are in no danger of being carried away in a euphoric rapture if they say a little prayer once in awhile.

Then I spot her, three rows back. She's down on the kneeler and her eyes are closed and in the diffuse light with her head tipped slightly that way she looks beautiful, but this purely aesthetic judgment doesn't begin to capture what makes her so compelling. It's her utter stillness. She has gone somewhere with someone she loves and they are conversing in private and she will have to haul herself back to this world when she is done.

For a moment, I am tempted to flee. This meeting might have been my idea, but I'm no longer sure it was a good one. What I'm observing here is clearly not crazy but—just as clearly—intensely serious, on a whole different level than saying a little prayer once in awhile, and if I stay, if I talk to her, I may have to take what I've just seen with equal seriousness.

**I am forty**. I have never seen monks before, and despite my best efforts to resist their draw, I am magnetically attracted in the same way I was attracted, years ago on a road trip through Pennsylvania, by the Amish and their horse-drawn plows. Why do I find these monks so intriguing? Most people who call themselves Christians are indistinguishable from me. They wear the same kind of clothes, live in the same kinds of houses, drive the same freeways, watch the same movies, buy the same stuff. The radically alternative lifestyle of these monks makes the hippies of my youth look tame.

I am here with my professor's wife, who has become a friend—no, more than a friend: a spiritual guide. She's a lifetime Catholic, a traditional Catholic, so it surprises me a little that she is so connected to these strange monks, who run a gift shop where books by the pope intermingle on the shelves with Protestant, Jewish, Muslim, Hindu, and Buddhist titles. I'm puzzled; I always thought Catholics believe they are the One True Church and everyone else is a heretic. But then how would I know? Pretty much everything I think I understand about Catholics was taught to me by my Lutheran mom, who sternly disapproved of anything having to do with the pope.

**I am forty-one,** and have for some time been going to weekday Mass on my way to the campus where I now teach. I keep a low profile and take my cues from the other early morning faithful. Much of what goes on is physical. I'm surprised, because I never thought religion had much to do with the body. There is a dance-like rhythm to it—genuflect, kneel, stand, kneel—that feels choreographically wedded to the liturgy.

Slowly, as the liturgy becomes more familiar to me, I find myself missing it when I can't be there, wanting to be present even though I can't participate. I see that the center of the Mass, the Eucharist, is the fulcrum around which everything else turns. For a long time I am too shy to go up, instead kneeling in my pew with head down and eyes closed, listening to the shuffle of people moving past me, the priest intoning, "The body of Christ, the body of Christ." For some reason, the hush, the shuffle, the chanted words always make me cry, and I sense that this has as much to do with the physical, the presence of the faithful around me, as it does with the spiritual presence that hovers over us like incense.

Inevitably, the day arrives when I join the throng, crossing my arms over my chest when I get to the priest holding the plate of hosts, as I have seen other non-Catholics do. For several long moments, I stop breathing as he leans forward to trace a cross on my forehead in blessing. This, too, makes my heart swell and weep. I am amazed that this sacramental stuff can sweep me around so powerfully, even as a nonparticipant on the periphery.

Especially since I am still struggling with the whole God question.

**I am forty-three,** and about to become a Catholic. It has been a long road, particularly because I had to obtain an annulment of my first marriage before I could proceed. The "Tribunal"—a committee of patient priests charged with reading my lengthy life story, plus the testimonies of five witnesses regarding my capacity for making good choices back then—have submitted their final report: as a "grossly immature" teenager, they are convinced, I was incapable of making a solid, adult decision to marry when I did.

Embarrassingly true.

Now there is only one more hurdle to pass: before I can officially become a Catholic, I must remarry my present husband in a ceremony conducted in the sanctuary by a priest. So today we are assembled at the Old Mission: my husband, the kids, and our two witnesses—who else but my professor and his wife? The priest, who has been of great help during this long ordeal, is happy to see me, and he signals me to follow him back into the sacristy for a moment so that we can talk alone before the small ceremony begins. There among the hanging vestments, the half-burned candles, the big sinks that are used for washing out the goblets and plates used for Communion, he confesses that he's not completely sure of the ritual required in this circumstance—that normally all this is done on Easter Vigil with the rest of the catechumens in a fairly lengthy and elaborate program that involves bare feet, white robes, etc. We scratch our heads—somehow, we've reached an anticlimactic moment without meaning to—and then he says, "What about the Apostles' Creed? Can you say it from memory?"

Can I say it from memory? Me, whose dad was the Memory Work program director? Me, who won that fine white Bible with my name stamped in gold on the cover? Proudly, I begin: "I believe in God the Father Almighty, Creator of Heaven and Earth, and in Jesus Christ, his only Son, our Lord..." I stop for a moment, stunned to realize that I actually *do* believe, that I am no longer in limbo, that all these long years of backing and forthing on the question of God's existence have finally come to an end. I gulp and go on to declare my faith in the "Holy Catholic Church, the communion of saints, the forgiveness of sins, the resurrection of the body and life everlasting." The priest and I look at each other, momentarily stumped about what comes next in this little do-it-yourself confirmation ceremony we've come up with. "Amen," I add firmly.

He nods, then traces a cross on my forehead with his thumb the way he's blessed me at the altar for nearly two years by now, the non-Catholic who is always coming to Mass, and then we break into mutual grins, and I hug him. He nods, pats my shoulder, then steers me toward the small door beyond which my husband, my children, and my two patient friends wait for us in front of the altar.

**I am forty-five**, a solo pilgrim on a round-the-world quest—for what, I can't yet say. Only that, much as I love being Catholic—a serious Catholic, a daily-Mass Catholic—it's somehow still not enough. Some mysterious thing has been patiently waiting for me for years by now, aching right at the edge of my consciousness, and if I don't figure out what it is, middle-aged as I already am, then when will I ever?

Which is why I am by myself—no husband, no kids, no friends—in the Old City of Jerusalem on Orthodox Easter. As I head toward the open doors of the Church of the Holy Sepulchre, the bells begin to toll—deep, harsh, earthshaking bells. The huge sound bowls me over, and I pause uncertainly. People surge past me on their way to join the massive throng pressed together in front of the Chapel of the Angel, and—still uncertain, but irresistibly drawn—I follow them.

The entry way is guarded by a muscular Greek priest who is holding back the mob and turning every few moments to bark out wake-up calls at those inside. You can't get in there until someone comes out; people could very easily be trampled in the rush. I am being lifted off the ground, both feet, by the press. It is getting hard to breathe.

The packed line moves forward inch by inch. Occasionally I can see people backing out of the Chapel of the Angel, crossing themselves and crying. A middle-aged man with a sturdy baritone begins to sing from somewhere deep within the crowd and everybody joins him. I recognize the Byzantine Easter Vigil hymn I heard in Athens the night before. "Christ is risen from the dead, trampling down death by death, and upon those in the tombs, bestowing life!" These Greek pilgrims sing with all the force of the choir on Easter Sunday morning at Christ Lutheran in Southern California.

Suddenly I am standing in front of the priest. A long moment of muscle-straining tension, then he gives me a rough shove inside the chamber. The abrupt cessation of pressure is disorienting, and I stare around me in a tremulous daze at candles, icons, silver lamps. This is the place, I tell myself, where the white angel gave Mary Magdalene the astonishing news. In *there* (stooping, I peer through the entryway to the Tomb itself) Christ's body was laid. I go in, and miraculously nobody comes in behind me.

A great slab of pale orange marble glows before me in the flickering candlelight. I kneel and spread my arms along its smooth length, let my cheek rest against its strangely warm surface. This tiny chamber, I think, is like a brave little heart beating on, decade after decade, at the center of this immense Crusader fortress. I kiss the stone; it tastes like salt; I kiss it again, experimentally, like a fifteen-year-old girl trying out her awesome new powers on the first boy who has ever asked her out.

Suddenly, I am flooded with a strong sensation of presence, not carnal, but exquisitely personal. I've felt this before, though not for many, many years. The same destabilizing, euphoric, launching-into-mystery I had on that crazy night with the Calvary Chapel kids three decades before. The night God got loose from the church and into me.

**I'm forty-seven.** My dear friend, my professor's wife, is standing beside me. The monks themselves are quietly listening as the two of us make our promises before the gathered community and our husbands and our children that we wish to adopt their way of living with God as best we can, given the fact that we will never abide within the walls of this monastery. We are wives, mothers, women working in the world. But what we are becoming through this small ceremony today is very much like what the monks themselves are hoping to become: we are asking to be "oblates," an ancient term that means "gift." We are offering up to this community and to God the persons we are and the persons we will eventually be.

I think of the convoluted pathway I have taken to get to this moment. What I am pretty sure I've finally figured out is that God—the Mysterium Tremendum, the Numinous, the Holy of Holies, the Great I Am—is too much for me on my own. That left to my own devices, I cannot handle that unadulterated blast of Power and Glory without panicking. That I need the container of monastic wisdom and practice—the calm, loving obedience of, as one wise monk put it, "Holy Monotony," to live in such close proximity to Yahweh.

And also that the holy ground of church is one of these necessary containers, a way to be with God day after day, week after week, without risking the loss of reason. The church, that holds Christians together and keeps us moving in the direction we were created to go. The church: a bed of forest mulch, sheltered under ancient branches, lit by a blue mountain sky, and harboring Great Beings.

# Chapter 10

# TED LEWIS: REDISCOVERING THE LYRICS OF FAITH

> "I forgot the lyrics of Christianity, but was still moved by the music."
> —Ted Lewis

Before relating Ted Lewis's story, let me express a hunch (without any numbers to prove it): a higher percentage of people leave faith who have a substantial history of family members who were leaders in faith than of people who were among the few, perhaps even the first, in their known family history to embrace faith. There is something about growing up with a legacy of faith that puts a cosmic target on you. Certain forces in the universe want you, you especially, to fall away.

This may just be another way of saying that growing up in the church can be dangerous to faith. Since it is seen in the Western world as almost an obligation of late adolescence and early adulthood to rebel against the views and values with which one has been raised, growing up religious can make one ripe for giving up religion.

This may have been a factor in Ted's life.

## LEAVING THE FAMILY TREE OF FAITHFULNESS

Ted says, "I was gifted with a rich religious heritage. Ministers and Bible teachers were on both sides of my family. I grew up with Christian beliefs and loyalties as a fish in water. I was not to remain content, however, with this inheritance." (Note his use of "inheritance," a key word for Kathleen Norris as well.)

Ironically enough, Ted's discontent lay in wanting *more* spirituality in his life rather than wanting less. A self-confessed Romantic by nature, he was (and is) a natural quester, always looking for something more—more intense, more genuine, more satisfying. He was a striver and all his striving eventually wore him out.

In his early twenties Ted increasingly found his Christian faith unsatisfactory, as is seen in his journal entries at the time. He alternates between being angry with God and wondering if anything like God even exists to be angry with. "Where the hell are you, Lord? My mind's eye is weary from looking. We've been playing hide-and-seek for some time and I can't find you nowhere."

He wrote in one of those journals, "I think I do not want salvation anymore—at least I don't *feel* as though I want it." And feelings are important to him.

Instead, he said he wanted to simply accept life "as it is," to "just let life happen." Sustaining all the beliefs and values associated with Christianity created more pressure, and more requirement for proof, than he could sustain. In an affirmation that is somewhere between a Christian truth and a generic cliché, he wrote, "Everything is holy! Nothing is more holy than other things."

And God? Well, God is just too vague and uncertain. A journal entry spoke of "my anger towards you (God) for being so distant and silent and ambiguous." This is a version of perhaps the oldest heart cry of people struggling with faith—from Job to Psalms to the medieval "dark night of the soul" to Mother Teresa to you and me—"Why, God, are you not more plain? Why do you not feel nearer? Why don't you do something about this?" (my phrasing).

He found Christian friends too easily satisfied. When he shared his struggles with one acquaintance, he discovered the fellow is only interested in personal peace and happiness—God as a narcotic, a dispenser of bliss. Ted wrote, he "scared the heaven out of me!" Ted later expressed his preference for "growth through tension rather than a static existence with no tension."

He was tired of what seemed like the mere trappings of faith and happy to be rid of them. "I don't really act like a Christian anymore. I don't pray or go to church or meditate on verses, don't worship. I just ain't pious anymore. But the irony is that I feel no void in me, only a beautiful space."

Ah yes—"a beautiful space." Another word for freedom, a feeling that Leavers often report. Faith and the church come to represent guilt, repression, restriction, judgment, intellectual and emotional struggle, and, simply put, a heavy load of "baggage." For a time after Leaving it all, there is often a much welcomed sense of being freed of a burden. The same emotions that people report when first coming to faith are also reported by many who Leave it—the old is past, all things become new. Leaving can itself feel like a conversion experience.

Sometimes that feeling lasts; sometimes it doesn't. For Ted—and for many Returners—it doesn't.

A month after declaring himself free, he wrote, "I'm just a bundle of longings!" Longing usually indicates dissatisfaction—a state of restlessness, not rest. Ted indicates his life became "an emotional rollercoaster." He said at this time, "Outwardly I have work, friends, folk dancing, poetry—plenty of beautiful 'highs.' Inwardly, my moods and longings seem out of control. Everything is an existential crisis."

"Control" is a key word in Ted's pilgrimage. On the one hand, he accepted the modern mantra that before all else one must be an individual in charge of one's own life. On the other, he wondered whether thinking one's self the final master of all things even in one's own life was not a form of foolishness.

The Romantic in him wrote the following bit of verse:

> *what sweet relief if I would bring all my beliefs*
> *within the radius of my own reach*
> *no longer to bow*
> *but be the master of them all*

Nothing could be more Romantic, more American—from the lips of children ("You're not the boss of me") to the lips of Frank Sinatra ("I did it my way") to the lips of modern sages ("I'm speaking my own truth").

## A COMMUNION OF THE SELF

Ted describes a strange (and disconcerting) ritual he created one Easter during this time. He designed and enacted his own Eucharist, a Eucharist of defiance rather than of worship (or, perhaps, of worship of his own sovereignty). He says he thought of it as a way to "honor my inner Prometheus, to express my gut-felt defiance toward God, and thus channel my anger artistically."

At midnight he "brought matches, bread, grape juice, a beer glass, and loose quarters" to a place underneath a freeway overpass. "I lit and blew out three matches which represented the Three Denials [of Peter] by the warming fire. After pouring juice in the glass and kissing it Judas-like, I heaved it at a cement buttress. Having not taken a sip, I had said, 'This is my blood which is shed for thee' (that is, Jesus' blood for me). I then recovered a sharp shard and drew blood from my cheek, and again said, 'This is my blood which is shed for thee.' ('Thee' now being Jesus.) The bread was used to sponge up the blood so the bleeding could clot. I crumpled the bread and scattered it for the pigeons, thinking it would at least be life for others. Finally, like the thirty pieces of silver, I tossed my quarters to the sidewalk below."

It is not clear to me whether this event was an act of blasphemy or of contorted devotion—or perhaps both. Ted sees it as part of an ongoing dialogue with God. He wrote later that this "cathartic venting of my feelings was a way to enter 'the fires of conflict and chaos in my life *in order to* bring about greater good.'"

This defiant expression of freedom from God and at the same time near-obsession with God is typical of the self-contradictory nature of people who travel to the edge of faith, unsure of God and of themselves. His question, "Where the hell are you, Lord?," is that of an earnest seeker (a Yearner). During the same season, however, he wrote, "I no longer relate to this Jesus Christ." Did he still have faith? He answered the question himself in his journal at the time. "I honestly don't know. From the looks of it, I'd have to say 'no.'"

## FINDING SOMETHING BIGGER THAN SELF

So what contributed to his Return?

A central factor was the fading attraction of seeing himself as the sole arbiter of what is true and good and meaningful. It is simply too big a job for a single human being, or even a collection of human beings. It might seem heroically Promethean, but in fact the attempt is both comic and tragic, the mouse roaring that it is king of the beasts.

As he was distancing himself from faith, Ted had felt a "beautiful space" in his life, free from the pressure of trying so hard to explain, to understand, to believe. Just take life as it comes, he told himself, "everything is holy," "be master" of your beliefs, create your own rituals, do it your way. But that "beautiful space" came to seem increasingly empty—not freedom after all, but a kind of narcissistic illusion. A dead end. (It is reminiscent of Wendell Berry's observation that sometimes when we think we are flying we actually are only falling.)

Meanwhile, Ted was dipping into Judaism as a viable alternative to Christianity. It seemed to him a far more beautiful religion than Christianity; it was more earthy, holistic, less controlling, without all the baggage. The Christian doctrine of atonement was a barrier for him, and he was deeply attracted to how the enduring elements of Jewish faith made it a mature tradition that had "come of age."

He then had an epiphany on a hike by the river one day with a friend. His endless quest to discover his new truth had become a lifeless idol, a spiritual fetish in which he pictured himself as a heroic searcher after truth. He had not heard of postmodernism at this time, but in hindsight he sees his life then as an example of the postmodern assertion that we do not discover truth or reality, we create them ourselves, each of us manufacturing a unique world. He no longer found that description believable.

In fact, he no longer found it even desirable. "The notion of being on a search all my life, never settling because of wanderlust, began to look very unappealing to me." Instead of Prometheus—heroic rebel against the gods—he increasingly felt like Sisyphus (my comparison, not Ted's), the mythic man condemned to roll the rock endlessly up the hill, only to have it roll every time back down to the bottom—a reality of Ted's own making, but not one of his liking.

He desired and needed a less subjective understanding of truth. And he knew "what I did *not* want, namely a smorgasbord of tasty beliefs over which I remain in complete control." He didn't want a self-made spirituality, he didn't want simply to "be a good person"—the two destinations of many Leavers. He wanted something outside himself that was true and good and beautiful. And he found it again in the faith which he had previously disparaged.

Ted moved from "no one can tell me what to do" to "I'm grateful that Someone has told me what to do." (My words, not his.) He even uses a dreaded word—"orthodoxy"—to describe what then attracted him. Orthodoxy now looked confirming rather than confining. It had the ring of truth to it.

Ted says he also learned to value "listening"—to God, to others, not just to himself. Listening, in fact, became central to his calling in life—as a mediator and reconciliation facilitator.

## THE MARRIAGE OF HEART AND HEAD

Ted now says that during his time away from faith, "I forgot the 'lyrics' of Christianity, but was still moved by the 'music.'" The rational part of him was suspicious of the direct teachings of the Bible and the church—the lyrics—but there was even in the wandering time an attraction to the music, that is the deep pull of a way of seeing reality that emphasized grace and mercy and love—and located the source of these things outside himself.

Ted has both a romantic and a rational side. Reason alone—self-directed—would have insisted on a lifelong search for certainty that would never be satisfied. The emotions and imagination insisted on something ultimate, some place of rest for the soul. He read and reread people like C. S. Lewis, a man who also struggled in his youth to put together the head and the heart, and who finally succeeded—and thereby found joy.

Ted's journal entry described the rest of the day after that fateful hike with his friend: "By noon I read through Ephesians (my least favorite book during my searching years) and started reading *Pilgrim's Regress* (for the third time). By mid-afternoon I was playing the Jude 24 benediction song on the piano ('Now to him who is able . . .'), and found myself weeping profusely. The 'lyrics' were reaching me.

"By evening I knew that something big had occurred which was more than what I myself had made happen. I felt as though I had been hunted after and was finally caught, only to find myself in agreement with the new terms of surrender. I wanted to bow. No longer did I want to be the master of my beliefs. In fact, I don't even like calling beliefs *mine*!"

"Hunted" and "caught" might be distasteful images for some. But Ted's use of the words echo the image of God in Francis Thompson's nineteenth-century poem, "The Hound of Heaven" (the poem Anne Rice cited). God pursues us tirelessly, like a bloodhound, even as we flee him. There's no place to hide from God's love. Ted didn't like calling his beliefs "mine," because "mine" suggests they are merely personal opinions, when instead he sees them as universal truths, facts to which we wisely bow and upon which we build our lives.

The "lyrics" of faith were reaching him because he now saw they were one with the "music" of faith. "Deep down I knew that this wanting was not at the expense of either my intellect or my imagination. I wrote, 'Every part of me has finally breathed out a single, true "yes" to the truth of Christianity.' C. S. Lewis, as the subtitle of *Regress* suggests, had shown how Reason and Romanticism can be wedded.'"

Faith, Ted sees, is a whole-person experience—heart and head, body and will—and it is the story not of reality as we create it, but of how the world actually is.

The next day after his moment of Return, a Sunday, Ted went to an evening service at a local church and took his first true Communion in a long time.

## Chapter 11

## BRAD GERMANY: BAD TO WORSE TO BEST

"As I sat there with this image of this boy with the weight of the world ready to overcome him, for the first time I felt sadness for him—a sadness for me. I was robbed of my childhood innocence. The more I sit in that thought, the more I want to hold that boy—to protect him from the pitfalls of life, the evils in the world. I needed a protector but I didn't know where to go."

—Brad Germany

Brad Germany's story illustrates how many stories of Leaving and Returning share common themes and even events. Brad and Lecrae Moore, whose story we heard earlier, were born a year apart, both in Houston. The pattern of their lives is eerily similar. Similarity however is not identity, and the differences in any two lives are more important than the echoes. Still, I think the echoes worth pointing out here at the beginning of Brad's story, if for no other reason than to avoid belaboring them later.

In broad strokes, each of them was raised without a father, whom they missed intensely; was sexually abused while very young; desperately sought male approval and relationships; acted destructively, even criminally, to get that approval; numbed themselves from their childhood trauma with alcohol, sex, and drugs; eventually found God, but not peace or health; was supported and guided by steadfast friends and mentors; entered therapy to deal with the obstinate pain of their past and present; learned they needed to be honest about being victimizers as well as victims; eventually established a healthier relationship with God and with the church; and now share their life wisdom and faith in order to help others.

That's the larger pattern, but God is in the details.

## SUBSTITUTES FOR LOVE

Brad has no memories of a united family, his father and mother having divorced very early in his life. Soon after the divorce, his mother moved him and his three siblings to the Deep South. He was raised as a Bible Belt Baptist in the Mississippi Delta and his life revolved around church. "As far back as I can remember, church was a big part of my childhood. Aside from Sunday school and church on the weekends, my brother and I were involved in all types of church functions. We were in the kids' choir and practiced every Wednesday before the service that night. Church camps were a regular thing, and we also participated in a Bible verse competition group who traveled around and competed with different churches. I was even baptized as a child . . . . twice."

A church kid and in the choir, but no "choir boy" in behavior. "From an early age, I was a wild man. I was always getting injured or in trouble for something, and not just minor offenses either. At five I was hit by a car that nearly killed me. At eight I had burned down our barn and my brother barely made it out. At ten I was introduced to sex. And at twelve, I was introduced to one of my most cherished relationships—alcohol."

The wild behavior was in part the result of a father-sized hole in his heart. "I always had a desperate need for belonging and to be accepted. I strongly desired male companionship and I was starved for attention from a father figure. . . . Although I would grow up to resent my father, the few days a year we would see him meant everything to me."

There is a whole category of destructive, even deadly, human behaviors that could be labeled "substitutes for love," in many cases substitutes for the love of a missing father or mother. Brad sampled many of them.

The first eight years of his life were spent mostly on a farm. At that time, after his mother divorced her third husband, they moved to "the big city." It was only about fifteen thousand people big, and only ten miles from the farm, but it made all the difference in the world to a young boy. Now there was the possibility of friends. "I was so desperate for that sense of belonging that came from male companionship that I began to seek out relationships in older boys in the neighborhood. Of course those boys didn't want a young kid tagging along all the time, so I began to act out in order to gain attention. I would smoke cigarettes, I would chew tobacco, I would roll people's yards with toilet paper, I would steal bikes, I would sneak out of the house and I would do just about anything in order to feel like I was part of the crew."

One of those older boys, whom Brad considered "my greatest friend," introduced him to pornography, grooming him to then be sexually abused. When he tried telling his mother about it, she brushed it off, blaming him for being where he ought not to be. It was the beginning of years of acting out sexually.

Things got worse. His mother marrying for a fourth time led to them moving again. "For an eleven-year-old boy this was a nightmare." Now again friendless and the target of bullying, he turned to alcohol and drugs to numb the pain. They became his decades-long companions, causing more pain than they numbed. Eventually he could not conceive of daily life without them. "Alcohol and drugs were never my problem . . . they were my solution."

## DIVINE APPOINTMENTS

The pattern was set—reckless living ("reckless" meaning, literally, without thought), multiple addictions, deep woundedness and trauma were the repetitious plot of his early adulthood. By twenty-nine, "I was a complete wreck and lucky to be alive." Well acquainted with detox centers and emergency rooms, he found he couldn't stay sober even during his three and a half years in prison. When he got out, "I had exhausted all my resources and it was obvious that no one wanted to be around me. I was all alone and hopeless. My twin brother was the only person who would take a call from me."

That brother picked him up on a street corner and took him and a mutual acquaintance to get something to eat. The acquaintance offered to let Brad sleep on his sofa if he would accompany him daily to a group called Cocaine Anonymous and agree to accept a sponsor. Having few choices left in life, Brad agreed. A meeting was arranged with the sponsor for the next morning at Starbucks. Walking in, Brad bumped into an old buddy he had done drugs with years before, and hadn't seen in almost a decade. He thought this would lead to getting high together again, just like the bad old days.

"I told him I was there to meet my drug sponsor. He smiled and said, 'I've been waiting for years for you to stumble through the doors of one of our meetings. I'm your sponsor.'" At that, he "literally picked me up, and said, 'Let's go home.'" Home indeed.

You are free to consider this a coincidence if you wish, but Brad's view is that God just might have had something to do with it. God, once more, was using a human agent to do divine work. If a Leaver Returns, look around for the guide.

This is not the point at which Brad returned to God, but it was an important stop along the way. "Although I was not a believer in God at the time, this would mark my first belief that there was a power greater than myself pursuing me in a profound way." The way back to God always starts *before* the Returner decides to Return.

This was followed by a few years of regular attendance at AA meetings, getting married, and finding the support from his wife and friends that he desperately needed. It wasn't, however, faith. He thought he had a good relationship with God, but came later to realize that it was more a relationship with AA and the people in his group than with his Maker.

In fact, with the prodding of a Christian counselor he found out that he was actually quite angry with God. "During my first meeting, I spilled my guts to this counselor. I told him all the grimy details of my past. Then this man who I've never met before, proceeded to tell me that God had written my story out of love. I was so angry that I cursed the man and left his office."

A man who has experienced as much pain in his life as Brad, did not want to hear that God had allowed it, even authored it, out of love. It seemed not only irrational but insulting and it sent him further away from healing for a long time. "At that point I wanted nothing to do with God; however, I continued to go back each week and press on. Years went by and I became withdrawn from my sober community and was left angry and isolating. After a brief relapse, a new counselor eventually asked if we could start bringing God into our conversations and I agreed. Through hard discussions and a lot of reading and writing, I began to not see God as this punitive figure, but rather as a Father who was trying to get my attention. A God who was trying to show me who He is and how He saved sinners . . . even me. My life had been 'messy' at best, yet God still pursued my heart."

## MINISTERED TO BY PRISONERS

There were more steps in Brad's road back to faith than we have space to enumerate, but here are some of the key ones.

He actively sought out the life stories of other Christians to see what he could learn from them. He had a quasi-mystical experience in which hearing the message of John 3:16 coincided with looking at his watch and seeing that it was 3:16 PM. He gained full custody of his eight-year-old daughter and became an active member of a Dallas church.

But he still felt something wasn't what it should be. He saw many believers who had a deep emotional connection to Jesus. He longed for that for himself, but didn't feel it. A lifetime of suppressing his feelings, because so many of them were painful, was keeping him from feeling deeply about God. In fact, he realized that he still didn't fully trust that God was good and that God's goodness extended to himself. He hadn't gotten fully past wondering where God was when he was abused as a child.

Help came from unexpected places. He was recruited into a prison ministry, entering it reluctantly because he lacked confidence that he could answer prisoners' questions about faith. And he found that the one supposedly ministering is the one ministered to—at a house for men transitioning out of prison. "I tell them about my trust issues with God and reveal my desperate need for prayer. So many men who were recently released from prison poured out tremendous love and biblical knowledge on me at that moment. It was a perfect time for the Spirit to move through those men to help open my heart."

And the work begun that night among the former prisoners continued through a song. "As I began to drive home, I clicked on the radio and for some rare occasion I turned to worship music. There was a song by Hillsong United that came on. It was called 'Another In the Fire,' and the Lord profoundly spoke to me in that truck ride home."

The song made clear to Brad that suffering and danger had always been a part of the story of faith, and that where there is suffering, there is God. "The song is about Shadrach, Meshach, and Abednego and when king Nebuchadnezzar put them in the fiery furnace. But the story tells us a fourth image was in there with them, putting a hedge of protection around them. . . . God revealed to me that he had never forsaken me. He had never once betrayed me. God spoke clearly to me and said, 'Brad I was with you during the abuse. . . . I wasn't . . . allowing evil to have its way with you. I was there in the fire with you and taking that punishment as well.' In an instant, an enormous weight was lifted off of me. I instantly mourned and grieved—not a normal response for me. I was able to see God in that moment as always good and forever trustworthy."

After a lifetime of stuffing his emotions, Brad allowed in that moment for the love of God and his love for God to flow freely. He immediately called his friend Anthony, a man who had stuck by him through thick and thin, and they rejoiced together.

## FORGIVING THE LITTLE BOY

Brad had one more step to take, and it was perhaps the hardest. He had to come to terms with a secret sin, a sin so dark that it created a visceral sense of self-loathing even to think about it. "You have to realize the amount of work I put into burying those shameful acts inside of me. When the thoughts of it would arise, I would literally shiver in disgust and shame, so why would I ever talk about revisiting those events?"

His sin was doing unto others as had been done unto him. He had been a victim of sexual abuse; as a result he had been an abuser of others. If what was done to him was heinous, then was he not himself heinous for doing similar things? This was a part of his life he had always resisted revealing even to therapists. "Normally around stuff with sexual abuse, I tend to get irritable or angry. It's possible I am angry because something I've hated about myself has surfaced, and instead of sitting in the shame I use anger as a tool to get me away from it."

He decided he had to talk this through with his counselor. "This time I actually sat in it and allowed myself to do something different—to feel. I was completely paralyzed, left feeling empty and alone. I honestly couldn't describe the feeling I was experiencing, but it went on for days."

But the God who was there when he was abused as a child, was also there in his paralysis. In fact, God took him back to his childhood. "During those days, God kept showing me this great image. It was quite vivid. I saw a shadowy figure of a small child—an adolescent boy. It's apparent this image was me, and I'm all alone and potentially lost. To each side are walls of raging water that are parted like the Red Sea. It's a massive site and I'm so small. At any moment, I could be consumed. But God is above me in the sky. His majesty is over it all. He is this awesome display of power covering everything—looking down upon me, holding the water back. As I sit with this image of myself—this lost boy, powerless and weak—I don't find myself hating this boy in this moment. I just feel empty or blank. It's an unfamiliar feeling because I've always felt so much contempt for this version of me that I saw as pathetic and worthless. But God is present. He is watching over my present darkness and seeing what road I would choose."

And the road Brad would choose, after decades of painful wandering, was to return to God—the God of the Bible verses he had memorized as a child, the God of the summer camps, the God of the songs he sang in the children's choir, the God of his two baptisms.

He continues his story of envisioning himself as that little boy. "As I sat there with this image of this boy with the weight of the world ready to overcome him, for the first time I felt sadness for him—a sadness for me.

I was robbed of my childhood innocence. It was taken from me and I let it continue to happen for such a long time. The more I sit in that thought, the more I want to hold that boy—to protect him from the pitfalls of life, the evils in the world. I needed a protector but I didn't know where to go."

After many a twist and turn, Brad found that protector. He let go of the shame of his secret sin. "The Holy Spirit spoke to me and told me that my past child abuse doesn't get to define me. How it played itself out in other sinful ways still does not define me. With that being true, my past means nothing. The power I gave it for my lifetime was stripped. Romans 8:1 speaks for me: 'therefore there is no condemnation for those who are in Christ Jesus.'"

Brad still thinks about that little boy, only now in a new way. "God gave me a new vision of that young child. Except this image was not of a lost boy who is desperate and scared. I see a boy full of life and freedom. He is dancing with all the innocence a child should have. What other sinful, broken people did to me in my past does not get to define me any longer. The enemy has won for so long because I've allowed my past to dictate my worth. I am not my past. I am made new."

Brad sees himself as a new character in a renewed story. He has decided his first counselor was right to say that God's love was there throughout. "Now I truly get to see how God wrote my story out of love. The reward was worth the scars."

And he sees that he now has a job to do. "God didn't sanctify and clean me up for my sake, but for His. He put me on display for the good of others, so I don't hide behind my scars any longer. I use them as a trophy and as a symbol of love and relationship with Jesus. I'd much rather walk through tragedy and experience God, than live a life in comfort and only know Him in my mind. Today, it's not about who I am, it's about whose I am. I am called to not just represent Christ, but to re-present Him to others. And there's no other way I know how to do that except to testify."

## TRAVELING TO THE EDGE—AND BACK

This last story is less a story of Leaving than one of feeling that one has been Left. It does not quite fit the pattern of the others, but it is a kindred story.

## Chapter 12

## RETURNERS

by LESA ENGELTHALER

> "The barn's burnt down
> but now I can see
> the moon above."
>
> —BASHO, HAIKU MASTER

A FEW YEARS AGO, God decided to change our relationship. He began by saying no, instead of yes, to my requests, one right after the other. Admittedly it was frustrating for this doer. Much worse was when it appeared that God had had enough of my constant, "so what about this idea?" chatter and didn't bother to answer at all.

It would not let up. Like the civil defense tornado siren in our neighborhood, I could not shut out the deafening silence of God.

I don't remember the exact day it started. I am not sure I recognized it instantly. I kept reading the Bible and asking for guidance, but the heavens were silent. Then, one night in the shower with hot water and hot tears running down my face, I said it out loud, "God, are you there?" And, like a letter returned unopened marked *Undeliverable*, I never knew why, but God was gone.

I had never experienced such silence from God. Sure, I had been distant from him, but the distance had always been mine, born of my rebellion or indifference. This was different. I was reaching out to God but couldn't feel his presence.

I had spent thirty-plus years as an activist *for* God. When God said no to my efforts to serve him—and then went silent—it was dark like a black sky with no stars, aptly describes by some as a dark night of the soul.

It broke my heart. It shook my faith. It lasted for over three years. And there was absolutely nothing I said, shouted, pleaded, or reasoned that made any difference.

Comedian Susan Isaacs tells of a similar experience: "All my life I had felt God's presence . . . even when I pushed him away he remained the still, small squatter I could not evict. Now I could hear nothing, feel nothing, know nothing. The squatter had vacated."

Mother Teresa describes the pain this way: "I am told God loves me—and yet the reality of darkness and coldness and emptiness is so great that nothing touches my soul. . . . What tortures of loneliness. I wonder how long will my heart suffer like this?"

In his powerful memoir about the Vietnam War, *The Things They Carried*, Tim O'Brien writes, "Stories are for those late hours in the night when you can't remember how you got from where you were to where you are." When I could not go forward in my relationship with God, I spent many late-night hours going back—a trip I embarked on only because I had no other choice. It seemed that God had commandeered the darkness.

As the childhood stories tumbled out, I unearthed two realizations about myself that were true before the dark night and proved even truer afterwards. From my first sit-in in junior high protesting school uniforms to recently volunteering until 2 AM with a nonprofit to help ferret out sex traffickers—I was born an "all-in" activist.

Secondly, a beautiful part that I had "flushed down the toilet" with the marijuana of my youth slowly resurfaced. God created me an artist. I embroidered my jeans not out of rebellion, but because I am . . . *Jackson Pollock*. My true self longs to get my hands dirty in creating beauty. On a silent retreat, I had time to reflect on the graciousness of my dad hanging my gigantic modern art canvases in our quaint not-modern New Jersey home. The memories came flooding back, as I sat by the tiny pond in my own backyard, of my obsession with Edgar Allan Poe in the seventh grade.

I penned plenty of my own darkly bent poems, much to my family's worry, but I also discovered that the pen could be as mighty as the sword.

I began to realize that my true self was good. In fact, the creator made quirky me in his image. And yet, growing up or getting old, somewhere along the way I believed the lie that being me, just me, was counterproductive to serving God.

I thought that God had had enough of my shenanigans and pulled up stakes.

## MINISTRY GOT TRICKY

The problem was amplified by the fact that I had ministry leadership roles in our church and community. In the midst of my "not hearing from God" time, it was tricky to know how to lead, or even if I should. In the silence, I had time to reflect on my so-called leader image and lifestyle choices that I had morphed into.

I cut back on some of my volunteering, but I did lead a group of women from my church on a trip to Nicaragua to work with a nonprofit that helps women and girls escape sex trafficking. A dark-night side effect became apparent on the first day. Though I had led dozens of trips, being unsure of my relationship with God made me uncomfortable teaching from the Bible. So, I asked various members to lead morning devotions, and that was the extent of our Bible study.

Afterwards, in a meeting for our trip evaluation, some women expressed that they had wished for more prayer and spiritual emphasis as a team. I left the meeting as quickly as I could, climbed in my Camry, and wept. It made me wonder if I should be leading at all.

## TO SHARE OR NOT TO SHARE

When people said to me, "But God was there in the dark all along, right?" I wanted to say, "Have you been in the dark lately? I mean the kind with no light. Where you can see nothing. Nada. If he was there, what does it matter, because I could not see *him*."

On occasion, I worked up the courage to offer an honest reply to the "How are you doing?" question. "Actually, not so good," I would say. "God seems really silent lately."

Choosing to share honestly did not always go well, however. I remember one woman saying, "Just remember that Moses had to wander for forty years in the desert." I offered a weak smile but wanted to shout, "Do you really think that is helpful?"

Yet other times, fellow dark-night strugglers came out of the woodwork when I was honest. At a women's church retreat, I was asked to share about my experience. I gripped the microphone with sweaty hands and spilled my story. After the talk a small support group of sorts formed spontaneously. We exchanged wordless hugs and tears. Later, one woman passed me a note with a sobering message: "It has been five years for me . . . you are not alone."

One summer, I had coffee with two college students home for the break. When they asked how I was, I responded candidly. "Well, lately God is silent." Immediately one replied, "That sucks." The other said, "I am there right now." That led to a long, no-easy-answers conversation.

A year into my dark night I had a startling realization. What if, while working so hard for God, my faith had become all about me? What if, even my restlessness to go on mission trips was more about my accomplishments than anything else? To hear God speak over my ego, I wondered if I needed to create space for solitude. It was humbling for a "doer," but I took a break from most of my ministry commitments.

## CHURCH

Eventually, I didn't attend church every Sunday. I loved the community of Christians whom God had given me. But having to be "on" at church exhausted me. God provided people who were church for me during that stretch. I became close with four women who invited me to start meeting with them. With most folks I refrained from sharing my struggles because it seemed to make people uncomfortable. But these women never flinched when I poured out the things that were breaking my heart. J. R. R. Tolkien warns, "Faithless is he that says farewell when the road darkens." When the road darkened for me, their unconditional love helped me remain faithful.

But community wasn't enough to pull me through. I needed to explore some new spiritual practices, and in some cases, return to old ones that had been absent from my life for too long.

## SPIRITUAL DIRECTION

By the second year I decided I needed outside help. I had been to marriage counseling and seen a therapist for childhood hang-ups, but the dark night issue was different. I didn't need a psychologist—I needed spiritual support. This hang-up was with God.

I learned about a local spiritual director. I was leery but desperate to hear from God. During the dark days, time spent with Dr. Linda Gotts was one of the most life-giving experiences. She shared about her own dark night, listened without judgment to my raging, and asked if she could pray Scripture over me. During our sessions Dr. Gotts helped me to see God's love for me in the silence and even in his refusals to grant my requests.

In hindsight, there were many people that God used as guides, or as C. S. Lewis calls them, "carriers of Christ," to lead the way in the dark. Now passed, Dr. Gotts was one of those guides.

Perhaps you are new to the phrase dark night of the soul. Before Dr. Gotts passed, I asked her for some simple terms for me to share.

**Me:** "Describe the part of the dark night where God seems silent?"

**Dr. Gotts:** "During a dark night of the soul, profound shifts can take place, shifts that we do not initiate or know how to make happen. Instead of experiencing God's love and peace and sensing his presence during prayer, it is as though God is silent and no matter what we do or how much we pray, nothing seems to help.

"In a dark night, one is faced with a reality that demands changing or adjusting to a current situation that does not change quickly or easily. We are faced with psychological, spiritual—and sometimes physical—challenges that seem unsolvable or insurmountable. God appears to have removed himself, and it feels as though we are left to handle the challenges alone."

**Me:** "So then, what is a person supposed to do?"

**Dr. Gotts:** "As time goes on, without a sense of God's presence or peace, we begin to realize that we cannot do all we believed we could do, and that the activities and striving we have typically done are no longer satisfying or fruitful. The way it used to work no longer works. This is a huge shock! As we face our own limitations, we must go through a grief process, letting go of many of our previous assumptions and simplistic beliefs."

## SCRIPTURE

During my struggle I became uncomfortable reading the Bible. I grew up memorizing tons of verses, and while I loathed the process, I loved how the Bible's poetic cadences rolled off my tongue and its beautiful images filled my head.

In the silence, I continued to read my Bible most days, but often the words, rather than being beautiful, seemed dagger-like. The apostle Paul felt unbearably accusing, and I could not stomach God's seeming harshness in the Old Testament. King David's psalms were safe.

One whole summer I camped out in the Psalms of Ascent with the companionship of Eugene Peterson and his grace-filled classic, *A Long Obedience in the Same Direction*.

My spiritual director advised me to stay awhile when I found a Scripture passage that helped. At some point I quit questioning what helped or what hurt.

Still, I can say that what did help were expressions of honest, raw disappointment with God. The prophet Jeremiah writes, "You have made me to walk in darkness. Even when I call out for help, he shuts out my prayers. You have covered yourself with a cloud so that no prayer can get through" (Lamentations 3:8).

But I was also reassured from the same beleaguered prophet. "Yet this I call to mind and therefore I have hope: Because of the Lord's great love we are not consumed, for his compassions never fail" (Lamentations 3:2).

## PRAYER

Even though I found a way to maneuver through Scripture, prayer as conversation was nonexistent. A friend asked what I meant by "when I pray God is silent." I replied, "What if right now, with us as close friends, you think we are having a conversation, you kept talking, sharing from your heart, and even asking me questions but I in turn said nothing? The whole time." She said, "Wow, that would be hard."

Morning prayers before work seemed contrived. Not knowing what else to do, I returned to childlike kneeling beside my bed at night. My prayers varied from short, "Here I am, Lord" to "How long, Lord?" to reciting familiar passages like the Twenty-Third Psalm.

Thomas Merton wrote, "The Dark Night, the crisis of suffering that rends our roots out of this world, is a pure gift of God." A good-out-of-bad gift of God's silence was an introduction to Merton, whose books now pile my shelves. His Prayer of Abandonment (from *Thoughts in Solitude*) became a nightly recitation.

> My Lord God, I have no idea where I am going. I do not see the road ahead of me. I cannot know for certain where it will end. Nor do I really know myself, and the fact that I think that I am following your will does not mean that I am actually doing so. But I believe that the desire to please you does in fact please you. And I hope I have that desire in all that I am doing. I hope that I will never do anything apart from that desire. And I know that if I do this you will lead me by the right road though I may

know nothing about it. Therefore will I trust you always though I may seem to be lost and in the shadow of death. I will not fear, for you are ever with me, and you will never leave me to face my perils alone.

My friend Justin relayed that when he was in seminary, he experienced a time when he could not hear from God or create prayers on his own. So, he prayed from the Book of Common Prayer. He said knowing such prayers were prayed by others gave him the words to say—when he had none. *I went a different route.* I bought a copy and used a fortune from a fortune cookie for my bookmark that read, "You will be pleasantly surprised tomorrow," as I made my way through the prayers.

Up until this time, for spiritual growth, I had mainly stuck with evangelical writers. During the dark night, I started and stopped at least twenty books before it hit me that I was going to have to broaden my pool of authors. I began asking people of other Christian traditions what they had read in hard times.

I discovered several new author companions, such as Christian mystic Evelyn Underhill, and old saints like St. John of the Cross (with whom the term "dark night of the soul" is closely associated), Ignatius of Loyola, Mother Teresa, and modern-day ones like Barbara Brown Taylor and Parker Palmer.

Frederick Buechner was one of a handful of Christian authors I could read during those excruciating years. In Buechner's novel *Godric*, about a twelfth-century English holy man, I found a curmudgeonly kindred spirit.

Godric spoke of his experience with prayer in a way that I could understand. Here are samples from throughout the novel:

"I breathed my words into the chill, grey stone, but the lips of him I prayed to, like the stones themselves, were still."

"'I prayed to him in Rome,' I said. 'It was like calling down an empty well.'"

"What's prayer? It's shooting shafts into the dark. What mark they strike, if any, who's to say? It's reaching for a hand you cannot touch. The silence is so fathomless that prayers like plummets vanish in the sea. You beg. You whimper. You load God down with empty praise. You tell him sins that he already knows full well. You seek to change his changeless will."

"Yet Godric prays the way he breathes, for else his heart would wither in his breast. Prayer is the wind that fills his sail. Else waves would dash him on the rocks, or he would drift with witless tides. And sometimes, by God's grace, a prayer is heard."

## SILENT RETREAT

During the dark times I tried something that I had never done. I went on a silent retreat. If God was silent, I reasoned, maybe silence was what he wanted from me. I found one at a Jesuit Center nearby.

The silent retreat was one of the most significant healing practices for me. I passed the quiet hours curled up on the bed in my tiny room or stretched out on a lawn chair in the sun by the edge of the lake. I did not hear God specifically, but I could feel his love in the lapping of the waves, the circling of the seagulls, and the purple and yellow of the wildflowers.

I learned about voids from the priests. I learned that the void of God's presence was perhaps designed for my good. The retreat center's rule of silence was something I had never experienced. I didn't have to have an appropriate response—I could just be. I learned to recognize the wonders of silence and solitude—the void of my own voice—as a gift. I would never have known about voids, though, if I had continued doing my faith the same old way.

## MY SIN?

And yet, as my dark night lingered, I couldn't help wondering, *did I bring this on myself?*

More than one person suggested that I was the problem. Akin to the bumper sticker "If God seems far away, guess who moved?"—they advised I simply needed to confess my sin. If shame was what they wanted, I felt it. Like a one-a-day multivitamin I was raised on the daily confession of 1 John 1:9. During this time, many a sleepless night, I pleaded it, "If we confess our sins . . ." And yet, the apostle John's "He who is faithful and just" remained far away.

I love to travel. When I was not able to see God in everyday life, I became a bit stir crazy to hit the road physically and, to be honest, spiritually. It was indicative of my reading list at the time: *On The Road, The Alchemist,* and *A Walk In the Woods*, to mention a few. I became obsessed with tales of those who had walked the Camino de Santiago. I had no idea if it was escapism or if God was to be found somewhere out there. I prayed, "Lord, please don't let me go off the path."

After a few years, unhealthy desires to find relief elsewhere grew stronger. One afternoon at a session with Dr. Gotts, I plopped down and said, "How does sin play into the dark night?" Dr. Gotts never flinched. "Temptation is one of the parts of the dark night."

Oddly, praying for deliverance brought me closest to God. After so much time in the darkness, I felt as though I was in a spiritual coma, and strangely enough wrestling with sin made me realize that at least I was alive.

Eugene Peterson's words reassured that God would not abandon me.

"All the persons of faith I know are sinners, doubters, uneven performers. We are secure not because we are sure of ourselves but because we trust that God is sure of us. Neither our feelings of depression nor the facts of suffering nor the possibilities of defection are evidence that God has abandoned us."

## UNEXPECTED GUIDES

As I said earlier, there were people who were God to me—by just being with me—during the dark night. Many of them I had not known before and yet were "carriers of Christ" to me.

One such gift was bestowed in a parking lot. As time went on, some relationships were strained. The people who remained in my life became even more precious. Since he was fifteen years old, Prentice and I have been friends. I interviewed him for a news article when Prentice was coaching kids basketball at a recreational center and we had kept in touch.

When Prentice was a senior in high school, I found out that he had never picked up his senior photos because he couldn't afford them. I called Darren the school photographer and arranged to pick up Prentice's photos. Walking me out to my car, Darren asked me how I knew Prentice and then I asked Darren about his own life. He told me he was quitting the photography business to work for a nonprofit that helps struggling city kids. I asked why. He said he had previously been a pastor and felt called to return to ministry. As we stood in the parking lot, Darren grabbed my hand and said, "Let's pray." He prayed for Prentice, for me trying to help him, and for struggling youth in our city. The redemptive comedy of heaven bestowed a gift. For the first time in years, I heard God's voice in the prayers of a photographer, who used to be a preacher.

## WRITING LIFE

I am a journalist. I report about what God is doing in the world.

When your relationship with God is zilch, it is ridiculous to think you can report credibly on what you think he is doing in the world. I met a brilliant author and writing teacher, Sharon Anderson, who suggested I stop publishing articles and write stories. So, I wrote about my childhood and unedited stories about not hearing from God. I sent dozens of them to Sharon, who graciously read them all. The gift of her time was a gift from God.

I have shoeboxes full of journals. During the dark night I scribbled more than I realized in my journals. To help make sense of my struggles, a friend suggested that I look back over my entries. I had never reviewed a page from those years. I knew it would be depressing or worse, whiny. But at a deeper level, I was terrified that I'd see that it really had been my fault: I sinned, I wandered, I strayed.

I don't let anyone read my journals. But I figure if you've gotten this far, you might also have been through a dark night of the soul or are in the *darkness* right now. If that's you, please read my entries. I want you to know that you are not alone.

## 2008

—Isaiah 50:10 says, "Let him who walks in the dark who has no light, trust in the name of the Lord and rely on his God." You know I have trust issues. Verse 11 warns, "All you who light fires and provide yourselves with flaming torches . . . This is what you shall receive from my hand: You will lie down in torment."

I know how to "light fires" and provide for myself. Help me Lord to know what trusting you in the darkness means. Isaiah says it is torment to live relying on myself.

—I have known you as my Abba since I was eight years old! Is it just a matter of enduring the dark valley, obeying when I cannot see, trusting although you are silent? Is that it, Lord? You know my breath prayer, "Abba, I belong to you." I say it again.

—Lord, I truly do not know what's wrong with me. Please show yourself to me or show me what I am doing wrong, so I can do something about it. Many anxieties, but it is more of a sadness, or doubt or lack of your presence. I confess my part, my sin, and beg for you to return.

—I abhor people like me, so negative. And yet if I dared say what I was really thinking, it might be like a flooded river pressing on an already-patched dam that's relieved to finally give way and not exist anymore.

2009

—Our church women's retreat was excruciating. Holding back saying how you really feel is exhausting. One night, I stayed awake listening to a woman snore, and for hours, tried to combat the doubts. My breath prayer has shifted somewhat. I said it over and over, "What the hell is wrong with me, God?"

—Maybe you are silent, so I will learn to shut up. You felt that someone had to begin the process, the quieting of my useless chatter. So, you closed the heavens? I wonder.

—Last night, I went to visit a neighbor who is in the psych hospital because she tried to kill herself. I wanted to assure her that you would be with her. Instead, I told her about the novel I was reading.

2010

—At Cedar Creek Lake, in a cabin called Water's Edge. I needed to get away to think about what I have been going through the last two years. I want to learn from it but really, I just want to get through it. And I think you are different than I was taught. Much wider, vaster than I knew.

—I would like to do next year differently. I bet you would like that, too.

—I am writing not because I want to or have something to say, but because I am hoping you will show up somewhere in the lines on these pages.

—God, I want to be okay. I like to be around people who are okay. I don't like needy. No one likes needy. Will I go too far, over the edge? It feels like I might.

One of my final journal entries for 2010:

—Broken cisterns. The Bible warns that when we dig our own wells, they are broken and cannot hold water. You say that you are the living water. I don't know what that means.

## PECTORAL CROSSES

In our thirties, a group of friends and I devoured Susan Howatch's series on the Church of England. In the first novel, *Glittering Images*, the main character, Ashworth, reveals to Father Darrow the demons he faces and his possible loss of faith. Beloved character Darrow presses a large pectoral cross into Ashworth's hand and says, "The cross bars their path. No demon can withstand the power of Christ." In solidarity with Father Darrow, I purchased at the time a rather large gold cross necklace, for a Protestant, and wore it proudly for years. It eventually landed in a drawer.

One fall during the dark night, I meandered the aisles of St. Rita's Christmas Bazaar, again in need of something to ward off the demons or simply bring back *the power of Christ*. I spotted a pearl necklace from a woman who made rosaries. The charm that dangled from the pearls read in tiny print, "Be Still." Another gift of the darkness was considering the thought that God's silence was an invitation to "be still" in a more intimate relationship with him. I purchased the necklace and asked the artist to help me put it on. It was a new kind of pectoral cross.

## THE STARS

Annie Dillard writes, "You do not have to sit outside in the dark. If, however, you want to look at the stars, you will find that darkness is necessary." I don't know why, but during that time being inside felt claustrophobic, whereas the outdoors soothed. I started going out in my backyard late at night. I would climb up on top of our picnic table and lay back looking up at the clear, dark night.

The spiritual darkness too provided the gift of space to see the "stars," the wonders in life, as if for the first time. I never would have noticed the breath-stealing beauty—around me or inside me—without the painful darkness of the night. Or the exhilarating gift of attempting to be my true self, a free spirit, artist and poet, all of whom I thought did not fit into the Christian faith. I had been hiding behind a false self for too long. I also thought that when God stopped my activity for him, that he did not approve of loud, activist me. I was wrong. And when I could no longer feel God's presence in a building on Sunday morning, he showed himself in the view from my own back porch.

## IMMANUEL, GOD WAS WITH ME

I remember the day God came back. I was in my car. The windows were rolled down and the radio volume up loud. A new habit to drown out the silence. Carlos Santana. I heard only one word not from the lyrics but it was meant for me—Immanuel. I knew the meaning of the word, "God with us," like I know the smell of the honeysuckle blooming off my back porch.

It still pains me to talk about the years of God's silence. So why tell the dark parts? When I brave the naked truth about the years of God's silence, there is sometimes an unexpected and yet powerful reaction. Without missing a beat, the responder simply refers to their own dark night as if they, too, have climbed Mt. Everest and survived. We are instantly soul sisters, blood brothers. It makes the risky telling worth every word.

Today, I am grateful to feel his presence again. It makes me tear up even as I write the words. I also know that there is much more mystery to God than I ever realized. I often find myself saying, "You know, I don't know."

Conservationist Wendell Berry makes a fitting analogy from nature: "It may be that when we no longer know what to do, we have come to our real work, and when we no longer know which way to go, we have begun our real journey. The impeded stream is the one that sings."

# III. WHAT THESE STORIES TELL US

A Native American storyteller says, "Stories are the ointment of the healer." If we do not learn from the important stories we hear, we will miss our needed healing—individually and collectively. Following is a chapter that explores common themes in the stories we've heard, and another that offers some thoughts on what the church might learn from them.

## Chapter 13

## COMMON THEMES IN STORIES OF RETURN

> Therefore tell the people: This is what the Lord Almighty says: "Return to me," declares the Lord Almighty, "and I will return to you."
>
> (Zechariah 1:3, NIV)

All good stories teach us something. We have listened to the stories of folks who have left the Christian faith and the church and later returned. So what can we learn from these particular stories? The social scientists, with their surveys and statistics, tell us that many people are leaving both faith and the church, and some of them suggest why. What do the handful of stories in this book tell us about both why people leave and why many come back? And how relevant are their stories to your story and mine?

I am going to suggest a fairly long list of factors that I think recur in the stories of Returners. Interestingly enough, many are the flip side of factors for why people leave faith in the first place. For instance, a bad experience with a Christian or group of Christians is often cited as a reason for Leaving, and a good experience with a Christian or group of Christians is often cited as an important factor in Returning. What follows is far from exhaustive. For every *shared* reason for Returning, there are multiple unique ones.

### "THE HOUND OF HEAVEN"

As a person of faith myself, and as one who greatly values the church as a whole, I want to be clear that I believe that ultimately any return to faith is the work of God. People do not simply "choose" to return as an independent exercise of the will. Nor are any of the factors discussed below adequate in themselves to "explain" why people return. Most explanations in most all matters of faith are, at best, incomplete.

If someone returns to faith, it is because God has worked in their lives. We might call this the "hound of heaven" phenomenon. As referenced directly by some of the storytellers above, Francis Thompson, a late nineteenth-century poet, wrote a poem of this title that explores the relentless pursuit of each of us by God's love. The Hebrew word for this kind of love is *hesed* and it is much more than affection or an attitude or even a valuing. *Hesed* is an active, pursuing love that will not rest or give up on the one who is loved, no matter that person's way of thinking or living.

The opening of the poem describes many a Leaver:

> I fled Him, down the nights and down the days;
>    I fled Him, down the arches of the years;
> I fled Him, down the labyrinthine ways
>    Of my own mind; and in the midst of tears
> I hid from Him, and under running laughter.
>    Up vistaed hopes I sped;
>    And shot, precipitated,
> Adown Titanic glooms of chasmed fears,
>    From those strong Feet that followed, followed after.

Throughout the poem, as the speaker seeks out earthly pleasures and earthly substitutes for God, he hears God's feet following steadily and relentlessly after him in a kind of heavenly haunting. So it is with all Returners, whether they recognize it at the time or not.

But if the Holy Spirit is the source of all Returning, that Spirit makes use of many very earthly circumstances and people to accomplish divine purposes. What follows are some of them.

## A CHANGE OF HEART AND FALLING BACK IN LOVE

As I have explored in other writing (see *The Skeptical Believer*), one does not lose one's faith as one loses a sock. It is not hidden in a drawer or under the bed, waiting to be noticed. Losing one's faith is an act of falling out of love. As with any human love, it is the end result of an often-long process of moving slowly away from something or someone one once highly valued. It involves many little decisions, often unconscious, and many little acts of neglect.

Returning to faith is discovering (better, experiencing) reasons—often little reasons at first—to love again what one once loved. It is, to use an imprecise phrase, "a change of heart."

We use the word "heart" to describe that wide and woolly area of the human experience that deals with the emotions, affections, intuitions, and will—among other things. (Other cultures, including those of the Old Testament, use different internal organs for the same things.) A "change of heart" leads us into love and out of love, including love of God. So in a general—and not particularly helpful—sense, a return to a faith one has left requires a change of heart. And that involves a reorientation of valuing and understandings and priorities and ways of living. A kind of revolution, but also a kind of coming home.

Kathleen Norris's "change of heart" was linked to a return to her grandmother's house and church—an acceptance of her own "inheritance." Rosaria Butterfield's began with being treated kindly by Christian strangers. Dan Wakefield cites the biblical description of the prodigal son—"he came to himself"—and applies it to his own life. Others do the same—discovering that they are able to love again the things they once loved but then abandoned.

All of which leaves still the question, what contributes to such a change of heart, to a renewal of love?

## NECESSARY DISILLUSION: THE INADEQUACY OF THE REPLACEMENT STORIES

An observation attributed to G. K. Chesterton goes as follows: "When men stop believing in God, they don't believe in nothing; they believe in anything." This is clever, with some truth to it, but is too dismissive. As noted earlier, most people who leave an established religious faith do not become atheists and do not believe in either "nothing" or just "anything." They often take with them values grounded in religion—such as compassion, justice, service—and seek secular foundations for them. If one wants to help those people return to faith, one needs to take their replacement commitments seriously.

In time—sometimes a long time—many Leavers find those replacement stories inadequate at best, complete failures at worst. A step in Returning for many is disillusionment, a necessary and positive step if what one is disillusioned with is less true and good than the things of God one left behind.

The stories of Returners are replete with examples of adopted substitutes for God that did not hold up in their lives. Dan Wakefield placed great faith (and time and money) in psychiatry as a source of truth and happiness—and found it a failure (though he advocates for more useful forms of psychotherapy). Ted Lewis had to become disillusioned with the common American ideal of being totally in charge of one's own life and creating one's own truth. In one sense, Lesa Engelthaler had to become disillusioned, ironically, with basing her faith on being hyperactive for God.

Many with an intellectual or artistic bent leave faith for a general approach to life that Anne Rice called "atheistic humanism." Whether specifically atheistic or not, this view emphasizes reason (often misunderstanding its limitations), imagination, and creativity. For people like Norris and Wakefield, it often begins in college, where young people discover for the first time a much larger life of the mind than they have ever known, one that often disregards or even disparages religion. Christian Wiman and Norris centered their lives around poetry, Rice around novels, Wakefield around journalism and fiction, Lecrae around music, Butterfield around social activism, A. N. Wilson around the life of the mind and writing in various genres.

None of these people ever rejected their love of words and ideas and creativity, but all of them found aestheticism and the secular humanities alone an inadequate foundation by themselves for ultimate meaning. The great hope of many since the eighteenth century in the West, accelerating in the nineteenth and twentieth, has been that art and the intellect can and should replace religion as the source for ultimate meaning. Many Returners have found that hope an illusion.

Similar things can be said for other substitutions: politics, social activism, hedonism, career success, self-fulfillment, designer spirituality, and so on.

For many Returners, all these replacements for God simply prove too shallow. They lack adequate profundity, adequate significance, adequate meaning. Secularism as a whole leaves out too much of reality—both perceived and intuited. It explores only the sands on the beach, not the depths of the ocean.

## THE CALL OF "SOMETHING MORE"

A recurring theme among Returners is the persistent and finally irresistible call of transcendence, of "something more" to reality and to their own lives than the merely physical and temporal. One of the most basic convictions (faiths, one could say) of secularism, especially for intellectuals, is that reality is entirely material, explainable only and exclusively in terms of physical processes. Not only are human emotions, intuitions, longings, and imaginings entirely fleshly matters of different areas of the brain, so is the very concept of the spiritual and the transcendent. Anything deemed "spiritual" can be explained by some interactions of chemicals, down to the atomic level.

Some secularists, of course, are not this dogmatic. They reject the specific claims of Christianity, but hold out, often quite vaguely, for some "higher power" or reality beyond what we can accurately describe. And many Leavers adopt such a position, rather than crass atheistic materialism.

But both straight-up, flat-world materialism and vague "higher power" substitutions for God eventually seem like weak tea to many Leavers. Christian Wiman's phrases—"a reality beyond the one we ordinarily see," "some excess of life," and "reality spilling its boundaries"—speak to this shared sense that the Christian vision of reality makes better sense of our experience than its secular competitors.

The "something more" factor applies not just to abstract worldviews, but also to the common measures of happiness and success in everyday society. America defines success in life in terms of the four "p's": possessions, pleasure, prestige, and power. Leavers often pursue one or more of these with passion. For the young especially, being "happy" seems like a good in itself. Who does not want to be happy? What's wrong with prioritizing being happy? Religion in general and Christianity in particular seem like a "no fun" approach to life. It is easy to abandon for more attractive models.

But Leavers often find that meaning and significance are more important than any of these and that the link between the four "p's" and long-lasting happiness is tenuous at best. Wiman and Norris did not find it in artistic success. Lecrae found it neither there or in fame and possessions. Brad Germany, among others, did not find it in alcohol, drugs, or sex.

Essentially, the "something more" factor speaks to the unerasable human hunger for meaning and significance. We need it to matter that we exist. We need to have reason to believe that our lives are significant. For many, secular thought and experience simply do not provide that.

Neither, for Returners, do "designer spirituality" or the "be a good person" substitute. Many Leavers recognize the value of "spirituality" and believe they can have it on their own terms. They often concoct a spiritual cocktail of their own making—a little bit of meditation, a dash of yoga, add some secular saints like Albert Schweitzer, John Lennon, Charles Darwin, and Ruth Bader Ginsburg, throw in a pinch of environmental consciousness, veganism, and commitment to nonviolence and you have a personal religion fit for modern times.

Okay, let me start over. The above description is snarky and demonstrates the lack of tolerance for which we Christians are famous. I actually have respect for anyone wise enough to try getting beyond pure materialism, even by crafting a spiritual response of their own. It simply doesn't work in the long run for many Leavers. It feels too much like pulling yourself up by your own bootstraps. It feels ungrounded, convictions without foundations. (If all values are culturally-created opinions, for instance, on what basis does one criticize anyone else for being unjust?) Leavers have tasted some expression of the real thing, even if they have abandoned it, and substitutes come to feel less real.

Leavers often think they can keep the best parts of their former faith and jettison the rest. The best part for many are the high ethical standards which, ironically, form the basis for most secular calls for social justice (and which they criticize Christians, often rightly, for not keeping). This is the "good person" strategy. What is important, they say, is not being religious, it's being a good person.

There are a couple of problems with this approach for many Leavers. First, it is very difficult, some would say logically impossible, to build a foundation under the concept of "good" in our relativistic age without reference to some ultimate source such as God for defining and sustaining the good. (Materialistic Nature, for instance, recognizes only "is," not "ought.")

Second, given enough time, many reflective and self-aware people come to the accurate conclusion that they are not particularly good. Not mass murderers or virulent racists, certainly, but also distressingly susceptible to indifference to the suffering of others. And, overall, too easily satisfied with their state of goodness. Many Returners come to the conclusion that they are sinners after all—secular abhorrence of the concept notwithstanding—in need of something stronger than good intentions or home-brewed spirituality.

One can distinguish between meaning and significance. Meaning is largely conceptual—thinking accurately, which is to say truthfully, about how things are. Significance is incarnational—worked out *and felt* in how one actually lives. You can believe correctly and still have minimal significance if your life does not follow what you believe. *Understanding* what is true (meaning) gives the potential for the *actions* of a life to be *significant* (meaning that shapes a life). Meaning and significance together yield wisdom, a life conformed to how things actually are and therefore well-lived.

Many of these Returners found this larger wisdom in writers and artists—past and present. They repeatedly testify to being shaped by reading Dante, Dostoevsky, Shakespeare, George Herbert, Pascal, Kierkegaard from the more distant past, T. S. Eliot, Bonhoeffer, Flannery O'Connor from the twentieth century, and contemporaries such as Carson McCullers, Eudora Welty, Robert Coles, and Annie Dillard. It is not that these writers continually and explicitly advocate for God, but that they take the idea of transcendence seriously, and that they explore the possibility of that which is beyond time and space also infusing and giving meaning to time and space. They also, with their considerable intellects and creativity, give the lie to many secular characterizations of religion as for ignorant, irrational people.

All of our storytellers came to realize that their desire for meaning and significance required more than their post-faith lives could offer. Wiman, Norris, Rice, and Lecrae realized that art and aesthetics alone could not provide adequate meaning. A N Wilson discovered the same regarding trendy intellectual movements. Fame and fortune and pleasure also didn't work for any of them. These realizations pointed them all back toward the God on whom all meaning and significance depends.

Essentially the "something more" factor is an acknowledgment of the failure of replacement stories. Leavers have left the Christian story in which they were, to varying degrees, participating as characters. They believed there were better stories on which to build their lives. They tried those better stories and found them wanting. It wasn't that there was no truth in them at all; there simply wasn't enough truth to give their lives the sense of meaning and significance that they needed. They needed "something more."

## INTERROGATING THE STEREOTYPES

Every grouping of human beings—in fact everything human—can be reduced to stereotypes. We do it constantly because it makes life simpler and because we are lazy and often ignorant. Currently we are most aware of stereotyping when it comes to issues of injustice and unequal treatment of others: racism, misogyny, homophobia, classism, and the like. But stereotyping is universal and as common as grass when it comes to religion—both how the nonreligious conceive of the religious and vice versa. A key factor in Returning is getting past common stereotypes of religion, in our case of Christianity.

What are some of these? A few were cited earlier: the perception of the church and Christianity generally as hypocritical, judgmental, intolerant, self-righteous, and scandal-ridden. Add to that anti-intellectual, ignorant, irrational, unscientific, anti-progress, and all around unmodern. Throw in uncool, boring, and anti-pleasure and you have all the reasons to abandon and stay away from faith as one could want.

So is there any truth to these stereotypes? Of course there is. All this can be found within Christianity—past and present—and within the church. After all, there are two thousand years of Christian history and literally billions of people who have called themselves Christian—all of them human. Christians, more than anyone, believe that both personal and institutional evil and error are inescapable—and, furthermore, that each of us is responsible for evil and error. It's everywhere in the Bible—all are "sinners saved by grace"—and those who don't think it applies to them are simply obtuse.

Can Christianity take comfort or find excuse in the fact that many of the charges against it are stereotypes? Absolutely not. The church cannot afford to ignore legitimate criticism of its failures simply because that criticism is stereotypical. Nor is it sufficient to point out the obvious—that many of these same stereotypes apply to religion's critics, including to the secular elites. I am no less guilty of sin simply because there are other sinners.

The error in a stereotype is not that it is devoid of truth. The error is in applying a partial truth universally. Attributing the behavior of some members of a group, for instance, to all members of the group is a logical as well as an ethical failure. Those who have left faith often do so because they have universalized the particular failures of a church—and perceived failures of God—in their own experience. Coming back to faith and to the church requires them getting beyond those false generalizations.

Kathleen Norris had to get beyond, among other stereotypes, the legalistic judgmentalism of her paternal grandmother and embrace the loving, serving faith of her maternal grandmother. And she had to see that faith still at work in the old women of her grandmother's church. She had to get beyond the "no fun" stereotype of Christianity by experiencing the joy of service within the church. And beyond the stereotype that Christians are stupid by experiencing herself the wisdom and hospitality of the Benedictine monks.

Dan Wakefield had to experience the sacrificial service of both Catholics and Protestants in the Bowery of New York to undercut the stereotype of Christians as unconcerned about injustice and the poor. He had to encounter a pastor he could finally talk to in order to rehabilitate his view of Christian leaders. He had to discover a church that did not frighten or repel him.

Similarly with A N Wilson. He had to recall Bonhoeffer and rediscover Pascal and Dostoevsky, among many others, to get beyond the anti-Christian stereotypes among intellectuals. In order to counter stereotypes about the Bible, Paula Huston needed to hear from a respected academic that "There's a way to read the Bible that doesn't make God out to be a fool." Lesa

Engelthaler was helped in escaping her spiritual desert by reading Thomas Merton, Frederick Buechner, and Wendell Berry.

Lecrae, ironically, had to get beyond his own negative stereotypes of the Black church. And every Returner has to move beyond stereotypes of God, which are endless—God as angry punisher, God as legalist, God as indifferent to suffering, God as absent, but also beyond the stereotypes of God as indifferent to sin, God as buddy, God as cuddly, God as just one among many gods, Jesus as only a good man.

The single best way to get beyond any stereotype of others is to have direct experience with those being stereotyped—to experience their uniqueness and individuality, and to discover the inadequacy of the generalizations about them. This is certainly true for Returners. They are not likely to change course in life without having new experiences with faith and people of faith to give the lie to the stereotypes they have embraced. That is why an interaction with a healthy person of faith is so universally a part of anyone's pilgrimage back to faith—a point we will look at more closely later.

## A FULLER UNDERSTANDING OF FAITH

Getting beyond stereotypes makes possible a more accurate understanding of who God is, what faith in God requires of us, and how it is a gift that we are called to live it out communally in the church. Norris expressed her surprise when she discovered—with the help of both the church ladies and the monks—"how ignorant I was about my own religion." What she came to discover, as do most Returners, is that the Christian faith is a whole person, whole body experience—and that it is wider and deeper (recall Lecrae) than our individual experience of it.

Faith is a matter of the mind, the emotions, the will, and the body. Its wholeness makes it attractive and provides a coherent story in which to live. The needs of each of our Returners are both unique and shared with others. Some need better answers to questions posed by the mind. Wilson needed a C. S. Lewis, even though he belittled him while away from belief. Others, such as Lecrae, Wakefield, and Brad Germany, needed healing of life-distorting psychological and spiritual wounds. All of them needed to exercise their will to return to a God from whom they felt alienated. Returning for many also involves the healing of the body—from exhaustion, addiction, and abuse. And faith is then lived bodily—in worship (including music), in thought, in physical service.

A fuller understanding and experience of faith requires a more accurate understanding of the Bible—not a rule book (though it has rules), not a book of myths (unless one sees it, as did Lewis and Tolkien, as proclaiming the ultimate myth-that-is-also-historically true), not a weapon to hit people over the head with, not a *Guinness Book of World Records* with which to win arguments. To see it instead as the telling of the great story of God's love for his creation—a story whose plot is God made us, God loves, God calls us, and whose theme is shalom—all things flourishing in the manner in which they were created to flourish.

Norris saw this fuller understanding in the lives of the church ladies and monks, Lecrae experienced it starting with the discovery of Black believers in Egypt, Germany found it in the love of individuals and communities that accepted him just as he was, Rice in the whole world around her which "was filled to the brim with God." Seeing a truer and richer faith in the lives of others than in the life they left, they were able to envision the possibility in their own lives. And then to move, often slowly, from a vision to an embodied reality.

## TURNING POINT EVENTS

Some folks return to God quietly and without drama—as they may have left. For others, the turn toward God commences with a dramatic, perhaps even traumatic, experience. The experience often initiates or confirms their sense of needing to change the direction of their lives.

Sometimes these experiences are of a "something more" kind, such as the quasi-mystical events in the lives of Norris, Wakefield, and Germany. Norris cites sitting in her New York apartment, long before returning to South Dakota or to faith, and sensing her grace-filled grandmother "whispering into my ear" about goodness and sin. It didn't restore her faith instantly, or even quickly, but it was a step in the process.

Wakefield has a similar experience walking past the grave of his churchgoing ancestor, reminding him that he exists in a much larger history of faith that is part "of the whole intricate pattern of my journey and return." Anne Rice describes the dramatic things she experiences in her travels to the Rio statue of Jesus in Brazil, and on her trips to Israel and Rome. And she recounts a series of "small miracles" as part of her Return.

Brad Germany had similar experiences, from finding the convergence between John 3:16 and the time on his watch, to the shock of discovering that his old drugs and drinking buddy was now his recovery counselor, to a song on the radio about an Old Testament story that exactly applied to his life at a key moment. None of these events would convince a skeptic, but Germany, as with many Returners, found he couldn't build a life on skepticism.

Lecrae had numerous "turning point" events as part of his way back to faith. One was his trip to Egypt. Another was finding a therapist to address his boyhood wounds. A third was discovery that the friends he had tried to mislead knew all about his failures and loved him nonetheless. Yet another comes through the books he began reading by Black theologians and thinkers.

And then there were the two dramatic and one traumatic events in the life of Christian Wiman that he cites as keys to his return. The first was the drying up of his poetic juices, writing poetry being a central pillar of his secular religion at the time. No poems would not be a big deal for most of us, but it destabilized Wiman's world.

A second dramatic event was discovering the love of another human being. Why would this be part of a return to God? Because it set Wiman reflecting on the ultimate source of the intense experience of love he was undergoing. Purely secular explanations, including the psychological, were unconvincing. They simply were not adequate to the experience, and so human love played its part in directing him back to the Source of all Love.

And then the trauma—the diagnosis of cancer followed by its excruciating pain. Such an experience might crush the faith of some, but it can make a reflective person think of ultimate things—and few people are as reflective as Christian Wiman.

Why do people who have left, even disdained, faith often return? One reason is that life experiences point the way, either by revealing the inadequacy of a life without faith or by giving glimpses of the greater truth and richness of a life with faith.

Simply put, they live their way back to faith.

## RETURNING TO SOMETHING DIFFERENT AND BETTER

A well-known writer once titled one of his novels *You Can't Go Home Again*. That assertion is often cited, both by people who think it true and those who think it isn't. For those returning to faith and the church, I think it is both true and not true. You certainly can return to faith and to church, as their lives show, but it's very likely not to be exactly the same conception or expression of either as the ones you left. If one has a healthy experience of faith and church, one is unlikely to leave it in the first place. (People do not abandon their life-defining stories for no reason.)

Having left, one is likely to return only to a fuller, richer, truer expression of faith and the church than one abandoned. Coming home does not have to mean—and usually should not mean—coming back to exactly the same home. Recall the words of Christian Wiman: "If you believe at fifty what you believed at fifteen, then you have not lived—or have denied the reality of your life."

Sometimes Returners find God again and then seek out a church. Other times they reconnect with some form of church and thereby rediscover God. Often it is a mix of the two.

Though he answers "yes" to the question of whether he ever left Christianity, it seems that Lecrae never completely left belief in God. But he did leave the Christian community, not least because he felt it had left him, and he experienced grave doubts about whether God was good, cared about people like him, or was even interested in his creation. You might say he stopped believing in the biblical God even if he retained the conviction that there was "something more."

Essentially Lecrae left white, evangelical, neo-Reformed Christianity and the particular community of faith it defined. He could not have returned to it as such, even if it is one of many legitimate expressions of faith. What he returned to instead was what he conceived of as a broader understanding of God and the world church. Not broader in the sense of watered down or more pleasing to contemporary sensibilities, but broader in the sense of more fully reflecting for him who God is and what God's people look like.

Dan Wakefield returned to a church far different from the ones of his youth, but one that made Christianity possible for him again. King's Chapel allowed him to be a self-declared Christian—incarnation, resurrection and all—among the Unitarian Universalists. A. N. Wilson finds that walking around his neighborhood with palm fronds while singing with his fellow churchgoers is more meaningful than all the weighty intellectualizing of his secular friends.

Christian Wiman's halting return to church was an early, important, and preliminary step to his returning to God. God had been at work in his and his wife's lives, but it was a work in progress, not a completed one. He says, as we have seen, "Then one morning we found ourselves going to church," as though it was not even entirely a choice they made. "Once inside the church, we were discovering exactly where and who we were meant to be." Wiman needed God to nudge him back to church, and, at the same time, he needed church to participate in his rediscovery of God.

And it couldn't be just any church. It couldn't, for instance, be the hellfire faith and church of his West Texas childhood. With a man as hyper-reflective and full of contradictions as Wiman, many particular churches would simply have driven him away again. With his wife, he had to find an expression of the church that nurtured and deepened their faith rather than assaulted it.

Every Returner needs a community that challenges his or her faith—and life—but in a way that draws them in more deeply, not one that makes it harder to believe and live.

Brad Germany found that community in parachurch organizations before he was willing to try a traditional church again. Faith-based addiction rehabilitation organizations started with where he was at the time—which was at the bottom. He learned that he needed both God's help and the help of others, including former addicts and prisoners.

Kathleen Norris initially returns to church out of politeness to her grandmother's small town and then only sporadically. It took her ten years to join. But in those ten years and after she had repeated experiences that made faith more credible to her. She saw that it worked in the lives of the congregation. She found that many of her stereotypes were faulty. They welcomed her without quizzing her closely on what she actually believed. And they gave her things to do that she found worth doing, including, eventually, preaching.

And then there were the monks, present-day embodiments of the ancient church, demonstrating more clearly to her than any sermon what faith was and what the church could be. A return to faith almost always includes (and even requires) a return to community. We literally experience God in and through each other. If one disdains the church as a whole, one is very close to disdaining the God who created it.

So, yes, you can go home again. But in the case of faith in God and life in the church, it will often need to be a healthier, richer home than the one you left. One that gives you the responsibility of contributing to making it closer to what God intends.

## RESISTING A RETURN

Not everyone who returns to faith and the church comes back smiling. A common theme is determined resistance—often prolonged. Norris's resistance was dogged if undramatic, consuming years. Rosaria says, "I fought with everything I had. I did not want this. I did not ask for this. I counted the costs. And I did not like the math on the other side of the equal sign."

Many factors contribute to resistance to Return. One is simply the power of habit—habits of living and habits of thought. We get used to seeing the world and our lives a certain way, and it takes a lot to deflect that, much less to reverse it completely—even when we find our lives unhappy or self-destructive. Wiman remarks on "the fierceness with which we cling to beliefs that have made us miserable, or beliefs that prove to be so obviously inadequate"—an observation relevant to both Leaving and Returning.

Another factor is fear of rejection, especially by people whose good opinion we crave. Those who prize the life of the mind and the imagination are perhaps more susceptible to this than most. A. N. Wilson liked being thought smart and approved of by the intellectual elites. Rosaria Butterfield had to get past the stigma of being thought stupid and a traitor for her Return.

One of the more unpleasant metaphors in the Bible is that in Proverbs comparing a fool continuing in foolishness—whether in thoughts or actions—to a dog returning to its vomit. But human beings are stubborn creatures. And willful and self-absorbed and selfish and all kinds of unpleasant things. Wiman says recognizing his need for humility was important both in his returning to faith and in his ongoing attempt to live it. Humility—to the point for some of being broken—is necessary for overcoming some kinds of resistance.

## ADDRESSING EARLIER TRAUMA AND WOUNDEDNESS

As we have seen, for people to return to faith, they usually need first to address both things that contributed to their leaving and obstacles to their returning. One class of obstacles is unaddressed trauma, whether in childhood or later. Sometimes these traumas are directly related to their faith experiences, but often they are unrelated life traumas that nevertheless shape many aspects of their lives, including faith.

Lecrae, for instance, found he could not return to a healthy faith without getting help for both father wounds and sexual abuse in childhood. Likewise Brad Germany. And both had traumatic years of addiction to alcohol and drugs to overcome. Lesa Engelthaler found much needed help from a woman spiritual director who had experienced her own "dark night of the soul."

Wiman's youth was shadowed by family violence, including physical fights with his father, family suicides and the threat of his own, and before his birth the murder of his grandmother by his grandfather. He also had to deal with his father spending "months at a time" in his room because of depression and his parents' "nasty, protracted, ruinous divorce."

Some Returners, such as Lecrae and Wakefield and Germany, get formal, professional help from therapists. Others come to terms with such things with the help of friends and loved ones. And some undoubtedly return without ever adequately dealing with past trauma. In all cases, God is at work. Just as faith is a whole-person phenomena, so God is interested in the whole person—mind, emotions, will, and body.

## FAITHFUL COMPANIONS: GUIDES, FRIENDS, AND MENTORS

Very few Leavers make it back to faith alone. I have claimed that God is at work in all returning, but that work is most often done with human hands. If someone has returned to faith and to the church, look for who helped out along the way. And if there is someone who you would dearly wish to return, think about how you could be that person.

Guides and mentors can be dead as well as alive, far as well as near. Guides for Kathleen Norris include ancient saints and her deceased maternal Grandmother Totten. Her grandmother was an example when Norris was a child, and still an important example of the possibilities after she had passed. When Norris was considering if she could return to faith and to what kind of faith, Grandmother Totten was a model. As were the strong women in her grandmother's church. And the Benedictine monks hanging out on the Dakota prairies. And St. Gertrude, the thirteenth-century German nun.

Wiman's return was also aided by memories of a grandmother and an aunt with their "almost instinctive" relationship with God and "air of easy devotion." More immediately, he credits a pastor who was wise enough to avoid triggering Wiman's stereotypes of preachers. The pastor preached of the cross in terms of God's love, and when he ran into Wiman and his wife on the street he avoided glad-handed bounciness and churchy language, and, most importantly, he inquired after Wiman's severe struggle with cancer with genuine interest and compassion. In other words, the pastor treated him as a fellow human being, not as a client or target for salvation.

Lecrae and Germany cite friends who stood beside them in the darkest hours, who inspired them with their example, who spoke wisdom to them or simply were present in their times of pain. In both cases, spouses were among those who played that role, as they often do. As with others, Lecrae also had strong memories of a grandmother—Big Momma—and her example of faith and service.

## III. WHAT THESE STORIES TELL US

For Rosaria, her way back began with Ken and Floy Smith and their extended hospitality, and continued with many models and mentors in her new church. Anne Rice cites the warmth and open arms of her New Orleans Catholic family. When she returned to them a pagan, she expected to be rejected, and when she was loved instead it contributed to her reconsidering the possibility of being a believer herself.

A. N. Wilson, on the other hand, discovered most of his guides in books (as Lecrae discovered additional guides in Black theologians and thinkers). When he thought about who had contributed most to Western civilization and who had most nearly lived the kind of life he himself would want to live, he thought of religious writers, scholars, artists, poets, activists, martyrs, and faith leaders. They made it impossible for Wilson to any longer cling to the negative stereotypes of faith and church that secular intellectuals trafficked in. Something similar was true for Wakefield.

Paula Huston discovered a guide, mentor, exemplum, and friend in the wife of the professor who claimed it's possible to read the Bible in a way that doesn't make Jesus and faith in Jesus appear foolish. Like Norris, she also found that the Catholic monks—strange to most Americans—modeled a "radically alternative lifestyle" of commitment to God in daily life that appealed to her.

And sometimes a whole community can be the example. It was true for Norris and for Germany. It became true also for Lecrae and Wiman and Wakefield. Where two or three are gathered together, we are told, God is present. When it's two or three dozen or two or three hundred or more—living out the gospel together to best of their ability, being the good news to their neighbors and to each other—the effect on one's own faith can be profound.

A biblical example is helpful here. Shortly after the resurrection, Christ appeared to some of the disciples. Thomas, who was not present, said soon after that he could not believe without proof. Two things happened. The other disciples did not kick him out of the community, and Thomas did not choose to leave. He stayed and the others accepted him and believed for him while he was unable to believe. When Christ later showed himself to Thomas, Thomas was, no doubt, ashamed of his disbelief, but tradition tells us he then carried the gospel east to as far as India, where he died a martyr.

The lesson here is plain—we need each other; we believe in only One triune God, but we work out that belief together.

## KINDNESS, CARING, AND CASSEROLES

Perhaps it is simply a subset of the last category, but a powerful force for Returners is simple kindness. The root meaning of "kind" is sharing the same nature. In the human context, this meaning expresses itself in valuing and, in many cases, in serving. To be kind is essentially to say, "We are alike; you are as important as me; allow me to treat you accordingly."

As artists and thinkers and spiritual leaders (and mothers) have told us from the beginning, we human creatures are not adequately kind to one another. We fail to recognize—or at least to act on—our shared natures and common human experience. Kindness is one of the fruits of the spirit listed in the New Testament, but it is not often preached on.

Those who return to faith consistently tell of experiences of kindness from Christians that befell them on their way back. I cited many of them above and in each of the preceding chapters.

This realization comes with some unsettling questions for those within the household of faith:

Who have we shown kindness to that did not expect it from us?

Who have we invited into our home besides family and established friends?

Who have we invited to join us for coffee or lunch after church?

When will we stop using busyness as an excuse for indifference?

Who is included in this "neighbor" who we are commanded to love as we love ourselves?

Is the good Samaritan just a character in another nice Bible story?

Why am I tempted to delete all these questions from my manuscript?

Kindness creates a path. It is the simplest form of blessing. It helps people flourish. It leads people to—and back to—God.

## GOD WORKING BEFORE THE RETURN

In every case we have looked at, there is evidence, often seen retrospectively, that God was at work before, often long before, the Returner even thought about Returning. This is part of our opening assertion that it is God who brings people back to faith. God works with human will and through human agents, but no one returns to faith apart from God's wooing.

Just to cite a few of many possible examples, God leads Kathleen Norris back to Lemmon, South Dakota long before she entertains the possibility of returning to faith. She thinks she is leaving the big city for the infinitesimal village because, among other things, it will be a good place to write poetry.

She goes to her grandmother's church out of politeness and nostalgia. She thinks she goes to the monastery because she wants to hear a fellow poet speak. Later, in each of these things, she sees the hand of God.

Lecrae thinks he goes to Atlanta during college to see the city and check out women at the conference. He thinks he goes to Egypt because he has been advised to rest. He thinks he has fooled his friends about his failures, when actually they are waiting patiently for the chance to help him.

Wiman thinks the drying up of his poetry is some kind of human blockage. Initially, he thinks of Danielle as another woman in his life, not the one who will teach him about the depths of love and accompany him back to church. He is tempted to think of his blood cancer diagnosis as simply a death sentence, potentially evidence that life is arbitrary and meaningless. After his return to faith, he sees God's fingerprints on each of these things.

Norris says directly that God was at work in her life even when she was fleeing him—the hound of heaven again. Even those choices and actions that brought chaos into her life proved useful, because the chaos and unhappiness created the conditions that made her open to a return to God, to something more. Lecrae says similar things.

Anne Rice spends much of her career writing about vampires while herself a devout atheist. Only after returning to faith does she understand the extent to which her novels were exploring spiritual questions—one's that eventually opened her up to a return to God. And God used travel, as he did in Lecrae's and Dan Wakefield's life, to keep transcendent realities matters for contemplation.

Some Christians work too hard at identifying every detail of their lives as clear evidence of God at work. They seem almost desperate to fit each moment into a great pattern, like they're holding a puzzle piece and looking at the completed picture of their life on the cover of the box. That seems to me to spring more from fear and insecurity than from faith and confidence.

I'm talking instead about learning to recognize and trust evidences that God actually cares about you and works for your good—for shalom in your life—in time and in eternity. We get balancing truths in Scripture—that all things work together for good (you know the qualifiers) and that we see as through a glass darkly. The first counsels hope and confidence, the second counsels humility and perseverance.

## ACTS OF FAITH SUPPORTING THE FEELINGS OF FAITH: GIVING RETURNERS SOMETHING TO DO

Many Returners describe their way back as an ongoing process, ongoing still, not a flash return in a single moment. Kathleen Norris reports that she still remains uncomfortable calling herself a Christian in public because she now understands what the implications and responsibilities of such a self-naming ought to entail. While in that limbo state of coming home but still perhaps a few blocks away, many report that being given jobs to do by the community of faith helped them discover that they were in fact believers again.

For Norris this involved helping the church ladies do the service work of the church needed for weddings, funerals, pot luck dinners, and other seasonal activities. It also involved engaging in acts of worship—singing hymns in church, retreating and praying and meditating with the monks, reading the Bible even when she didn't know how much of it she believed. It surprised her when a monk described her to another as a woman of faith, and yet that was what she found herself becoming. Her church even eventually asked her to preach, an indication that they accepted her as a sister in Christ, one who could teach them things, even if she was not entirely confident about her status herself. Speaking the truth aloud helped her believe the truth.

Christian Wiman returned to writing poetry as he returned to faith. He used poetry to explore what faith is and isn't, including his own. He acknowledged that "God doesn't give a gift without giving an obligation to use it." And using the gift deepened his faith.

Dan Wakefield used his own gift of teaching in his church and, later, in workshops on spiritual memoir writing across the country. Brad Germany found that his own experience in prison was useful in ministering to men themselves in prison and in halfway houses. Likewise his own healing from addiction made him useful in leading other men out of addiction.

If you want to help someone in the midst of Returning to faith, give them something faith-related to do. For Returners, using a gift results in the strengthening of faith. It puts hypothetical faith to practical use, transforming the merely theoretical to the actual.

## III. WHAT THESE STORIES TELL US

### YEARNING FOR HOME: THE "IN THE BONES" PHENOMENON

Some of the reasons for returning to faith are practical, definable, and even verifiable. Others are more nebulous and intuitive—such as the "in the bones" phenomenon. Just as the sense of "something more" to reality and life is impossible to quantify, so the feeling that faith and the church are home—the place you are meant to be, the place that best accounts for and nurtures you as a whole person—is a feeling that one cannot adequately explain even to oneself.

Augustine famously asserted that the heart is restless until it finds its rest in God. Christian Wiman didn't believe that for much of his life and yet after widely exploring the world he said the following while still away from God: "I've just made my fortieth move in fifteen years," adding, "There is something missing from all this motion, some hunger that all this seeing never sates." He only finally finds a resting place when he returns to resting in God.

The same restlessness and relief from restlessness characterizes many Returners. Wakefield says that leaving atheism made him feel like an "exile," one who needed to find a home. Norris comes to see a return to faith as accepting her "inheritance." She was from a long family line of faith, something she wished to escape in her twenties and thirties, but something that would not let her go and to which she eventually returned, finally admitting "this is who I am."

## Chapter 14

## KEEPING THEM WITH US, DRAWING THEM BACK

### SOME THOUGHTS FOR THE CHURCH

> "The Truth is not something you can just think or say. Truth does not belong to the Smarty-pants; it belongs to the fully alive human being, who increasingly conforms himself to Love."
>
> —Jordan Castro

I CLOSE THIS BOOK of stories with optimism and a bit of hesitancy. I want to offer some reflections on how we as "the church" (or "the Church") can do better in keeping folks with us and drawing those back who have left us. The optimistic me says God desires this, God has made and will preserve the church, and this community—living out the story of faith together—is a great and necessary good.

The hesitancy has to do with expertise regarding advising the church. I have none. Others have thought much longer and deeper about what the Bible says about the church, how to build the church, what worship should look like, how the church can be good news to the world around it, and so on. So I offer only personal reflections based on a lifetime of being in churches and on interacting with folks like those in the stories in this book that we have had the privilege of hearing. It took courage for them to tell them, and we are the better for having heard. So what can we learn?

The basic question I would like to address now is simply, "How can we do better?" What are characteristics of a healthy Christian community—broadly and locally? What kind of church would keep more Leavers with us and draw more Returners back?

I want to make clear that I believe it a mistake to blame the church for all leaving, or even most of it. People choose to leave the church and the faith for their own reasons—many of them poor ones. The very gospel itself—as is clear in the New Testament—is offensive. It offended people and the wider culture then and it does the same now. Some branches of the church have addressed this by adjusting the gospel message to be more appealing, and, in the process, have often made it less the gospel. Doing so in the name of "love" has actually made it less loving, because it has made it less true.

At the same time, other expressions of the church have too often been unfaithful to the gospel in other ways—making it less beautiful, less relevant, less good news. If one is looking for blame, there is plenty to go around for both those who choose to leave and for the church that does not adequately model faith in a way that encourages them to stay. But we should not be looking for people to blame; we should be looking for ways, with God's help, to live out the gospel as fully as we can. As Norris said, "The only hypocrite I have to worry about on Sunday morning is myself."

So here, simply, are some reflections—not at all exhaustive, not unique to me, not fully developed. Limited, but maybe useful.

They are details of a broad assertion: the foundational goal for any local church and the church as a whole is to live out the story God is telling the world in as full and loving and committed a way as possible, depending on God's strength, wisdom, inspiration, and revelation, not on their own. As declared earlier, the plot of that story is that God made us, God loves us, and God calls us. And the theme of the story is shalom—all created things flourishing because of being and doing what they were made to be and do.

I believe certain characteristics are necessary for the church to be a place of shalom. This list is only a start. Add your own reflections.

## WINSOME

Many people would start such a list with an intellectual quality, such as "true." I'll get to true, which of course is essential, but I will start with a more affective characteristic because I think its lack is one of the things that block Leavers from perceiving that the gospel is, in fact, true. If we want to keep believers within the church and draw back those who have left, we should strive to preserve and embody the natural winsomeness of the gospel. (This winsomeness does not derive from accommodating to the world's values and desires, but from living well God's purposes for his creation.)

Since the meaning of "gospel" is "good news," the church needs to present and live it as such. "Taste and see that the Lord is good," says the psalmist (34:8). The Old English root of the word "winsome" (wynn) means pleasure or delight. Somehow the church too often fails to convey the winsomeness of God and the gospel.

Rightly lived, faith will be something people want to believe rather than something they ought or have to believe. Some leave the church because they no longer believe in the existence of God. But many others, such as Lecrae, leave because they no longer believe in the goodness of God, nor of his church. Each church needs to ask itself, "Have we somehow blunted the perception that God and the gospel are good and greatly to be desired?"

The ancient culprits for distorting the winsomeness of the gospel are legalism, condemnation, self-righteousness, hypocrisy, and abuse of power. More recent additions to the list, especially for the young, are intolerance and indifference to justice. There are of course many others, including things cited in the stories we have heard.

Some have said that the gospel is bad news before it is good news in that it tells us we are sinners and not adequate in ourselves (repugnant to the secular gospel of self-affirmation and fulfillment). True, but that is only the diagnosis part of the gospel. The delightful part is that Christ has overcome that bad news. It is simple realism to point out our brokenness, the good news is that healing and joy (shalom) are available for all.

How does one—as a parent or a friend or a church—convey such a message? Only by living it out in the details of our own lives.

Where to start? With Jesus' answer to the question, "Which is the most important commandment in the law of Moses?"

"'You must love the Lord your God with all your heart, all your soul, and all your mind.' This is the first and greatest commandment. A second is equally important: 'Love your neighbor as yourself.' The entire law and all the demands of the prophets are based on these two commandments" (Matt 22:37-39, NLT).

Straightforward, but not of course easy to fulfill. This answer requires understanding the gospel more fully than we usually do, and living it out in actions as well as beliefs.

I would add a few other things, having more to do with personality than theology. They are not commanded in the Bible, but they are characteristics of individuals in my life who have kept faith winsome for me: laugh easily, hold on to nonessentials loosely, stay curious, accept mystery and risk, act compassionately, be open to learning more and differently.

And one thing the Bible does command—love easily and widely, sometimes extravagantly. Make love an action, not just an abstract conviction. Love is valuing to the extent of being willing to sacrifice for. Splash it on folks who do not necessarily deserve it.

If we get even a start on such things, the life of faith will strike those watching as winsome—a source of pleasure, an experience of delight. They will be more reluctant to leave us and more willing to come back.

## BELIEVABLE

Being winsome also makes faith more believable. Too often we think that it is enough for something to be true for it to be believable. Yet many true things are not believed in this world, as has always been the case. And of course the reverse as well.

Believing, as I have claimed repeatedly, is a whole-person phenomenon. It involves not only the intellect, but also the emotions, will, and even body. The intellect must be satisfied to some degree (or at least quieted), but so must be the emotions and the will. If something is merely true but an offense to the emotions, the will sets itself against it. And the body will stiffen (and release certain brain chemicals) in support of that resistance.

The Christian faith is committing one's life to the story that God is telling the world. It involves accepting one's role as a character in that story and living accordingly. One will likely only find the story believable and attractive if it is more than an idea or a truth claim. It must ring true to us emotionally in order to woo our will, which is not, in our self-absorbed culture especially, particularly inclined toward it.

A believable faith is realistic—about human nature, about the human condition, about the social and intellectual context in which we live. And of course it is realistic about the character of God and the story God is telling.

For many people, if our telling and living of God's story is not winsome, it will not be believable. Christianity is commonly depicted as judgmental, self-righteous, intolerant, and on and on. And of course there are examples—in history and today—of these things. The only way of giving the lie to this depiction as a general truth—as is the case with all negative stereotypes—is to provide sufficient amounts of contrary evidence.

To do that we must seek to live out God's story in a whole-person, believable way. We must meet people's felt needs—from food shelves, to grief groups, to crisis pregnancy services, to social justice marches, and even to art displays and book clubs. If we do so, people are more likely to at least listen to our other moral imperatives and to our theological assertions. If we don't, they simply won't find our story believable.

## TRUE

Okay, now I get to the place where many would like to start. To be winsome and believable, we need also to defend the truth of our faith. The Christian story will not survive if it is only (I do not say "merely") emotionally satisfying or practically useful. (Or it will survive only as a distorted and therefore false version of the story.) It must be winsome but not at the expense of its truth. Its claims are much larger than that—literally infinitely large.

The story of faith insists there genuinely is a God—both transcendent and present in this world—that the Bible describes God accurately, though not of course completely, that the same Bible is reliable in conveying the story God is telling his creation, and that we are called to respond to that story—individually and collectively.

And of course much of the world says that none of this is true. Anyone who agrees that the story of faith is false will, and should, leave the church and not come back until they have changed their mind. (Better for everyone by far than to stay, become influential, and undermine the truth of the story in the lives of others.)

So a winsome and believable church needs to defend its truth claims. This means that apologetics in some form should be spread throughout its life. It should be, at various levels of sophistication, a part of educating and equipping everyone—children, youth, adults. It should arise in sermons, in Sunday school, in conferences, in reading and discussion groups.

It need not be academic or larded with jargon. The arguments of Paul are a good example—sometimes closely reasoned and even challenging to understand, but more often commonsensical, practical, logical, and based on experiences with God in Scripture and his own life.

## HONESTY

At the same time that we insist on truth, we should also insist on honesty. In teaching our youth, for instance, we must be honest in pointing out that ours is a minority view—in our culture and the wider world—and always has been. Even the majority of people who themselves heard Jesus rejected him—immediately or eventually. Too many young people raised in the church are unprepared for the dismissiveness and even hostility towards faith they encounter when they leave a Christian bubble. If they know it's coming, and if that have been equipped to defend their faith with their minds, they are much less likely to leave it.

We should also be honest about mystery and uncertainty. God tells us enough of the story to invite us, but chooses not to tell us everything we would like to know. Our theological assertions—our doctrines—are the application of God-given but still fallen reason in order to systematize the story. In doing so, we pray for the guidance of the Holy Spirit, we study the Bible, we listen to the history of faithful people thinking about these things, but we need to understand that the system is not synonymous with the story.

This doesn't mean that theology and doctrine and creeds are not crucial. They are because they can keep us from misreading and misinterpreting the story. Theology and story talk to each other. In a sense, they evaluate each other. God's big story (made up of many smaller stories) comes first and provides the raw material for potentially true and all-important assertions that can arise from understanding the story. Stories give the assertions a body, and assertions or doctrine give the stories a mind. Stories make the assertions understandable and believable and appeal to the whole person, assertions help guide our interpretations of the story.

There are many straight assertions in the Bible, but all of them happen in the context of the story in which they arise. We need to test the assertions against both the smaller and the bigger story.

## HUMILITY

And honesty should also include acknowledging that we may not always get it completely right. The Bible tells us that we human beings are looking in an imperfect mirror and therefore not always perceiving reality exactly as it is. But it then says that one day—though not in this life—we will understand perfectly.

All this calls from us a quality that the Bible commends throughout—humility. Humility does not call us to self-abasement—after all we are created only a little lower than the angels—but it does call us to a realistic understanding of ourselves and our world. Included in this healthy humility is an acknowledgment of our fallenness, our limitations, and our dependence on grace. This applies to our reasoning as much as to our behaviors.

I remind myself of this need for humility when encountering doctrinal and theological disagreements, especially when contested passionately. I invoke a principle coming down from the Middle Ages: in essential things, unity; in doubtful things, liberty; in all things, charity (love). Over the years, my list of theological essentials has grown smaller, but also firmer. Also firmer, I hope, is my willingness to interact lovingly with those who judge differently.

## CONFIDENCE

As important as humility is, however, it should be balanced with confidence (not to be confused with arrogance or pride). The church should accept that faith is entirely compatible with doubts and hard questions, but it need not glamorize doubt as though doubting is more heroic and intellectually respectable than believing. Scripture says "Seek and you will find." Honest seeking—honest doubting—should not insist on never finding.

Scripture is big on assurance, which it says is a foundation for faith. We can rest in the assurance that God is real, has revealed himself, and keeps his promises. The Bible tells the stories that establish that. The church should not shrink from boldly proclaiming it.

At the same time there is, as we've said, mystery and uncertainty. We cannot prove any of the things of faith in the same way that we can prove that the world is a sphere (though, personally, I can't myself prove that either, so I have to have faith in what others say). This used to bother me—a lot. Eventually I came to realize that most of the important things in life cannot be proved. I cannot prove to my wife and family that I love them (perhaps I'm faking it). I cannot prove that Rembrandt is a better artist than my grandchildren. I cannot prove that democracy is a better form of government than a totalitarian one. I cannot even prove to a severely depressed person that life is better than death. But I can offer reassuring evidence for all these things.

So, it no longer bothers me that I cannot prove—with numbers and equations and measurements—that God exists or that his story is true. But if I had been introduced to this reality at a younger age, it would have saved more than a few years of worry.

## RISKS, CHALLENGES, AND SOMETHING TO DO

There is much in the Bible that emphasizes the availability to the believer of comfort, protection, and justified hope. But there is also much that indicates that the life of faith can be filled with danger, challenge, and uncertainty. Faith is healthier and more attractive when people are made aware of both.

A winsome and true faith will not minimize its risks. Among them are unpopularity, stigmatization, loss of opportunity, and sometimes loss of life. There is also the risk of simply being wrong about one's ultimate commitment. Maybe there is no God, maybe there is no great meaning to life. Maybe it's as Samuel Beckett says—we "give birth astride of a grave, the light gleams an instant, then it's night once more."

But this risk of being wrong is inherent in every choice about the ultimate significance of human life. If you think that faith is more risky than other choices, I commend Pascal's wager to you. Look it up.

A faith that is honest with me about this risk (though it no longer strikes me, given the reward and the alternatives, as much of a risk) makes me more likely to accept it and stay in it.

The same is true when the church challenges me to live out my faith, when it expects things of me, when it tells me to get off my cell phone and do some of the things that faith calls me to do. (Actually, I don't own a cell phone, but that's irrelevant. My call is to close my damn computer, which my wife calls my fifteen-inch cell phone.)

Many people feel heroic in giving the church some money now and then. To me that is no more than sharing your wood, hay, and stubble. Of course I should give money, more than I do. The truth of the gospel *sets* you free, but proclaiming the gospel—locally and around the world—does not happen for free.

God's story doesn't primarily call you to be a nice person, not even a generous and kind person. Jesus says pick up your cross and follow me. After you're obedient, you'll have plenty of opportunities to be generous and kind.

Ironically enough, the church will be more winsome and believable and true when it is more demanding. When it gives people significant things to do. Run the thrift store, call on the sick, help fix the furnace, teach the five-year-olds, help out with the funerals and weddings, volunteer and engage in your wider community, encourage the pastors and youth leaders, tell a few of your friends about Jesus.

Any kind of faith in anything is strengthened by doing. That whole-person thing again, including the body. It will keep some of the Leavers and attract back some of the Returners.

## ANSWER THE QUESTIONS PEOPLE ARE ACTUALLY ASKING

The questions that people ask of faith and the church change over time. Too often the church is focused on answering the questions asked a generation or two prior. Some questions have been and will always be asked, such as

Jesus' question, "Who do you say I am?" There is no more important question than this for every church and every person. But other questions—and kinds of questions—rise to the surface in some eras and recede in others.

When I was first thinking for myself in the 1960s and later, the apologists of the time were responding to the modernist challenge, "You can't prove it." Their response, largely, was "Yes we can. Or at least we can provide good evidence." And I, personally, was ravenous for that evidence. I piled up evidence for God existing on one side (the God of the Bible) and evidence against God existing on the other, hoping somewhat desperately that God's pile would end up higher.

Many people today, especially the young, are not asking, "Can your prove it?," asking instead, "Can you live it?" Charles Taylor and many others claim that the operative questions today involve "authenticity." That is, "Does your life match your claims?" "Are your stated values demonstrated in what you do?" "The Bible, in both testaments, seems to emphasize caring for the poor, the widow, and the stranger—how are you doing on that?" "You claim that God loves and values everyone—without exception; do we see you loving and valuing everyone—without exception?"

One of the most common claims from Leavers, Nones, Dones, New Atheists, and Never-Weres is that Christians are hypocrites. It was also a common claim of Jesus regarding the religious leaders of his day. And, of course, hypocrisy we will always have with us, both among the faithful and among the scorners. Few people completely live up to their stated values.

One non-defensive answer to the charge is, "Of course we're hypocrites. Stay with us and help us do better. Stay or Return and model authentic faith among us. Be the change you are looking for." In many ways, the hypocrisy charge is a smoke screen, a lazy, nonreflective way to dismiss God because God's people are jerks. Some advocates for social justice are also hypocrites with questionable motives; does that mean we should abandon work for social justice? Countless individuals and churches are living the gospel authentically. Join with them.

The desire for "authenticity," however, goes beyond the issue of the church living up to its claims. It should influence in other ways the face we show to Yearners, Leavers, and Returners, and the world at large. Some will still want answers to the "Is it true?" questions. But most others are interested not in argument and evidence but in storied responses to their questions. Show me that the story you are telling is winsome, that it is good, that it is beautiful, that it is honest, that there is a place in it for me despite my wounds, my failures, my doubts, my hard questions. (For Returners return not after all their issues are resolved, but with many of them still percolating.)

## LISTENING BEFORE SPEAKING

Sometimes Christians talk too much. And too loudly and too aggressively and too smugly. Better to follow the biblical advice of being quick to listen and slow to speak.

Kathleen Norris said it was important during the early stages of her return to church that the folks did not press her closely on what she believed. Wiman praised the pastor they met on the street for avoiding churchy language and "bouncy" Christian enthusiasm. Rosaria Butterfield continued her relationship with Pastor Smith and his wife because he asked her questions about what she believed rather than focusing on telling her what he believed. Germany, perhaps, needed the useful vagueness of AA's "higher power" before he could handle the more accurate revelations of God in the Bible.

A sign of caring and kindness is soliciting another's story—of listening rather than lecturing. Returners are usually jumpy about returning to church. Welcome them, show them warmth and friendship, invite them into your lives. They will ask what *you* think when they're ready.

## ONCE MORE ON SHALOM

As I have suggested, the single word and concept that most fully embodies everything this exploration of Leaving and Returning is about is the word "shalom." Do a word study on it. Shalom is the central theme of the story God is calling us to. When any created thing is doing what it was created to do, it is in a state of shalom.

People primarily associate shalom with peace, but it is much more than simply the absence of conflict. It is also the root for related words that translate as wholeness, health, order, prosperity, justice, protection, well-being, and much more.

Shalom is always falling apart in a fallen world. People leave faith and the church because of ruptures in shalom. But God is calling us to be always repairing and extending shalom. If the church is seen as contributing to shalom in the lives of the individual, of the church and local community, and of the wider world, it will thrive, even if the culture grows more and more hostile to it. If it doesn't, it won't.

To the degree that the church lives out God's intention for it, there will be fewer Leavers and more who Believe Again.

May it be so.

# EPILOGUE
# A WORD TO POTENTIAL RETURNERS

"Let us examine our ways and test them, and let us return to the Lord."
—Lamentations 3:40, NIV

"I have swept away your sins like a cloud. I have scattered your offenses like the morning mist. Oh, return to me, for I have paid the price to set you free."
—Isaiah 44:22, NLT

"So walk on air against your better judgement"
—Seamus Heaney, "The Gravel Walks"

This book has been written for anyone interested in the topic announced by the title. But my last word is directed to those who may find themselves in its stories: a Yearner who lives in the borderlands, or a onetime believer, who then walked or fled away, and is now wondering about believing again. Is it desirable? Is it possible?

I have asked these questions myself. I was raised in faith and in the church, dozens of them as we wandered hither and yon as a family. I was born into the story, accepting my place in it at the age of five. I never left it entirely, but I wandered to the edge. I made faith an object of contemplation, of intellectual probing, something to be tested abstractly regarding its truth claims. Like the disciple Thomas, I wanted proof as I decided whether to continue to believe.

I did not have church wounds. My father, the pastor at many of the churches I attended—mostly in Texas and California—was a fundamentalist in theology, but not in temperament. He had been—and was still—too much a hell-raiser himself to be harsh about the lifestyle of others, including his kids. Unlike many, I am not bitter about my experience in fundamentalist churches, though I have long since looked elsewhere for a community. As I have written before, I'm grateful that my fundamentalist Sunday school teachers and youth leaders cared about my soul. My secular friends and influences didn't think I even had one.

I was reflective about the things of God from early in life. I wondered if it was okay that I liked the taste of the grape juice taken at communion, and whether I was wrong to want to lick the not-quite-empty cup. I spent a lot of energy thinking about the relationship between my own behavior and whether the baseball Dodgers—my companion religion—would win or lose. Later the questions became more serious—and so did the doubts.

My assumption was that there were good answers to all my questions, if not directly in the Bible, then surely in the books and sermons and lectures of faithful people, especially the heavy thinkers—past and present. I spent years looking, earnestly but with decreasing confidence. But momentum kept me within the church and within faith. If I couldn't prove it was true, then I also didn't find that anyone had proved to me that it wasn't. So I never became a Leaver. Basically, I was a Yearner wandering in the hinterlands of belief.

But mine was an attenuated, theoretical faith at best. Far less real and alive than Jayne's, my wife's. I was Kierkegaard's metaphorical donkey, standing between two piles of hay—belief and disbelief—and starving because I couldn't decide which one to eat.

What I discovered—precisely from reading people like Kierkegaard and Pascal and many others—is that faith is not a puzzle to be solved; it is a story to be lived. God is writing the story and calls me to be a character in it. The story has a plot and a theme and it offers me both meaning and significance. It also involves risks of all kinds—intellectual, relational, for some people physical. (But then what thing of great value doesn't?) It does not offer me an easy life, nor does it protect me from suffering. It only gives me the possibility that even pain can be meaningful—and redeemed.

This vision of faith emphasizes God's love for us and for the creation. At its core is grace—embodied in Jesus, the Christ. I found it winsome. In the end, I found it irresistible. I have not found a story that offers me more. I commend it to you.

Admitting you belong to God, not to yourself or your desires, is not an easy thing in a culture that idolizes individualism, self-fulfillment, and creating your own reality. It's more countercultural than anything tried by any generation in American history, an act of rebellion, in fact, against the gods of this world.

It won't make you popular. It will disappoint some of your friends, maybe even some of your family. It might hurt your career. Its consequences may surprise even yourself.

But, if you decide it's worth the risk, welcome home.

# SUGGESTED READING

RESOURCES ON AMERICAN RELIGION as it relates to the topics addressed in *Believing Again* (especially faith development and declines in religious participation) are endless—books, articles, and ongoing studies. Those listed below are simply a place to start—either works I found helpful or which are often recommended. Readers can consult their bibliographies for many, many more related resources, both popular and academic.

Berger, Peter. *A Far Glory: The Quest for Faith in an Age of Credulity*. New York: Anchor, 1993.
———. *The Sacred Canopy: Elements of a Sociological Theory of Religion*. New York: Anchor, 1990.
Burge, Ryan. *The Nones: Where They Came From, Who They Are, and Where They Are Going*. Minneapolis: Fortress, 2021.
———. *20 Myths about Religion and Politics in America*. Minneapolis: Fortress, 2022.
Davis, Jim, and Michael Graham (with Ryan Burge). *The Great Dechurching*. Grand Rapids: Zondervan, 2023.
Fowler, James. *Faith Development and Pastoral Care: Theology and Pastoral Care*. Minneapolis: Fortress, 1987.
———. *Stages of Faith: The Psychology of Human Development and the Quest for Meaning*. New York: HarperCollins, 1981.
Hunter, James Davison. *To Change the World: The Irony, Tragedy, and Possibility of Christianity in the Late Modern World*. New York: Oxford University Press, 2010.
Marriott, John. *A Recipe for Disaster: Four Ways Churches and Parents Prepare Individuals to Lose Their Faith and How They Can Instill a Faith that Endures*. Eugene, OR: Wipf and Stock, 2018. Note: This author has various other books on topics related to losing faith.
Smith, Christian, and Melinda Lundquist Denton. *Soul Searching: The Religious and Spiritual Lives of American Teenagers*. New York: Oxford University Press, 2005.
Stone, Lyman. "Promise and Peril: The History of American Religiosity and its Recent Decline." American Enterprise Institute, 2020. https://www.aei.org/research-products/report/promise-and-peril-the-history-of-american-religiosity-and-its-recent-decline/.

Taylor, Charles. *A Secular Age*. Cambridge: Belknap, 2007. (See also James K. A. Smith, *How (Not) to be Secular: Reading Charles Taylor*. Grand Rapids: Eerdmans, 2015.)

Taylor, Daniel. *The Myth of Certainty: The Reflective Christian and the Risk of Commitment*. Downers Grove, IL: InterVarsity, 2000. First published 1986.

———. *The Skeptical Believer: Telling Stories to Your Inner Atheist*. St. Paul: Bog Walk, 2013.

Wuthnow, Robert. *The God Problem: Expressing Faith and Being Reasonable*. Berkeley: University of California Press, 2012.

The following are organizations that have long conducted ongoing research into religious life in America:

Barna Group
https://www.barna.com/

Gallup
https://www.gallup.com/Search/Default.aspx?q=religion

The General Social Survey (GSS)
https://gss.norc.org/

Lifeway Research
https://research.lifeway.com/

Pew Research Center
https://www.pewresearch.org/topic/religion/

## INDIVIDUAL AUTHORS

Following are the primary sources for stories by published writers told throughout *Believing Again*. All quotations come from these sources. An internet search of names will lead to many additional interviews, articles, and author websites.

### Rosaria Champagne Butterfield

*The Secret Thoughts of an Unlikely Convert: An English Professor's Journey into Christian Faith*. Pittsburgh: Crown and Covenant, 2012.

*Openness Unhindered: Further Thoughts of an Unlikely Convert on Sexual Identity and Union with Christ*. Pittsburgh: Crown and Covenant, 2015.

*The Gospel Comes with a House Key: Practicing Radically Ordinary Hospitality in Our Post-Christian World*. Pittsburgh: Crown and Covenant, 2018.

### Lecrae Moore

*Un-Ashamed*. Nashville: B&H, 2016.

*I Am Restored: How I Lost My Religion but Found My Faith*. Grand Rapids: Zondervan, 2020.

Kathleen Norris
*Dakota: A Spiritual Geography*. New York: Ticknor and Fields, 1993.
*The Cloister Walk*. New York: Riverhead, 1996.
*Amazing Grace: A Vocabulary of Faith*. New York: Riverhead, 1998.
*The Virgin of Bennington*. New York: Riverhead, 2001.

Anne Rice
*Christ the Lord: Out of Egypt*. New York: Knopf, 2005.
*Christ the Lord: The Road to Cana*. New York: Knopf, 2008.
*Called Out of Darkness: A Spiritual Confession*. New York: Anchor, 2008.

Dan Wakefield
*Returning: A Spiritual Journey*. Boston: Beacon, 1984.
*How Do We Know When It's God? A Spiritual Memoir*. New York: Little, Brown, 1999.
*Spiritually Incorrect: Finding God in All the Wrong Places* (co-authored with Marian Delvecchio). Nashville: Skylight Paths, 2003.

A. N. Wilson
Wilson has written dozens of books. There are many articles reproduced online on his return to faith. Following are articles that consist largely of his own words:
"Why I Believe Again." *The New Statesman*, April 2, 2009. https://www.newstatesman.com/religion/2009/04/conversion-experience-atheism.
Steer, Roger. "A N Wilson's Return to Faith." *Christianity*, May 15, 2009. http://www.rogersteer.com/a-n-wilson%C2%B4s-return-to-faith/.

Christian Wiman
*Ambition and Survival: Becoming a Poet*. Port Townsend, WA: Copper Canyon, 2007.
*My Bright Abyss: Meditations of a Modern Believer*. New York: Farrar, Straus and Giroux, 2013.
*He Held Radical Light: The Art of Faith, the Faith of Art*. New York: Farrar, Straus and Giroux, 2018.

Selected volumes of poetry:
*Every Riven Thing: Poems*. New York: Farrar, Straus and Giroux, 2010.
*Once in the West: Poems*. New York: Farrar, Straus and Giroux, 2014.
*Hammer Is the Prayer: Selected Poems*. New York: Farrar, Straus and Giroux, 2016.
*Survival Is a Style: Poems*. New York: Farrar, Straus and Giroux, 2020.
*Zero at the Bone: Fifty Entries Against Despair*. New York: Farrar, Straus and Giroux, 2023.
An article:
"White Buffalo: Keep your mind in hell, and despair not." *Harper's*, November 2024.

www.ingramcontent.com/pod-product-compliance
Lightning Source LLC
Chambersburg PA
CBHW032127160426
43197CB00008B/549